THE DELICIOUS AND SIMPLE COOKIES COOKBOOK

SIAN I RICHARDSON

Copyright © 2023 Sian I Richardson

All rights reserved.

CONTENTS

INTRODUCTION

HOW TO USE THIS BOOK

GENERAL BAKING ADVICE

A FEW IMPORTANT THINGS TO NOTE

Cookie Baking Tips

INGREDIENTS

Dairy + Eggs

Cooking Oils

Salt + Spices

Sweeteners

Flour

Leavenings

Nuts

Chocolate

Vanilla

EQUIPMENT

Measuring Equipment

Utensils

C1. THE CLASSICS

1) Soft Chocolate Chip Cookies

2) Brown Butter Chocolate Chip Cookies

3) Thin and Crispy Chocolate Chip Cookies

4) Thin and Crispy Double Chocolate Cookies

5) Peanut Butter Cookies

6) Sugar Cookies

7) Brown Sugar Cookies

8) Chocolate Sugar Cookies

9) Brownie Cookies

10) Chocolate Crinkle Cookies

11) Snickerdoodles

12) Ginger Cookies

13) Oatmeal Raisin Cookies

14) Thumbprints

15) Sablés

16) Bourbon Sablés with Chocolate

17) Shortbread

18) Cut Out Cookies

C2. BROWNIES + BLONDIES

19) My Favorite Brownies

20) Fudgy Brownies

21) Cakey Brownies

22) Cream Cheese Brownies

23) Turtle Brownies

24) Rocky Road Brownies

25) Swirl Brownies, Two Ways

26) Marshmallow Peanut Butter Brownies

27) Peanut Butter Crunch Brownies

28) Chocolate Basil Brownies

29) White Chocolate Brownies

30) White Chocolate Swirl Brownies, Two Ways

31) White Chocolate Red Velvet Brownies

32) White Chocolate Brownies with Toasted Sesame Caramel

33) Blondies

34) Brown Butter Blondies

35) Espresso Caramel Blondies

36) Cinnamon Roll Blondies

37) Banana Crunch Blondies

38) S'mores Blondies

C3. FRUITEXTRAVAGANZA

39) Olive Oil Sugar Cookies with Blood Orange Glaze

40) Lemon Sugar Cookies

41) Orange Almond Shortbread Cookies

42) Raspberry Rye Cookies

43) White Chocolate, Rosemary, and Apricot Cookies

44) Banana Poppy Seed Cookies

45) Banana Cream Pie Bars

46) Cream Cheese Pumpkin Pie Bars

47) Danish Pear-Apple Bars

48) Mixed Berry Crumble Bars

49) Strawberry Crème Fraîche Bars

50) Red Wine Cherry Cheesecake Swirl Bars

51) Grapefruit Cake Bars

52) Lemon Oat Bars

53) Citrus Pie Bars

C4. THE NEXT LEVEL

54) Lavender Cookies with White Chocolate–Crème Fraîche Glaze

55) Smoky Butterscotch Cookies

56) Palmiers with Apricot and Cardamom

57) French Meringues

58) Meringues with Cacao Nibs and Caramel Swirl

59) Double Chocolate Espresso Cookies

60) Espresso Cheesecake Bars

61) Black and White Cheesecake Bars

62) Chocolate Hazelnut Bars

63) French Silk Pie Bars

64) Mud Pie Bars

65) Crème Brûlée Cheesecake Bars

66) Boston Cream Pie Bars

67) Carrot Cake Bars with Meringue

C5. TIME TO PLAY

68) Macarons

Rhubarb Caramel Filling

TROUBLESHOOTING TIPS

Oven Temperature

"Aging" the Egg Whites

Food Coloring

Sugar Brands

Feet

Mistakes

Letting Go

69) Chocolate Macarons

Chocolate Ganache Crunch Filling

Coffee Cacao Nib Filling

70) Neapolitan Cookies

71) Roll-Up Cookies, Two Ways

72) Half-and-Half Cookies, Two Ways

73) Kitchen Sink Cookies

74) Chocolate Sandwich Cookies

75) Scotcharoos

76) Caramel Bars with Candied Peanuts

77) Chocolate–Peanut Butter Pretzel Bark

78) Caramelized White Chocolate Pistachio Bark

C6. PAN-BANGING COOKIES

THE PAN-BANGING METHOD

The Story

Some Notes

79) Chocolate Chip Cookies

80) Oatmeal Chocolate Cookies

81) Rum Raisin Cookies

82) Triple Chocolate Cookies

83) Rocky Road Cookies

84) Toasted Sesame Cookies

85) Peanut Butter Cookies

86) Ginger Molasses Cookies

87) Snickerdoodles

88) Sugar Cookies

89) Banana–Espresso–Cacao Nib Cookies

90) S'mores Cookies

C7. MIX + MATCH

91) Brownie Cookies with Cardamom Buttercream Filling

92) Peanut Butter Cookies with Peanut Butter Filling

93) Snickerdoodle Cookies with Pumpkin Buttercream

94) Ginger Cookies with Salted Caramel Ice Cream

95) Oatmeal Cream Pies

96) Sugar Cookies with Raspberry Ripple Ice Cream

97) Brownies with Coffee Ice Cream

98) White Chocolate Brownies with Hazelnut Ice Cream

99) Chocolate Chip Cookies with Ice Cream and Sprinkles

100) Chocolate Malt Ice Box Bars

C8. EXTRAS

Pie Dough Base

Rough Puff Pastry

Brown Butter

Pastry Cream

Lemon Curd

Caramel

Crème Fraîche

Marshmallows

Marshmallow Fluff

Ermine Buttercream

No-Churn Ice Cream

Whipped Cream

Candied Nuts

Candied Cacao Nibs

Caramel Shards

Music to Bake To

CONVERSIONS

BIBLIOGRAPHY

Introduction

When I was fourteen years old, I embarked on what is now known in my family as the "cookie years." Each day I'd step off a hot school bus, walk a half block to my back door, throw my book bag somewhere in the kitchen, and get to work: mixing, whisking, and baking until my mom took over the kitchen so she could get dinner started. The story I told my mom about my afternoon baking compulsion was that I was setting out to make the perfect, quintessential cookie, but really the whole project started as an excuse to eat cookie dough.

Initially, my mom was dubious about the whole affair, as day after day dozens of cookies covered our countertop. Ninth grade was one of those years—the textbook story of a young girl in the awkward transition to womanhood. After dinner I would head to my room, recording tear-stained journal entries with an overarching junior high theme known to many: I felt like I just didn't fit anywhere. I never shared those tears with my mom, but maybe she could sense I needed an emotional outlet because she let me keep baking. Or maybe it was because I was so engaged with mixing and stirring that I didn't have time to fight with my sister or tease my brother. Or, just maybe, deep down inside, her motherly instincts whispered to her, and she saw something greater in me than I saw in myself.

I worked my way through our three cookbooks: *The Mount-Hope Redemption Church Cookbook, Better Homes and Gardens New Cookbook* (the classic 1976 edition), and the *Betty Crocker Junior Cookbook*. Day after day I tried out recipes, experimented with recipes, and crossed out recipes that failed me. I found myself intrigued more with the process than the outcome. If I had discovered Shakespeare at this point, his words would have rang true: "Things won are done; joy's soul lies in the doing."

While I had eventually developed a repertoire of recipes, my chocolate chip cookies received the most acclaim; they were made with shortening and a little butter, extra vanilla, and a sprinkling of chocolate chips throughout the batter. I passed them out to neighbors, sent them home with my grandma, and ate more than my share. I was pleased with the cookies, but also all my hard work that went into them. I felt content with the process of taking initiative, setting out to do something, and keeping at it even when it wasn't working, or I was tired of it.

My obsessive cookie-baking phase ended, fading away when summer came and I had to find employment; college wouldn't pay for itself. High school passed and I barely spent time in the kitchen. I never took time to learn how to cook for myself, or bake anything other than cookies and chocolate cakes from boxes. The passion that had stirred in my heart lay dormant. Occasionally, there would be a need to bake: cookies at holidays, or birthday cakes for friends. I would remember for a moment, when my hands patted dough and rolled it thin, the beauty of the color of sugar and butter and eggs combined, and the pleasure of watching the dough become a perfect rectangle on the counter. There was the thrill of peeking in the oven window, watching a cake rise and take shape before my eyes. With my feet firm on the kitchen floor and my belly nestled against the counter as I stirred and whisked, I felt grounded. Through these fleeting moments, the kitchen gods were pacing above, sending messages to me on the wind. I kept missing them; they were faint whispers, floating past me and through me, and then astray. "Prophesy to the wind, and the wind only, for only the wind will listen," T. S. Eliot lamented. (*Four Quartets* and "Ash Wednesday" wouldn't find their way to me, either, until years later.)

> "'A cookie,' Avis told her children, 'is a soul.' She held up the wafer, its edges shimmering with ruby-dark sugar. 'You think it looks like a tiny thing, right? Just a little nothing. But then you take a bite.'"
>
> –Diana Abu-Jaber, *Birds of Paradise*

My high school years ended, and I headed off to Winona State University, certain my future was in teaching English or writing poetry. I found myself working at the Blue Heron Coffeehouse, owned by Larry and Colleen Wolner, where I was hired as a barista for a few evenings and weekend days. I didn't know what I was walking in to; I had no idea this little shop with no air conditioning in the kitchen and limited counter space would be a refuge and light to me. Here was a safe space to learn and fail, a place to laugh and cry and spend long hours. Here was a place to study and hide and drink so much coffee. When I walked through the doors my first night of work, I still didn't hear the gods. But looking back, I'm sure their trumpets were blaring.

Larry and Colleen had just bought the store when I started, so in the beginning there was a brief stint in which I was the only employee. Business was slow at first but soon picked up, and one crazy evening, after looking sadly at the empty bake case, Larry asked me if I knew how to make cookies. I thought back to those afternoons in my parents' kitchen, making dozens upon dozens of cookies. I had moved on, and everything I had painstakingly taught myself was mostly forgotten. I fibbed a confident "Yes!" regardless.

Larry set me to work making chocolate chip cookies, and I mixed and stirred and hummed a little tune, happy to be creating again. The cookies, however, emerged from the oven in one gigantic blob, with butter streaks and flour patches galore. I'll never forget Larry's pursed lips and side eye as he gazed at the giant cookie disaster. He hunched his tall frame over the baking sheet, and flipping his ponytail carefully over his shoulder, he quietly commented, "Are you *sure* you know how to make cookies?" I flushed, but he set me to work again, kindly walking me through each step of the recipe. Then he had me make them again, and again. Soon I was making beautiful cookies, and then bars, and coffee cakes, and scones and muffins, too. Maybe in those initial moments the Wolners were desperate and took what help they had, or maybe their maternal instincts picked up on the whispers in the wind. Whatever the case, their diligence in teaching me and their trust that I could succeed fostered my lifelong love for baking.

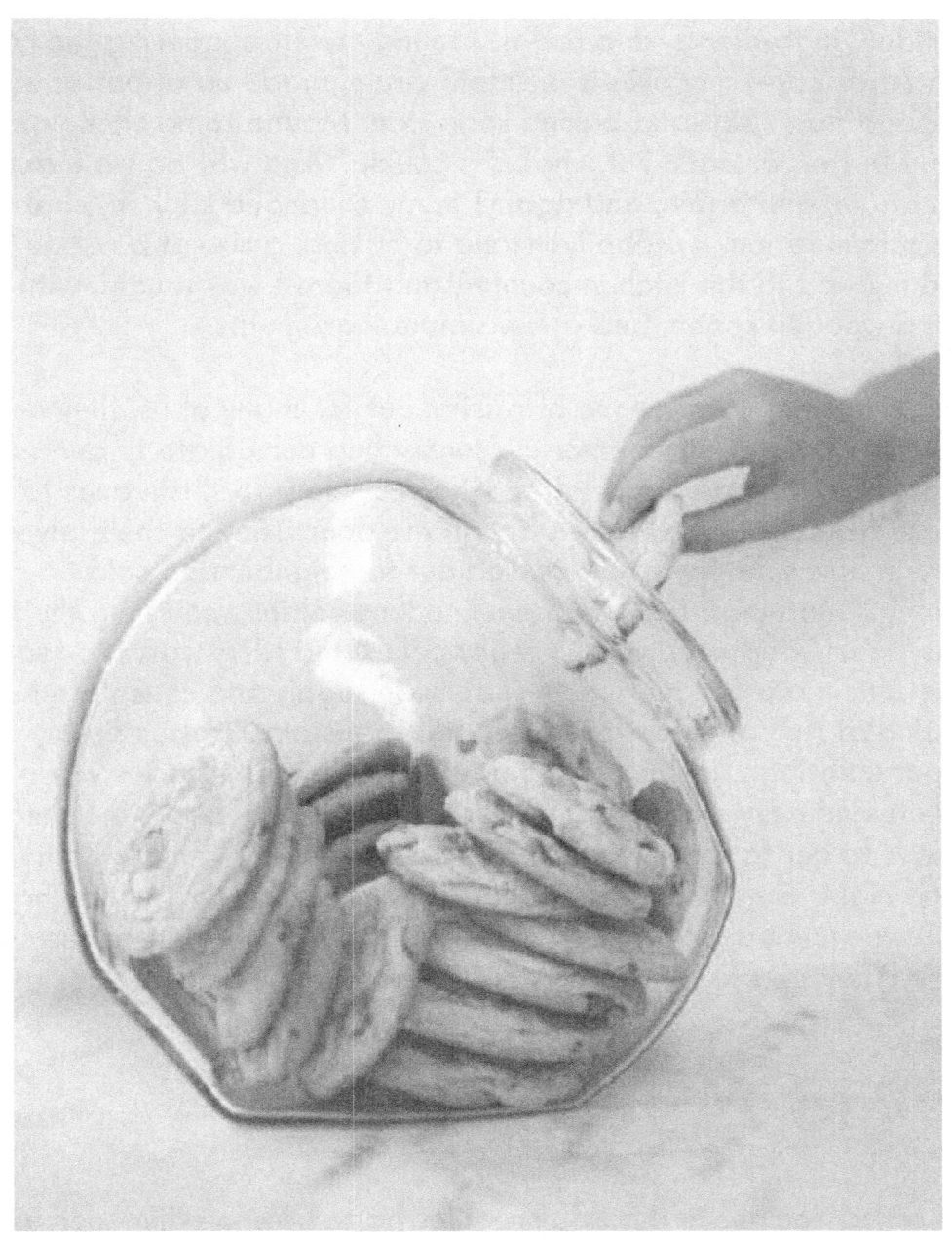

Cookie making was now part of my life, and in the years that followed, I spent time both personally and professionally honing my craft. And while I spent weeks and months playing around with technique, ingredients, and ratios, I found myself pondering the cookie itself. At its core, a cookie is a simple circle, made up of butter, sugar, eggs, and flour. Salt and baking soda, too. Maybe some chocolate, or peanut butter, or oats. But what *is* a cookie? And why do we make them again, and again, and again? In my childhood kitchen, cookies were a foundation, a stepping-stone to baking, a rite of passage. I found my way to the kitchen counter, and there I was taught, with a bowl, a wooden spoon, and a few simple ingredients.

Cookies are the cornerstone of pastry. But for many of us, they are also at the core of our memories, connecting our palate to our person. Cookies wait for us after school, anxious for little ones to emerge from a bus and race through the door. They fit themselves snugly in boxes, happy to be passed out to neighbors on cold Christmas mornings; trays of them line long tables, mourning the loss of the dearly departed. While fancy cakes and tarts walk the red carpet, their toasted meringue piles, spun sugar, and chocolate curls boasting of rich rewards that often fail to sustain, cookies simply whisper knowingly. Instead of pomp and flash, they offer us warm blankets and cozy slippers. They slip us our favorite book, they know the lines to our favorite movies. They laugh at our jokes, they stay in for the night. They are good friends, they are kind words. They are not jealous, conceited, or proud. They evoke a giving spirit, a generous nature. They beg to be shared, and rejoice in connection. Cookies are home.

HOW TO USE THIS BOOK

Most of the recipes in this book require basic baking skills, such as mixing butter, adding ingredients, and the like. A few are a bit more complicated or require more of a time commitment. Be sure to follow the baking tips in the pages that follow, and read through the ingredient and equipment lists for extra advice and reference.

This book is divided into eight chapters. The first chapter, "The Classics," is my personal cookie canon: the recipes I turn to over and over, the recipes I am passing on to my children and perhaps one day my grandchildren. They are the recipes that bring delight on bright, sunny afternoons and comfort on chilly winter evenings. Everything from Soft Chocolate Chip Cookies (page 29) to Snickerdoodles (page 48) can be found here.

"Brownies + Blondies" follow with aplomb, confident that they are just as important. I have several basic brownie recipes to meet everyone's cocoa longings, plus quite a few recipes to take brownies to new heights with swirls, curls, crunch, and more chocolate. "Fruitextravaganza" will meet all your berry needs, as well as citrus and stone fruit. Pie bars and cake bars abound, as well as Lemon Sugar Cookies (page 117) and Banana Cream Pie Bars (page 126), a personal favorite.

"The Next Level" is exactly what it sounds like: recipes extravagantly elevated for your holiday and dinner party needs. You'll find French Silk Pie Bars (page 174) and Crème Brûlee Cheesecake Bars (page 181) here. "Time to Play" is right behind with some trendy takes on classics. There are both easy recipes and some that are a little more time consuming. Neapolitan Cookies (page 200), Macarons (page 193), and Scotcharoos (page 215), a Minnesota classic, are located there.

Sixth on the list is "Pan-Banging Cookies," an entire chapter dedicated to my pan-banging ripple effect. Here you'll find the original recipe that started the whole #bangonapan affair, plus quite a few more recipes with crisp, ripply outer edges and gooey, melty centers. "Mix + Match" ends the cookie recipe portion of the book, with plenty of fillings to sandwich cookies and bars into new creations.

Finally, "Extras" closes the book, with recipes for No-Churn Ice Cream (page 289) and Caramel (page 283), among other basics you'll incorporate into the cookie and bar recipes.

GENERAL BAKING ADVICE

READ THE RECIPE First and foremost, it is vital to read the entire recipe through before beginning a baking project. It is essential to know all the ingredients, details, and timing at the start to help ensure the recipe succeeds. Once you feel confident about how a recipe works, you can then think about personalizing it.

MISE EN PLACE This is an important concept that literally means "put in place." It is the practice of having everything ready before baking begins: all ingredients measured, all pans greased and lined, the oven preheated, etc. This process keeps you from wasting time and resources and helps guarantee a good outcome.

USE YOUR SENSES It's my job when writing recipes to make sure each one is thoroughly tested and then help you navigate through as best I can. However, there are many variables that may pop up and cause issues as you proceed. If your oven isn't calibrated to the right temperature, your baked goods may not turn out as described. High altitude and humidity can affect baking. Feeling depressed or anxious can influence your concentration and could possibly alter how you read the recipe. If any or all of these situations occur, you will need to rely on your senses to help guide you. If your cookies are not golden on the edges in the time the recipe allots, let them bake a little longer. If your bars seem to be browning too quickly, check to see if they should be removed from the oven. Your eyes, nose, hands, and palate are all important tools in the kitchen.

REMEMBER THE GODS I've found that when I'm overconfident or assume that what I make will turn out perfectly just because I've made it a hundred time before, I am often unconsciously careless and make a mistake. My belief is that the food gods are silently watching, reminding me of my place in things. Regardless if it's myth-come-true or just coincidence, I've learned to approach my kitchen counter with humility and be mindful of the notion that how we approach our work affects how it turns out.

A FEW IMPORTANT THINGS TO NOTE

MEASURING FLOUR Throughout this book, 1 cup of flour equals 142 g (or 5 oz). This is on the higher end of the scale (a cup of flour can range anywhere from 4 to 5 oz, depending on the baker), but I found that after weighing many cups of flour and averaging the total, mine always ended up around this number. Because most people do scoop flour differently, I highly encourage the use of a scale when measuring ingredients to get consistent results.

MEASURING SEMISOLIDS Yogurt, sour cream, peanut butter, pumpkin purée, and the like are all examples of semisolids: ingredients that fall somewhere between a liquid and a solid. I always measure these types of ingredients in a liquid measuring cup, which gives a little more volume than a dry measuring cup because the cup is slightly bigger. If you are not using a scale to measure these ingredients, I highly recommend using a liquid measuring cup so your baked goods will turn out correctly.

A PINCH OF SALT is called for occasionally throughout these pages. It is a little more than $1/8$ teaspoon, but less than $1/4$ teaspoon.

EGG WASH To make an egg wash, use a fork to whisk 1 large egg, a pinch of salt, and 1 tablespoon [15 g] of water together in a small bowl.

LINING PANS WITH PARCHMENT PAPER Lining pans with a parchment paper sling results in an easy release. Cut two pieces of parchment paper the same size as the bottom of your pan, and long enough to come up and over the sides. Spray the pan with cooking spray, and then place the pieces of parchment in the pan, perpendicular to each other so each side has a bit of parchment overhang, making sure to push the sheets into the corners.

TEMPERING CHOCOLATE Tempering chocolate allows it to set properly and gives the chocolate a glossy, smooth finish. Throughout the book I use a "cheater's method" to temper chocolate, which is to melt most of the chocolate called for, and then finely chop the few ounces of chocolate left and stir it into the melted chocolate until it is also melted, so that the finished, melted chocolate ends up around 88°F [31°C]. This method isn't foolproof, but it's worked for me 99 percent of the time.

TAPPING VS. BANGING In a few of the recipes in the book, I call for the pan to be "tapped" against the oven rack. This motion helps set the sides of the cookies, giving them a nice edge. I find it is an important step in baking some of the cookies in this book, and the recipe will call for it if I think it is beneficial. This tapping motion is different than "banging" the pan repeatedly to make ripply edges, and that method is explained in more detail in "Pan-Banging Cookies" (see page 226).

Cookie Baking Tips

Here are a few tips specific to cookie baking, to help you through this book.

- Make sure to beat the butter and sugar together as directed. Most recipes call for a "light and fluffy" texture, which means beating these two ingredients together for 2 to 3 minutes. It is also important to have the butter at the temperature the recipe calls for. If no temperature is indicated, this means that it can be used cold.

- The best way to get cookies in a consistent, uniform shape is to use a cookie scoop or kitchen scale. The recipes in this book indicate what size each cookie should be for best results. You can weigh the dough individually and roll into balls, or use a scoop that portions out the correct size.

- After I am done mixing a dough in the stand mixer, I always take a spatula and give the dough a final mix, making sure that it is perfectly combined and that there are no streaks of butter or pockets of flour. Stand mixers can occasionally miss the very bottom of the bowl, and I check frequently to make sure that there are no stray ingredients lurking there.

- To flatten the cookies without the dough sticking to the bottom of the cup, gently grease a small square of parchment paper with cooking spray, and place that between the dough and the glass when flattening.

- Lining your pans and using the correct pan the recipe calls for will help ensure your cookies are baked evenly.

- If your cookies are consistently not turning out right—burning on the edges, not cooking through, splotchy, etc.—your oven could be the problem. Make sure you have an oven thermometer to check if your oven is heating properly, and check for any hot spots.

- It's often hard to wait to eat cookies, but letting them cool as called for will help them reach the right texture. So, if possible, resist the urge to dive right in.

STORING COOKIES Most cookies are best eaten the day they're made, or within a day or two of baking. If you can't finish off a baker's dozen in 24 hours flat, the good news is that you can freeze them! Make sure your cookies are cool, then place them on a lined sheet pan in a single layer. Let them freeze for an hour or two, then once they are frozen solid, move them to labeled freezer-safe bags or containers to store. They can be stored for 1 month in the freezer. Move them to the refrigerator the night before serving.

GIVING COOKIES Many people like to mail cookies as gifts or take them on long trips. If you are thinking of doing so, here are some tips. Fragile cookies and cookies that need to be refrigerated should not be mailed. Pick sturdy cookies that will hold up over the distance or bar cookies that don't crumble easily. Place the cookies in an airtight container, then pack the container in a mailable box filled with bubble wrap or other filler to keep them from bumping around. If the cookies are spending a few days in the box, you can wrap each one individually in the airtight container.

INGREDIENTS

The following is a list of ingredients used in this book. Most of these ingredients should be available at your local grocery store, but for the few that are specialty items or hard to find, I have included a resources section at the back of the book (page 298) to help you locate them.

Dairy + Eggs

BUTTER All the recipes in this book call for unsalted butter. If you are a fan of salted butter and decide to use it instead, you will want to use a little less salt overall in the recipe. European-style butter cannot always be swapped for regular butter; the high fat content can cause extra spreading or other problems. If European-style butter is used, it will be noted in the recipe. For grocery store brands, I prefer Land O'Lakes Unsalted Sweet Butter. I do not suggest substituting oils for butter.

CREAM CHEESE I prefer Philadelphia brand cream cheese in my recipes; I find it tastes best overall and gives baked goods a "creamier" feel.

CRÈME FRAÎCHE is a matured cream with a tangy flavor and smooth texture. It is used occasionally in this book, and there is a recipe for making it at home in the "Extras" chapter (page 284).

EGGS All the recipes here call for Grade A large eggs. In its shell, a large egg should weigh 2 oz [57 g]. For egg-rich recipes (such as Pastry Cream, page 280), I like to use local, farm-fresh eggs because they typically have beautiful, orange yolks. If the recipe calls for room-temperature eggs, you can place the eggs in a large bowl, cover them with warm water, and let them sit for 10 minutes. If you need to separate the egg whites and the yolk, it's generally easier to start with a cold egg because the yolk will be firmer.

HEAVY CREAM Look for a heavy cream that is pasteurized, not ultra-pasteurized, if possible, especially when making crème fraîche. Heavy cream is also known as double cream.

MILK I tested all the recipes in this book with whole milk. I don't recommend replacing most recipes with a lower-fat milk as this can possibly change the outcome of the recipe.

Cooking Oils

CANOLA OIL Canola oil is the most common oil you'll find called for in this book, because of its neutral flavor.

OLIVE OIL Use a good-quality extra-virgin olive oil so the flavor shines in the final product.

TOASTED SESAME OIL I love the flavor of toasted sesame oil, and while it is usually used in savory cooking, I've found pairing it with sugar is delicious. I have a few recipes in the book that include it.

Salt + Spices

FLEUR DE SEL This is a delicate, moist salt that is usually used as a finishing salt. Because the crystals are larger, the salt takes longer to dissolve, and the taste lingers a bit longer.

SPICES Make sure your spices haven't been sitting in your cupboard for years before using them. Although they appear to last forever, they do have a shelf life and can grow stale or rancid over time.

Spices retain their freshness for 6 months to a year.

TABLE SALT I use table salt rather than kosher salt in all the recipes in this book unless otherwise noted.

Sweeteners

BROWN SUGAR Light brown sugar was used for recipe testing in this book. If dark brown sugar is needed, it will be specified in the recipe.

CONFECTIONERS' SUGAR Confectioners' sugar is also known as powdered sugar and icing sugar.

CORN SYRUP Do not substitute dark corn syrup for light; it has a more robust flavor and is not a good replacement in these recipes.

GRANULATED SUGAR Granulated sugar (also known as white sugar) was used to test all the recipes in this book. Organic sugar can be substituted, but please note that it often has a coarser grain than regular white sugar, which means it won't melt as quickly as more finely ground sugar. If organic sugar is preferred, it can be processed in a food processor until it is finely ground before using.

> *A Note on Beet vs. Cane Sugar:* While scientists insist there is no chemical difference between beet and cane sugar, many bakers claim there is a noticeable difference in their baking outcome, citing that the beet sugar burns more quickly and less evenly, and many macaron enthusiasts swear the beet sugar affects their cookies in a negative way. For most cookie baking I haven't noticed a huge difference, but when I am working with sugar at high temperatures—for instance, making Caramel (page 283),

crème brûlée, or Macarons (page 193)—I use cane sugar. Many manufacturers do not specify what type of sugar they are using, but C&H is pure cane sugar.

SANDING SUGAR Sanding sugar is a large-crystal sugar that doesn't dissolve while baking. It is used mainly for decorating.

Flour

ALL-PURPOSE FLOUR All the recipes in this book were tested with Gold Medal unbleached all-purpose flour, unless otherwise noted in the recipe. Different brands of flours have varying levels of protein, ranging from low to high, which can result in very different outcomes when baking. I've found Gold Medal to be the best option for the recipes in this book.

I highly recommend a digital scale to measure flour and have provided weight measurements. I recommend the dip-and-sweep method for flour if you are not using a scale: Dip the measuring cup into the bag or container of flour, then pull the cup out with the flour overfilling the cup. Sweep the excess off the top with a knife, so that you have a level cup of flour.

ALMOND FLOUR Almond flour is also found in most grocery stores' baking aisles or can be ordered online. Look for blanched almond flour, which removes the almond skins before processing.

HAZELNUT FLOUR Hazelnut flour is found in most grocery stores' baking aisles or can be ordered online. If you can't find it, you can finely pulse skinned hazelnuts in a food processor.

Leavenings

BAKING POWDER I use nonaluminum baking powder when I bake, as brands with aluminum can give off the taste of metal. Baking powder can expire. To check if your baking powder is still potent, add a spoonful of it to a cup of hot water. If it bubbles, it is still good to use.

BAKING SODA In order for baking soda to rise, it needs to be paired with an acidic ingredient, such as buttermilk, sour cream, yogurt, vinegar, coffee, molasses, brown sugar, or pumpkin. You can also check baking soda for freshness the same way you would check baking powder.

Nuts

I usually toast nuts as soon as I purchase them and then store them in the freezer, as nuts can turn rancid. To toast nuts: Place an oven rack in the middle position and preheat the oven to 350°F [180°C]. Line a sheet pan with parchment paper and place the nuts in the prepared pan in a single layer. Bake for 5 to 10 minutes, until the nuts darken and are fragrant. Let them cool, and then store them in a plastic freezer bag in the freezer for up to 1 month.

Chocolate

BITTERSWEET/SEMISWEET CHOCOLATE When shopping for semisweet and bittersweet bar chocolate to use in baking, look for one that falls between 35 and 60 percent cacao, and don't use anything over 70 percent, as this can alter the taste and texture of the recipe. (*Bittersweet* and *semisweet* can be confusing terms, as both can mean chocolate with a cacao percentage of anywhere from 35 to 99 percent.) Most recipes in this book call for semisweet chocolate.

When melting chocolate, chop the bar into fine pieces. This will help the chocolate melt more quickly and evenly and will give it less opportunity to burn. Make sure that there is no water in your bowl when melting, or on your knife and spatula, as contact with water can cause the chocolate to seize, turning it grainy. Adding a tablespoon or two of hot water to the seized chocolate and then stirring it can sometimes save it.

To melt chocolate in the microwave: Place the chopped chocolate in a microwave-safe bowl, and microwave the chocolate on medium for 1 minute, then stop and stir the chocolate. Continue to microwave the chocolate in 20-second intervals, stirring after each one, until the chocolate is almost completely smooth. Remove the bowl from the microwave and then stir until completely smooth.

CACAO NIBS Cacao nibs have a complex, bitter flavor and are crunchy to eat.

CHOCOLATE CHIPS Chocolate chips have less cacao than bar chocolate, which allows them to hold their shape when melted. This does mean, however, that they are not always a good substitution for bar chocolate.

COCOA POWDER There are two kinds of cocoa powder: Dutch-process and natural. Dutch-process cocoa is treated; it is washed with an alkaline solution that neutralizes its acids and has a more mellow, nutty flavor and a richer color. Natural cocoa powder is left as is and is a very acidic, sharp powder. The recipes in this book all call for Dutch-process cocoa powder.

WHITE CHOCOLATE White chocolate is made from cocoa butter. Not all white chocolate is created equal, so use a brand you trust when baking with it. White chocolate chips do not melt well. White chocolate also melts more quickly than dark chocolate, so be sure to stir it more frequently than you would dark chocolate, especially when using the microwave.

Vanilla

VANILLA BEANS To use a vanilla bean: Use a sharp knife to split the bean lengthwise, and then scrape the seeds out of the bean with the dull side of the knife or a spoon. Use the seeds in the recipe as called for. The leftover pod can be dried and then finely ground in a food processor to make a vanilla bean powder.

VANILLA EXTRACT All the recipes in this book use pure vanilla extract, and I don't recommend using artificial vanilla, as the taste is, well, artificial.

EQUIPMENT

Measuring Equipment

DIGITAL SCALE A digital scale will ensure that ingredients are measured correctly. Throughout this book, I have weights listed for most ingredients. I have not included small measurements that are less than 4 tablespoons. A digital scale can also be used for portioning out cookie dough and dividing cake batter evenly between pans.

MEASURING CUPS AND SPOONS Dry measuring cups measure dry ingredients. I use metal cups that come in these sizes: $1/4$ cup, $1/3$ cup, $1/2$ cup, and 1 cup. I use metal measuring spoons for teaspoon and tablespoon measures: $1/4$ teaspoon, $1/2$ teaspoon, 1 teaspoon, and 1 tablespoon. For liquids, I use glass measuring cups with pourable spouts and measurements marked along the side of the cup.

Utensils

BENCH SCRAPER A bench scraper is a great tool used for so many things, from transferring ingredients to lifting dough off the counter, cutting dough, and cleaning the work surface.

FOOD PROCESSOR I use a food processor for pulverizing nuts and grating carrots quickly.

HEAVY-DUTY STAND MIXER If you do a lot of baking, I highly recommend investing in a stand mixer for both convenience and speed. The recipes in this book call for one, but a handheld mixer or sturdy wooden spoon can be substituted.

INSTANT-READ THERMOMETER An instant-read thermometer is an essential tool and is especially useful when making caramel. As its name suggests, it tells the temperature instantly, so you have a better chance of making your confections perfectly.

KITCHEN SCISSORS Kitchen scissors have many functions, like cutting parchment paper and pastry bag tips, as well as snipping dough.

KITCHEN TORCH I use my kitchen torch to caramelize sugar, brown meringues, and toast marshmallows.

MICROWAVE OVEN A microwave oven is a useful alternative to a double boiler for melting butter and chocolate, and also works well to heat milk.

OFFSET SPATULA Offset spatulas are used for spreading batter evenly and icing cookies and cakes. I use both large and small ones, and prefer them with a rounded edge over a straight edge.

OVEN THERMOMETER Many ovens are not properly calibrated, and this can greatly affect the outcome of your baked good. I have an inexpensive oven thermometer that I keep hanging on the middle rack of my oven.

PARCHMENT PAPER I use parchment paper for lining sheet pans when baking cookies and use it as a sling when making bars, for easy removal. I like to buy parchment paper from a restaurant supply store, where the sheets come precut and lie flat.

PASTRY BRUSHES Pastry brushes have so many uses—glazing, coating, and brushing away crumbs and excess flour. I use a natural-bristle brush; I've found they work much better than silicone, although they need to be replaced more frequently.

PORTION SCOOP Portion scoops are a great way to scoop cookies, helping to ensure consistent and even shapes. They are not essential, but I highly recommend them. Vollrath makes a reliable scoop that doesn't break easily.

RULER Rulers are useful for measuring when cutting bars. I have an 18 in [46 cm] long ruler that works perfectly.

SHEET PAN I use medium-weight half sheet pans (12 by 16 in [30.5 by 40.5 cm] with a 1 in [2.5 cm] rim), unless otherwise noted.

SILICONE SPATULA Spatulas are an essential kitchen tool with many uses: folding, smoothing, stirring, mixing, and scraping, just to name a few.

SKEWERS I use wooden skewers for testing when bars and brownies are done. A toothpick can also be used.

WIRE COOLING RACK Cooling racks help the bottom of baked goods stay crisp and also help speed up cooling times.

WIRE WHISK I use whisks for many kitchen tasks, such as beating eggs and combining dry ingredients.

ZESTER A Microplane zester comes in handy when a recipe calls for freshly grated nutmeg or gingerroot, or the zest of an orange or a lemon.

CHAPTER 1
The Classics

"I believe the nicest and sweetest days... bring simple **little pleasures,** following one another softly, like pearls slipping off a string."

—L. M. Montgomery, *Anne of Avonlea*

Soft Chocolate Chip Cookies

As much as I like crisp, rich chip cookies packed with dark chopped chocolate and sprinkled with sea salt, I am convinced there is still a need for a basic, soft chocolate chip cookie that doesn't require much work or pretention. At least, that's what my kids tell me on a weekly basis. After trying all the chocolate chip cookies in this book, they have declared this simple one to be their very favorite, and each time I make them, I have to agree.

MAKES ABOUT 20 COOKIES

2½ cups [355 g] all-purpose flour

1 teaspoon baking soda

¾ teaspoon salt

12 tablespoons [1½ sticks or 170 g] unsalted butter, at room temperature

¾ cup [150 g] granulated sugar

¾ cup [150 g] brown sugar

2 large eggs

1½ teaspoons pure vanilla extract

7 oz [198 g] semisweet or bittersweet chocolate, chopped into bite-size pieces, or 1¼ cups [226 g] semisweet chocolate chips

1) Adjust an oven rack to the middle of the oven. Preheat the oven to 350°F [180°C]. Line three sheet pans with parchment paper. 2) In a medium bowl, whisk together the flour, baking soda, and salt. 3) In the bowl of a stand mixer fitted with a paddle, beat the butter on medium speed until creamy, about 1 minute. Add the granulated and brown sugars and beat on medium speed until light and fluffy, 2 to 3 minutes. Scrape down the sides of the bowl, add the eggs and vanilla, and mix until smooth. Add the flour mixture and beat on low speed until just combined. Add the chocolate and mix into the batter on low speed. 4) Form the dough into 1½ oz [45 g] balls (2 tablespoons) and place 8 cookies on each sheet pan.

5) Bake one pan at a time, rotating halfway through baking. Bake for 8 minutes, until the cookies are slightly puffed in the center. Give the pan a slight tap in the oven. Bake the cookies until the edges are just turning golden brown but the center is still soft, 2 or 3 minutes more (10 to 11 minutes total). 6) Give the pan one final tap in the oven and then transfer the pan to a wire rack to cool. Let the cookies cool completely before removing from the pan. When pulled from the oven, the cookies will look puffed and light in color, but they will slowly deflate as they cool on the pan. Store cookies in an airtight container at room temperature for up to 5 days.

NOTE Using chocolate chips instead of chopped chocolate will make for a puffier cookie.

Brown Butter Chocolate Chip Cookies

While declaring in the previous recipe the need for just a simple chocolate chip cookie, I occasionally require some luxury in my daily life. These cookies demand a little more work, but you won't regret the effort, especially as the warm chocolate pockets hit your tongue and perfectly mix with the crisp, buttery edge. A tiny burst of salt will cause your closed eyes to flutter open in delight, and from that day forward these cookies will quietly call to you, like the song of the Sirens to the sailors, like the waves of the Sundering Seas to the Elves . . .

MAKES ABOUT 20 COOKIES

2 cups [284 g] all-purpose flour

1 teaspoon baking powder

1/2 teaspoon baking soda

12 tablespoons [1 1/2 sticks or 170 g] unsalted butter, at room temperature

3/4 cup [150 g] granulated sugar

3/4 cup [150 g] brown sugar

1 tablespoon pure vanilla extract

3/4 teaspoon salt

1 large egg plus 1 large yolk

8 oz [226 g] bittersweet chocolate, chopped into bite-size pieces

Fleur de sel, for finishing (optional)

1) Adjust an oven rack to the middle of the oven. Preheat the oven to 350°F [180°C]. Line three sheet pans with parchment paper. **2)** In a small bowl, whisk together the flour, baking powder, and baking soda. **3)** Slice 4 tablespoons [57 g] of the butter into four pieces, and place them in a large bowl. Melt the remaining 8 tablespoons [113 g] of butter in a medium skillet over medium-high heat. Brown the butter until it is dark golden brown and is giving off a nutty aroma, 2 to 3 minutes (for tips on browning butter, see page 280). Pour the browned butter (and any bits of browned butter stuck to the bottom of the skillet) into the bowl with the room-temperature butter, and stir until all the butter is melted and combined. Stir in the granulated and brown sugars, vanilla, and salt with a rubber spatula, mixing until combined. Whisk in the egg and the yolk until fully combined, about 45 seconds, until it is smooth and glossy. Let the batter sit for 2 to 3 minutes, and then whisk again for 45 seconds. Pour the flour mixture into the bowl and use the spatula to combine (it may take a minute to incorporate all the dry ingredients). Place the chopped chocolate over the dough and use your hands to knead it in until it is evenly distributed (you can use a spatula here, too, but I've found my hands make for quick work).

The dough will be very shiny, slick, and dense, and it will take a minute to incorporate the chocolate. 4) Form the dough into 1 1/2 oz [45 g] balls (2 tablespoons). Place 8 cookies on each sheet pan. 5) Bake one pan at a time, rotating halfway through baking. For soft cookies with a gooey center, bake the cookies until the sides are set, the centers are very puffed, and the dough is still light, 8 to 9 minutes. For cookies with a crispy edge and tender center, bake until the cookies are light golden brown around the edges and the centers are still slightly puffed, 9 to 10 minutes. For cookies with a crisp edge and firm center, bake until the cookies are golden brown around the edges and the centers have begun to collapse, 10 to 11 minutes. 6) Transfer the pan to a wire rack and let the cookies cool for 10 minutes, then move the cookies to the wire rack to cool. Sprinkle the cookies with fleur de sel, if desired, a few minutes after they emerge from the oven. Store cookies in an airtight container at room temperature for up to 3 days, but they're best eaten warm.

NOTE I like using a combination of chocolate; I use 5 oz [142 g] of Guittard semisweet or bittersweet baking wafers and 3 oz [85 g] of Vahlrona CARAÏBE feves. For a more developed flavor, the dough can be rested (or aged) for up to 48 hours in the refrigerator. Place balls of formed dough on a sheet pan lined with parchment and cover with plastic wrap. Cookies can then be baked as directed, adding a little baking time (about a minute) to the chilled cookies. These cookies will be plumper and won't spread as much.

Thin and Crispy Chocolate Chip Cookies

Crispy cookie lovers of the world, rejoice: I didn't forget about you and your need for a good chocolate chip cookie. This cookie is thin and crunchy, as its title boasts, with a rich, buttery flavor and just enough chocolate.

MAKES ABOUT 30 COOKIES

2 cups [284 g] all-purpose flour

1 teaspoon salt

½ teaspoon baking soda

1 cup [2 sticks or 227 g] unsalted butter, at room temperature

1½ cups [300 g] granulated sugar

¼ cup [50 g] brown sugar

2 large eggs

3 tablespoons water

1 tablespoon pure vanilla extract

4 oz [113 g] semisweet or bittersweet chocolate, very finely chopped (or ¾ cup [135 g] mini chocolate chips will work, too)

1) Adjust an oven rack to the middle of the oven. Preheat the oven to 350°F [180°C]. Line three sheet pans with aluminum foil, dull-side up. **2)** In a small bowl, whisk together the flour, salt, and baking soda. **3)** In the bowl of a stand mixer fitted with a paddle, beat the butter on medium speed until creamy, about 1 minute. Add the granulated and brown sugars and beat on medium speed until light and fluffy, 2 to 3 minutes. Scrape down the sides of the bowl and add the eggs, water, and vanilla, and mix on low speed to combine. Add the flour mixture and mix on low speed until combined. Add the chocolate and mix into the batter on low speed. Remove the bowl from the mixer and use a spatula to make sure the dough is completely mixed. **4)** Form the dough into 1 oz [28 g] balls (1½ tablespoons). Place 6 cookies an equal distance apart onto the prepared sheet pans. The cookies will spread quite a bit, so make sure they are a good distance apart. **5)** Bake one pan at a time, rotating halfway through baking. Bake until light golden brown, 15 to 17 minutes. **6)** Transfer the sheet pan to a wire rack; let the cookies cool for 10 minutes on the pan, then move them to a wire rack to finish cooling. The cookies will crisp up as they cool down. Store cookies in an airtight container at room temperature for up to 3 days.

Thin and Crispy Double Chocolate Cookies

Thin and crispy like the previous cookie, only chocolatier.

MAKES ABOUT 30 COOKIES

1³⁄₄ cups [249 g] all-purpose flour

1⁄3 cup [33 g] Dutch-process cocoa powder

1 teaspoon salt

1⁄2 teaspoon baking soda

1 cup [2 sticks or 227 g] unsalted butter, at room temperature

1¹⁄2 cups [300 g] granulated sugar

1⁄4 cup [50 g] brown sugar

2 large eggs

3 tablespoons water

1 tablespoon pure vanilla extract

4 oz [113 g] semisweet or bittersweet chocolate, very finely chopped (or 3⁄4 cup [135 g] mini chocolate chips will work, too)

1) Adjust an oven rack to the middle of the oven. Preheat the oven to 350°F [180°C]. Line three sheet pans with aluminum foil, dull-side up. 2) In a small bowl, whisk together the flour, cocoa powder, salt, and baking soda. 3) In the bowl of a stand mixer fitted with a paddle, beat the butter on medium speed until creamy, about 1 minute. Add the granulated and brown sugars and beat on medium speed until light and fluffy, 2 to 3 minutes. Scrape down the sides of the bowl and add the eggs, water, and vanilla, and mix on low speed to combine. Add the flour mixture and mix on low speed until combined. Add the chocolate and mix into the batter on low speed. Remove the bowl from the mixer and use a spatula to make sure the dough is completely mixed. 4) Form the dough into 1 oz [28 g] balls (1¹⁄2 tablespoons). Place 6 cookies an equal distance apart onto the prepared sheet pans. The cookies will spread quite a bit, so make sure they are a good distance apart. 5) Bake one pan at a time, rotating halfway through baking. Bake until light golden brown, 15 to 17 minutes. 6) Transfer the sheet pan to a wire rack; let cool for 10 minutes on the pan, then move the cookies to a wire rack to finish cooling. The cookies will crisp up as they cool down. Store cookies in an airtight container at room temperature for up to 3 days.

Peanut Butter Cookies

Chocolate chip cookies will always have the number-one place in my heart, but peanut butter runs a very close second. This cookie has extra peanut flavor thanks to the additions of candied peanuts, and has the perfect balance of softness and crunch.

MAKES ABOUT 24 COOKIES

2 cups plus 3 tablespoons [311 g] all-purpose flour

1 teaspoon baking soda

3/4 teaspoon salt

1 cup [2 sticks or 227 g] unsalted butter, at room temperature

1 cup [200 g] brown sugar

1/2 cup [100 g] granulated sugar

1 cup [215 g] creamy peanut butter

1 large egg

2 teaspoons pure vanilla extract

3/4 cup [105 g] Candied Nuts, Peanuts variation (optional, page 291)

1) Adjust an oven rack to the middle of the oven. Preheat the oven to 350°F [180°C]. Line three sheet pans with parchment paper. 2) In a medium bowl, whisk together the flour, baking soda, and salt. 3) In the bowl of a stand mixer fitted with a paddle, beat the butter on medium speed until creamy, about 1 minute. Add the brown and granulated sugars and beat on medium speed until light and fluffy, 2 to 3 minutes. Add the peanut butter and beat on medium speed until fully combined. Add the egg and vanilla and beat on medium speed until smooth. Add the flour mixture and beat on low speed until just combined. Stir in the candied peanuts, if using. 4) Form the dough into 1 1/2 oz [45 g] balls (2 tablespoons). Place 8 cookies on each sheet pan, and use the tines of a fork to make a crisscross shape over the top of each one (the cookies will flatten slightly when you do this, but you don't want them to flatten too much). 5) Bake one pan at a time, rotating halfway through baking. Bake until the cookies have spread and the edges are set, 9 to 10 minutes. 6) Transfer the pan to a wire rack and let the cookies cool completely on the pan. Store cookies in an airtight container at room temperature for up to 3 days.

Sugar Cookies

Growing up, my dad would always try to sneak little pieces of the sugar cookie dough while my mom was baking. It is a vivid childhood memory: watching his head peek around the corner, checking to see if her back was turned, and then making a dash for the bowl. She would yell and throw a towel at him, and my sister and I would giggle and hope he would share some with us while we followed him out of the kitchen (he always did).

MAKES ABOUT 20 COOKIES

2½ cups plus 1 tablespoon [364 g] all-purpose flour

¾ teaspoon baking soda

¾ teaspoon salt

¼ teaspoon cream of tartar

1 cup [2 sticks or 227 g] unsalted butter, at room temperature

1¾ cups [350 g] granulated sugar, plus ½ cup [100 g] for rolling

1 large egg plus 1 large yolk

1 tablespoon pure vanilla extract

1) Adjust an oven rack to the middle of the oven. Preheat the oven to 350°F [180°C]. Line three sheet pans with parchment paper. 2) In a medium bowl, combine the flour, baking soda, salt, and cream of tartar. 3) In the bowl of a stand mixer fitted with a paddle, beat the butter on medium speed until creamy, about 1 minute. Add 1¾ cups [350 g] of the granulated sugar and beat on medium speed until light and fluffy, 2 to 3 minutes. Add the egg, yolk, and vanilla, and beat on medium speed until combined. Add the flour mixture and beat on low speed until just combined. 4) Place the remaining ½ cup [100 g] of sugar in a medium bowl.
5) Form the cookies into 1½ oz [45 g] balls (2 tablespoons). Roll each ball in the sugar and place 8 cookies on each sheet pan. 6) Bake one pan at a time, rotating halfway through baking. Bake until the sides are set and the bottoms are light golden brown, 12 to 14 minutes.
7) Transfer the sheet pan to a wire rack and let the cookies cool for 5 to 10 minutes on the pan, then remove them and let them cool completely on the wire rack. Store cookies in an airtight container at room temperature for up to 3 days.

Brown Sugar Cookies

I will never say no to a simple sugar cookie, but adding brown sugar makes for an interesting twist on the classic white version. A teaspoon of molasses increases the dark brown sugar flavor without making it taste like holiday fare.

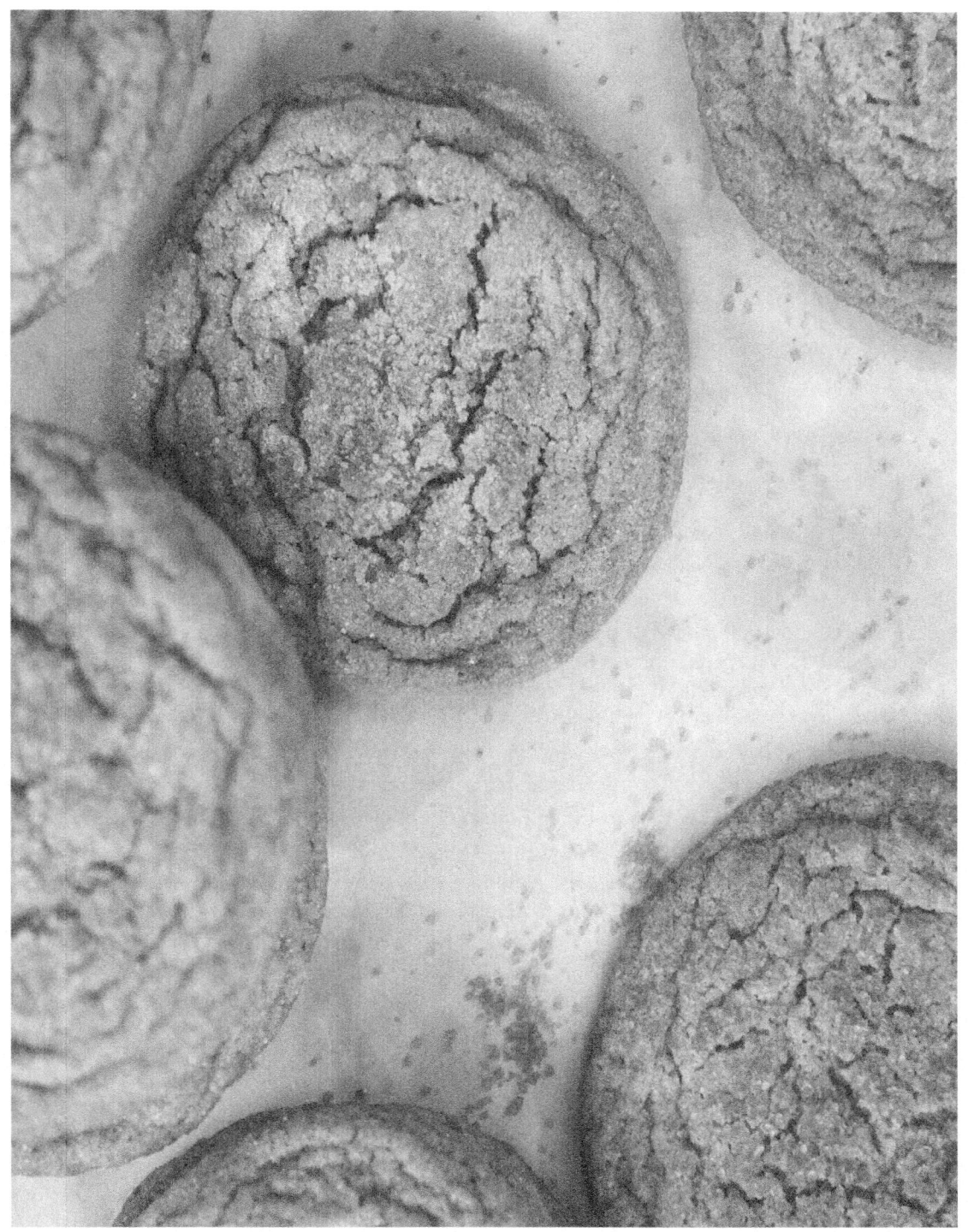

MAKES ABOUT 20 COOKIES

2½ cups plus 1 tablespoon [364 g] all-purpose flour

¾ teaspoon baking soda

¾ teaspoon salt

1 cup [2 sticks or 227 g] unsalted butter, at room temperature

1¾ cups [350 g] dark brown sugar

1 teaspoon molasses

1 large egg plus 1 large yolk

2 teaspoons pure vanilla extract

½ cup [100 g] granulated sugar, for rolling

1) Adjust an oven rack to the middle of the oven. Preheat the oven to 350°F [180°C]. Line three sheet pans with parchment paper. **2)** In a medium bowl, combine the flour, baking soda, and salt. **3)** In the bowl of a stand mixer fitted with a paddle, beat the butter on medium speed until creamy, about 1 minute. Add the brown sugar and the molasses and beat on medium speed until light and fluffy, 2 to 3 minutes. Add the egg, yolk, and vanilla, and beat on medium speed until combined. Add the flour mixture and beat on low speed until just combined. **4)** Place the granulated sugar in a medium bowl. **5)** Form the cookies into 1½ oz [45 g] balls (2 tablespoons). Roll each ball in the sugar and place 8 cookies on each sheet pan. **6)** Bake one pan at a time, rotating halfway through baking. Bake until the sides are set and the bottoms are light golden brown, 10 to 11 minutes. **7)** Transfer the sheet pan to a wire rack and let the cookies cool for 5 to 10 minutes on the pan, then remove them and let them cool completely on the wire rack. Store cookies in an airtight container at room temperature for up to 3 days.

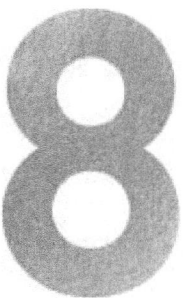

Chocolate Sugar Cookies

Sugar cookies are great, but chocolate sugar cookies are the bee's knees. These little circles are full of chocolate flavor, with crisp edges and a tender center.

MAKES ABOUT 20 COOKIES

2 cups [284 g] all-purpose flour

1/2 cup [50 g] Dutch-process cocoa powder

3/4 teaspoon baking soda

3/4 teaspoon salt

1 cup [2 sticks or 227 g] unsalted butter, at room temperature

1 3/4 cups [350 g] granulated sugar, plus 1/2 cup [100 g] for rolling

1 large egg plus 1 large yolk

2 teaspoons pure vanilla extract

1) Adjust an oven rack to the middle of the oven. Preheat the oven to 350°F [180°C]. Line three sheet pans with parchment paper. 2) In a small bowl, combine the flour, cocoa powder, baking soda, and salt. 3) In the bowl of a stand mixer fitted with a paddle, beat the butter on medium speed until creamy, about 1 minute. Add 1 3/4 cups [350 g] of the sugar, and beat again until light and fluffy, 2 to 3 minutes. Add the egg, yolk, and vanilla, and beat on low speed until combined. Add the flour mixture and beat again on low speed until combined. 4) Place the remaining 1/2 cup [100 g] of sugar in a medium bowl. 5) Scoop the dough into 1 1/2 oz [45 g] portions (2 tablespoons). Roll each ball in the sugar. Place 8 cookies on each sheet pan. 6) Bake one pan at a time, rotating halfway through baking. Bake until the sides are set and the top begins to crackle, 12 to 14 minutes. 7) Transfer the sheet pan to a wire rack and let the cookies cool for 5 to 10 minutes

on the pan, then remove the cookies and let them cool completely on the wire rack. Store cookies in an airtight container at room temperature for up to 3 days.

VARIATIONS
• *Cardamom Chocolate Sugar Cookies—Add 1 teaspoon of ground cardamom to the sugar used for rolling.*

• *Chocolate Mint Sugar Cookies—Add 1 teaspoon of mint extract along with the vanilla.*

• *Double Chocolate Sugar Cookies—Add 3 oz [85 g] of chopped semisweet or bittersweet chocolate after mixing in the dry ingredients.*

Brownie Cookies

This rich brownie cookie is thinner than the classic bar brownie, but all the necessary chocolate flavor is there. Sometimes I swirl in a teaspoon or two of peanut butter (see variation) just to take these over the top.

MAKES ABOUT 16 COOKIES

3/4 cup plus 1 tablespoon [116 g] all-purpose flour

3/4 teaspoon baking powder

3 large eggs, at room temperature

1 1/4 cups [250 g] granulated sugar

3/4 teaspoon salt

1 tablespoon canola oil

1 teaspoon pure vanilla extract

5 tablespoons [70 g] unsalted butter

8 oz [226 g] semisweet or bittersweet chocolate

1/4 cup [25 g] Dutch-process cocoa powder

1) Adjust an oven rack to the middle of the oven. Preheat the oven to 350°F [180°C]. Line two sheet pans with parchment paper. 2) In a small bowl, whisk together the flour and baking powder, and set aside. 3) In the bowl of a stand mixer fitted with a paddle, beat the eggs, sugar, and salt on medium-high speed until the mixture is pale and doubled in volume, 6 to 8 minutes. Turn the mixer to low speed and stir in the canola oil and vanilla until just combined. 4) While the egg mixture is beating, melt the butter and chocolate. Place the butter in a small, heavy-bottom saucepan set over low heat. Add the chocolate and melt together, stirring frequently, until smooth. Off the heat, add the cocoa powder to the chocolate and whisk until completely combined. 5) Add the warm chocolate-butter mixture to the egg mixture and mix on low speed until combined. Add the flour

mixture and mix on low speed until combined. Let the mixture sit at room temperature for 5 minutes. **6)** Use a small scoop or two spoons to drop heaping tablespoons of batter onto the prepared sheet pans, spacing them at least 2 in [5 cm] apart, fitting 12 on a pan. **7)** Bake the cookies one pan at a time, rotating halfway through baking. Bake until the cookies are puffed and cracked and the edges are set, 8 to 12 minutes. **8)** Transfer the sheet pan to a wire rack and let the cookies cool completely on the pan. The cookies are best the day of baking but will keep in an airtight container at room temperature for up to 2 days.

VARIATION
- *With Peanut Butter—Drop 1 heaping teaspoon of peanut butter on top of each brownie dough ball and use a knife to swirl.*

Chocolate Crinkle Cookies

I never knew I needed these cookies in my life; as a child I gravitated toward cookies that were shoved full of coated candy and sprinkles over a dusting of confectioners' sugar. Adulthood finally knocked some sense into me, and now these little crinkles are on regular rotation during the holiday months and quite a few hot summer days, too.

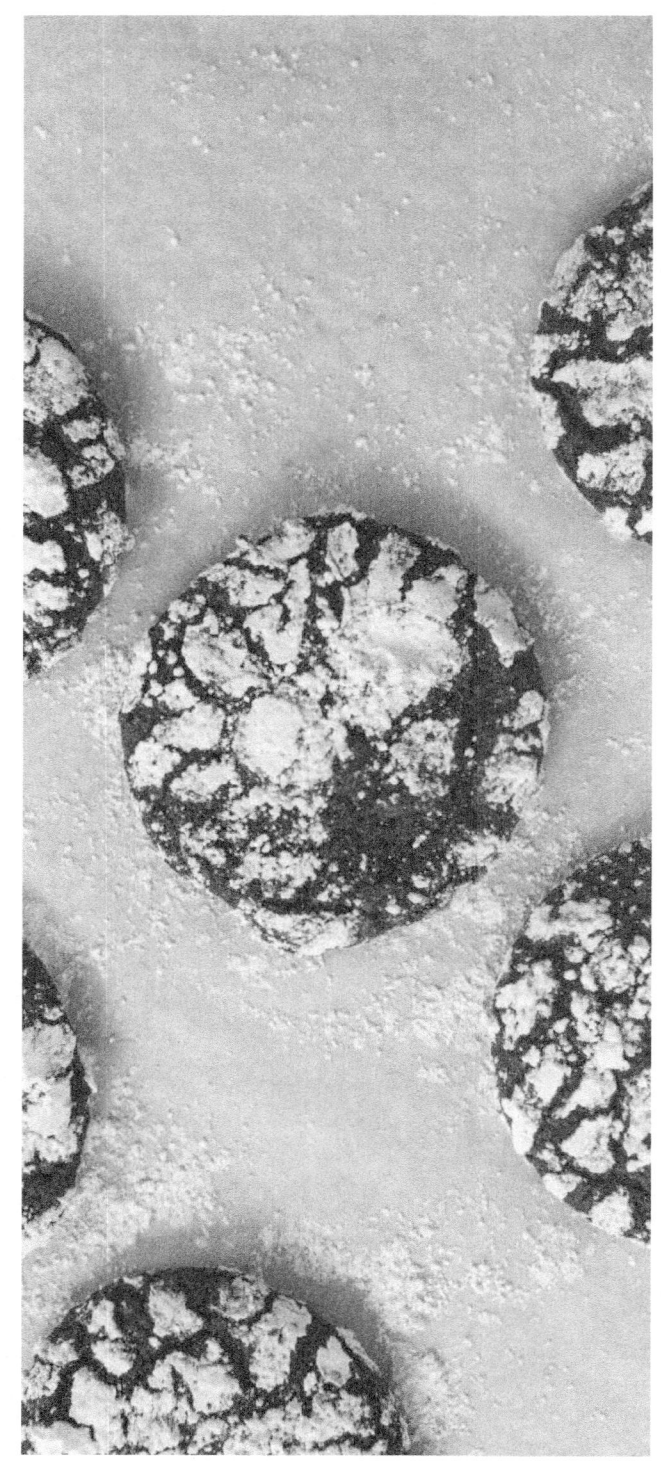

MAKES ABOUT 20 COOKIES

1 1/3 cups [190 g] all-purpose flour

1 teaspoon baking powder

1/8 teaspoon baking soda

3/4 cup [150 g] granulated sugar, plus 3 tablespoons [45 g] for rolling

1/2 cup [100 g] brown sugar

2 large eggs plus 2 large yolks, at room temperature

1 tablespoon canola oil

1 teaspoon pure vanilla extract

1/2 teaspoon salt

1/4 cup [57 g] unsalted butter

3 oz [85 g] semisweet or bittersweet chocolate

1/2 cup [50 g] Dutch-process cocoa powder

1/2 cup [60 g] confectioners' sugar

1) Adjust an oven rack to the middle of the oven. Preheat the oven to 350°F [180°C]. Line three sheet pans with parchment paper. 2) In a small bowl, whisk together the flour, baking powder, and baking soda. 3) In a large bowl, whisk together 3/4 cup [150 g] of the granulated sugar, the brown sugar, eggs, yolks, canola oil, vanilla, and salt. 4) Place the butter and chocolate in a small, heavy-bottom saucepan set over low heat and melt together, stirring frequently to prevent the chocolate from scorching. Continue cooking until the mixture is smooth. Off the heat, add the cocoa powder to the chocolate and whisk until completely combined, about 45 seconds. 5) Add the warm chocolate-butter mixture to the egg mixture and whisk together until combined. Add the flour mixture and use a rubber spatula to mix gently until combined. Let the mixture sit at room temperature for 10 minutes. 6) Combine the confectioners' sugar and the remaining 3 tablespoons [45 g] of granulated sugar in a small bowl. Scoop the dough into 1 1/2 oz [45 g] portions (2 tablespoons). Roll the dough in the sugar mixture. Place 7 cookies on each sheet pan. 7) Bake one pan at a time,

rotating halfway through baking. Bake until the edges are set and the cookies are puffed but still soft in the center, 8 to 9 minutes for very soft cookies, and 9 to 10 minutes for a cookie with firm edges and a tender center. 8) Transfer the sheet pans to a wire rack and let the cookies cool to room temperature. Cookies can be stored in an airtight container at room temperature for up to 3 days.

NOTE The dough is very sticky, so using a cookie scoop works best here; I like to drop the dough balls into the sugar and then gently roll them. Once they are covered, they are easy to pick up. If you don't have a cookie scoop, you can refrigerate the dough for 15 minutes or so to help it scoop easier.

11

Snickerdoodles

The definition of the word *snicker* involves such nouns as *chuckle, cackle, giggle,* and *boff.* I would like to note that those descriptions explain exactly what my kids do every time I say the word *snickerdoodle*—they find the name hilarious, and laugh with the warm sugar-and-cinnamon coating all over their faces and hands.

MAKES ABOUT 24 COOKIES

2½ cups [355 g] all-purpose flour

1 teaspoon cream of tartar

¾ teaspoon baking soda

¾ teaspoon salt

12 tablespoons [1½ sticks or 170 g] unsalted butter, at room temperature

2 oz [57 g] shortening or refined coconut oil

1¾ cups [350 g] granulated sugar, plus ⅓ cup [65 g] for rolling

1 large egg plus 1 large yolk

1 tablespoon pure vanilla extract

1 tablespoon ground cinnamon

1) Adjust an oven rack to the middle of the oven. Preheat the oven to 350°F [180°C]. Line three sheet pans with parchment paper. 2) In a small bowl, combine the flour, cream of tartar, baking soda, and salt. 3) In the bowl of a stand mixer fitted with a paddle, mix the butter and shortening together on medium speed until creamy, about 1 minute. Add 1¾ cups [350 g] of the sugar, and beat again on medium speed until light and fluffy, 2 to 3 minutes. Add the egg, yolk, and vanilla, and beat on low speed until combined. Add the flour mixture and beat again on low speed until combined. 4) Combine the remaining ⅓ cup [65 g] of sugar and the cinnamon together in a small bowl. 5) Scoop the dough into 1½ oz [45 g] portions (2 tablespoons). Roll the balls in the cinnamon sugar mixture. Place 8 cookies on each sheet pan. 6) Bake one pan at a time, rotating halfway through baking. Bake until the sides are set and the tops begins to crackle, 12 to 14 minutes. 7) Transfer the sheet pans to a wire rack and let the cookies cool on the pans to room temperature. Cookies can be stored in an airtight container at room temperature for up to 3 days.

Ginger Cookies

Ginger cookies will never fail to invoke memories of my Great-Aunt Frannie. Opening the door to her home meant breathing in the faint smell of ginger and molasses, no matter whether it was winter or spring, and her freezer was forever *packed* with a baker's dozen, plus some. While her version was sweet and full of snap, I've gone the opposite direction and made mine tender, with a bit of spice.

MAKES ABOUT 22 COOKIES

2½ cups [355 g] all-purpose flour

1½ teaspoons ground cinnamon

1 teaspoon baking soda

1 teaspoon ground ginger

¾ teaspoon salt

½ teaspoon grated nutmeg

Pinch cloves

12 tablespoons [1½ sticks or 170 g] unsalted butter, at room temperature

¾ cup [150 g] brown sugar

½ cup [100 g] granulated sugar, plus ½ cup [100 g] for rolling

⅓ cup [113 g] light molasses

1 large egg plus 1 large yolk

1 teaspoon pure vanilla extract

¼ cup [32 g] crystallized ginger, cut into tiny pieces

1) Adjust an oven rack to the middle of the oven. Preheat the oven to 350°F [180°C]. Line three sheet pans with parchment paper. 2) In a small bowl, whisk together the flour, cinnamon, baking soda, ginger, salt, nutmeg, and cloves. 3) In the bowl of a stand mixer fitted with a paddle, beat the butter on medium speed until creamy, about 1 minute. Add the brown sugar and ½ cup [100 g] of the granulated sugar, and beat on medium speed until light and fluffy, 2 to 3 minutes. Add the molasses and beat on low speed until well combined, stopping to scrape down the sides as needed. Add the egg, yolk, and vanilla, and mix on low speed to combine. Add the flour mixture and mix on low speed until combined. Add the crystallized ginger and mix into the batter on low speed. 4) Form the dough into 1½ oz [45 g] balls (2 tablespoons). Roll each ball in the remaining ½ cup [100 g] of granulated sugar, and place 8 cookies on each sheet pan. 5) Bake one pan at a time,

rotating halfway through baking. Bake until the cookies are puffed with cracks running along the tops, 9 minutes for soft cookies, and 10 to 11 minutes for a cakier cookie. Transfer the sheet pans to a wire rack and let the cookies cool completely. Store the cookies in an airtight container at room temperature for up to 3 days.

Oatmeal Raisin Cookies

Often, when chocolate is strutting around a bakery case, sending out its sexy, glossy vibes, the humble oatmeal cookie is completely overlooked. Small and round, filled with dried fruit and a handful of spices, this unassuming cookie doesn't always make a big splash. Its charm is subtle; it hums quietly while other confections roar. But, in all honesty, I'm fine with the majority of people passing by those raisin-filled circles because it just means there are more for me.

MAKES 20 COOKIES

1 1/3 cups [190 g] all-purpose flour

3/4 teaspoon baking soda

3/4 teaspoon ground cinnamon

1/2 teaspoon salt

1/4 teaspoon ground nutmeg

12 tablespoon [1 1/2 sticks or 170 g] unsalted butter, at room temperature

3/4 cup [150 g] brown sugar

1/2 cup [100 g] granulated sugar

1 large egg

2 teaspoons pure vanilla extract

1 1/2 cups [150 g] rolled oats

3/4 cup [105 g] raisins

1) Adjust an oven rack to the middle of the oven. Preheat the oven to 350°F [180°C]. Line three sheet pans with parchment paper. **2)** In a medium bowl, combine the flour, baking soda, cinnamon, salt, and nutmeg. **3)** In the bowl of a stand mixer fitted with a paddle, beat the butter on medium speed until creamy, about 1 minute. Add the brown and granulated sugars and beat on medium speed until light and fluffy, 2 to 3 minutes. Add the egg and vanilla and mix on medium speed until combined. Add the flour mixture and mix on low speed until just combined. Add the oats and mix on low speed until almost combined, then add the raisins and finish mixing on low speed. Using a spatula, stir the batter to incorporate any stray oats on the bottom of the mixing bowl. **4)** Form the dough into 1 1/2 oz [45 g] balls (2 tablespoons) and put 8 cookies on each sheet pan. **5)** Bake one pan at a time, rotating halfway through baking. Bake until the edges are light golden brown (the middle will still look slightly undercooked), 12 to 14 minutes. Give the pan a slight bang on the oven rack and then remove it from the oven. **6)** Transfer the sheet pan to a wire rack and let the cookies cool completely on the pan. Store cookies in an airtight container at room temperature for up to 3 days.

Thumbprints

There is some debate over where thumbprints originated, and many cultures have their own adaptation of this cookie. In Sweden, these little jam-packed treats are called *rosenmunnar*, which translates as "raspberry cave," and I think this is a perfect description. My version is made with hazelnut flour and strawberry, so it's not quite a perfect translation, but I think they are rather delicious regardless.

MAKES ABOUT 48 COOKIES

2 cups [284 g] all-purpose flour

1/2 cup [50 g] hazelnut flour (see page 19)

1/2 teaspoon salt

1/8 teaspoon baking soda

1 cup [2 sticks or 227 g] unsalted butter, at room temperature

3/4 cup [150 g] granulated sugar, plus 1/2 cup [100 g] for rolling

1 large egg plus 1 large yolk

1 teaspoon pure vanilla extract

3/4 cup [240 g] strawberry or other flavor jam

1) Adjust an oven rack to the middle of the oven. Preheat the oven to 350°F [180°C]. Line three sheet pans with parchment paper. **2)** In a medium bowl, whisk together the all-purpose flour, hazelnut flour, salt, and baking soda. **3)** In the bowl of a stand mixer fitted with a paddle, beat the butter on medium speed until creamy, about 1 minute. Add 3/4 cup [150 g] of the sugar and mix on medium speed until light and fluffy, 2 to 3 minutes. Scrape down the sides of the bowl and add the egg, yolk, and vanilla, and mix on low speed until combined. Add the flour mixture and mix on low speed until combined. Use a spatula to finish mixing and make sure the dough is evenly combined. **4)** Roll the dough into 1/2 oz [15 g] balls (about 2 teaspoons), and roll each ball in the remaining 1/2 cup [100 g] of sugar. Place 12 cookies, evenly spaced, on each sheet pan. Use your thumb (or a greased, rounded 1/2 teaspoon) to make an indentation in the middle of each ball of dough. Fill each indentation with a heaping 1/2 teaspoon of jam. **5)** Bake one pan at a time, rotating halfway through baking. Bake until the cookies are puffed, the sides are set, and the bottom is just beginning to turn light golden brown, 10 to 12 minutes. **6)** Transfer the pan to a wire rack and let the cookies cool on the pan. Store cookies in an airtight container at room temperature for up to 3 days.

NOTE I prefer Dickenson's Seedless Strawberry Preserves here, but other brands and flavors can be substituted with good results.

Sablés

With their buttery flavor, sandy texture, and sugar-coated edges, sablés will make you swoon with each bite. They are also the perfect slice-and-bake, make-ahead treat. Use European-style butter instead of the unsalted to make these extra buttery.

MAKES ABOUT 30 COOKIES

1 cup [2 sticks or 227 g] unsalted butter, at room temperature

1 cup [200 g] granulated sugar

½ teaspoon salt

1 large egg yolk

1 teaspoon pure vanilla extract

2 cups [284 g] all-purpose flour

1 cup [200 g] turbinado or sanding sugar, for sprinkling

1) In the bowl of a stand mixer fitted with a paddle, beat the butter on medium speed until creamy, about 1 minute. Add the granulated sugar and salt, and beat again on medium speed until light and fluffy, 2 to 3 minutes. Scrape down the bowl and add the egg yolk and vanilla, and mix on low speed until incorporated. Add the flour and mix on low speed until just combined. 2) Transfer the dough to a workspace and form the dough into a 12 in [30.5 cm] long log. Place the log on a large piece of plastic, a few inches longer than the log. Sprinkle the sanding sugar over each side of the log, covering the outside of the dough. Gently press the sugar into the dough with your hands. Wrap the log in the plastic wrap and refrigerate until firm, about 2 hours.

3) Adjust an oven rack to the middle of the oven. Preheat the oven to 350°F [180°C]. Line three sheet pans with parchment paper. 4) Slice the chilled log into ¼ in [6 mm] thick rounds. Space the rounds about 2 in [5 cm] apart on the sheet pans. 5) Bake one pan at a time, rotating halfway through baking. Bake until the edges are very

light golden brown but the centers are still pale, 14 to 16 minutes. **6)** Transfer the pan to a wire rack and let the cookies cool completely on the pan. Store cookies in an airtight container at room temperature for up to 4 days.

VARIATION
• *Pistachio Sablés—Mix $1/3$ cup [45 g] of chopped pistachios into the dough after mixing in the flour.*

16

Bourbon Sablés with Chocolate

Chocolate chip shortbread has made the rounds on social media, becoming famous for good reason. I decided to add chocolate to my Sablés recipe (page 56), along with a little splash of bourbon. The results are pretty little cookies that are crispy and buttery, with a perfect hit of booze and bittersweetness.

MAKES ABOUT 30 COOKIES

1 cup [2 sticks or 227 g] unsalted butter, at room temperature

1 cup [200 g] granulated sugar

1/2 teaspoon salt

1 large egg yolk

2 tablespoons bourbon

1 teaspoon pure vanilla extract

2 cups [284 g] all-purpose flour

2 oz [57 g] bittersweet or semisweet chocolate, chopped into small pieces

1 cup [200 g] sanding sugar, for sprinkling

1) In the bowl of a stand mixer fitted with a paddle, beat the butter on medium speed until creamy, about 1 minute. Add the granulated sugar and salt and beat again on medium speed until light and fluffy, 2 to 3 minutes. Scrape down the bowl and add the egg yolk, bourbon, and vanilla, and mix on low speed until incorporated. Add the flour and mix on low speed until just combined. Add the chocolate pieces and mix on low speed until just combined. **2)** Transfer the dough to a workspace and form the dough into a 12 in [30.5 cm] long log. Place the log on a large piece of plastic a few inches longer than the log. Sprinkle the sanding sugar over each side of the log, covering the outside of the dough. Gently press the sugar into the dough with your hands. Wrap the log in plastic wrap and refrigerate until firm, about 2 hours. **3)** Adjust an oven rack to the middle of the oven. Preheat the oven to 350°F [180°C]. Line three sheet pans with parchment paper. **4)** Slice the chilled log into 1/4 in [6 mm] thick rounds. Space the rounds about 2 in [5 cm] apart on the sheet pans. **5)** Bake one pan at a time, rotating halfway through baking. Bake until the edges are very light golden brown but the centers are still pale, 14 to 16 minutes. **6)** Transfer the pan to a wire rack and let the cookies cool completely on the pan. Store cookies in an airtight container at room temperature for up to 4 days.

Shortbread

Shortbread has many aficionados, but like all intense passions, there is a great divide among enthusiasts about principle and purpose. Many fanatics argue over whether to cream butter and sugar together initially, or work the butter into the flour toward the end of mixing. I found I preferred the latter method, which resulted in a crisp, golden, perfect triangle of a cookie. But fear not, beloved—there is room for compromise, as this cookie can be made both ways to the delight of all.

MAKES 16 WEDGES

2 large egg yolks

1 teaspoon pure vanilla extract

2 cups [284 g] all-purpose flour

½ cup [100 g] granulated sugar, plus more for sprinkling (optional)

½ cup [60 g] confectioners' sugar

½ teaspoon salt

1 cup [2 sticks or 227 g] unsalted butter, at room temperature, cut into 1 in [2.5 cm] pieces

1) Adjust an oven rack to the middle of the oven. Preheat the oven to 450°F [230°C]. Line a sheet pan with parchment paper. 2) In a small liquid measuring cup or bowl, use a fork to mix the egg yolks and vanilla together. 3) In the bowl of a food processor fitted with a blade, pulse the flour, granulated and confectioners' sugars, and salt together. Scatter the butter over the top of the flour mixture and pulse until the mixture looks like wet sand, 8 to 10 one-second pulses. Pour the egg yolk mixture over the top of the flour mixture, and pulse until the dough is smooth and starts to pull away from the sides of the processor, about 10 more one-second pulses. 4) Scrape the dough out of the processor and move it to the prepared pan. Pat the dough into a 10 in [25 cm] circle, smoothing the top with the bottom of a measuring cup. Score the shortbread into 16 wedges with a knife, cutting through the dough, and use the tines of a fork or a wooden skewer to poke holes in each wedge (the holes are purely decorative, so you can design them however you desire). Sprinkle the

shortbread generously with granulated sugar, if desired. **5)** Place the shortbread in the oven and turn the oven temperature down to 300°F [150°C]. Bake until the shortbread is pale golden and firm to the touch, 45 minutes to 1 hour. Remove the pan from the oven and let the shortbread cool for several hours. Cut the shortbread at the scored marks. Shortbread can be stored in an airtight container at room temperature for 4 to 5 days.

To make the shortbread the opposite way, in a stand mixer: Beat the butter on low speed until creamy. Add the sugars and mix together on medium speed until light and fluffy, 3 to 4 minutes. Scrape down the sides and add the egg yolks, vanilla, and salt, mixing on low speed until combined. Add the flour and mix on low speed until combined. Continue with the above directions.

VARIATIONS
• *Lemon Shortbread*—Add 1 tablespoon of grated lemon zest to the flour mixture.

• *Espresso Shortbread*—Add 1 teaspoon of espresso grounds to the flour mixture.

Cut Out Cookies

Cut out cookies come in handy many times throughout the year: Christmas, of course, but also Halloween and Valentine's Day and birthdays and just because. This dough is very forgiving, rolls out smooth, and can be rerolled multiple times with good results.

MAKES ABOUT 5 DOZEN COOKIES

4 cups [568 g] all-purpose flour

1 teaspoon salt

3/4 teaspoon baking powder

1/4 teaspoon baking soda

1 1/2 cups [3 sticks or 339 g] unsalted butter, at room temperature

3 tablespoons unrefined coconut oil, at room temperature

1 3/4 cups [350 g] granulated sugar

1 large egg plus 1 large yolk

1 tablespoon pure vanilla extract

SIMPLE GLAZE

2 cups [240 g] confectioners' sugar

1 tablespoon unsalted butter, melted

1 teaspoon pure vanilla extract

Pinch salt

3 to 6 tablespoons [45 to 80 g] water

1) In a large bowl, whisk together the flour, salt, baking powder, and baking soda. 2) In the bowl of a stand mixer fitted with a paddle, mix the butter on medium speed until creamy, about 1 minute. Add the coconut oil and mix again on medium speed until smooth. Add the granulated sugar and mix again on medium speed until light and creamy, 3 to 5 minutes. Add the egg, yolk, and vanilla, and mix again on low speed until combined. Add the flour mixture and mix on low speed until completely combined. Use a spatula to fold in any dry pieces of dough that may be lingering on the bottom of the bowl. 3) Divide the dough in half. The dough can be used immediately, or wrapped in plastic and refrigerated for up to 2 days (let the dough come to room temperature before rolling).
4) Adjust an oven rack to the middle of the oven. Preheat the oven to 350°F [180°C]. Line several sheet pans with parchment paper. 5) On a floured surface, roll the dough somewhere between $1/8$ in [4 mm] and $1/4$ in [6 mm] thick (the thinner the cookie, the crisper it will be, so this will depend on your preference). Use cookie cutters to cut out shapes, then slide a spatula underneath the dough and move the shapes to the sheet pans, leaving 1 in [2.5 cm] of space between the cookies. Chill the pan of cookies in the refrigerator for 15 minutes before baking. Dough scraps can be rerolled and cut out again. 6) Bake one pan at a time, rotating halfway through baking. For a

softer cookie, bake for 12 minutes; for a crisper cookie, bake until light golden brown around the edges, 14 to 16 minutes. Transfer the pan to a wire rack and let the cookies cool completely before glazing.

FOR THE GLAZE

1) Place the confectioners' sugar in a medium bowl. Add the melted butter, vanilla, salt, and 3 tablespoons of water, and stir to combine. If the mixture is very thick, add 1 tablespoon of water at a time until the desired consistency is reached. 2) Spread the glaze on the cooled cookies. Once the glaze is set, cookies can be stored in an airtight container at room temperature for 3 days.

CHAPTER 2
Brownies + Blondies

"All the variety, all the charm, all the beauty of life is made up of light and shadow."

—Leo Tolstoy, *Anna Karenina*

My Favorite Brownies

This recipe is from my first book and I haven't changed it at all, because I am highly devoted to it. Imagine if boxed brownies and all their chewy goodness were actually chocolaty and delicious—that's what I set out to do here. I was ecstatic to see people making this recipe and enjoying the results, so I didn't have the heart to tinker with it at all. I have added some variations in the recipes that follow if you do have my first book, so you can change things up if you so desire.

MAKES 12 LARGE OR 24 SMALL BROWNIES

1 cup plus 2 tablespoons [160 g] all-purpose flour

3/4 teaspoon salt

1/2 teaspoon baking powder

4 large eggs, at room temperature

1 1/2 cups [300 g] granulated sugar

1/2 cup [100 g] packed brown sugar

1/2 cup [112 g] canola oil

2 teaspoons pure vanilla extract

8 tablespoons [1 stick or 113 g] unsalted butter

8 oz [226 g] bittersweet chocolate, chopped

1/4 cup [25 g] Dutch-process cocoa powder

1) Adjust an oven rack to the middle of the oven. Preheat the oven to 350°F [180°C]. Grease a 9 by 13 in [23 by 33 cm] baking pan and line with a parchment sling. 2) In a small bowl, whisk together the flour, salt, and baking powder. 3) In a large bowl, whisk together the eggs, granulated and brown sugars, canola oil, and vanilla. 4) Place the butter and chocolate in a small, heavy-bottom saucepan set over low heat and melt together, stirring frequently to prevent the chocolate from scorching. Continue cooking until the mixture is smooth. Off the heat, add the cocoa powder to the chocolate and whisk until completely combined.

5) Add the chocolate mixture to the sugar-egg mixture and whisk until smooth. Add the flour mixture and stir with a spatula until just combined. 6) Pour the batter into the prepared pan and bake for 22 to 27 minutes, until the sides of the brownies have set, the top is starting to crackle and look glossy, and a wooden skewer or toothpick inserted into the center comes out with crumbs. The batter on the toothpick should not be wet but should have a good amount of crumbs clinging to it. 7) Transfer the pan to a wire rack and let cool completely. Use the parchment sling to gently lift the brownies from the pan. Cut them into bars and serve. Store brownies in an airtight container at room temperature for up to 2 days.

Fudgy Brownies

While My Favorite Brownies (page 68) are a middle-of-the-road affair, this fudgy version finds itself falling off the cliffs of chocolate insanity. Extra chocolate, cocoa, butter, and eggs may be the culprits. These are best eaten in small bites.

MAKES 12 LARGE OR 24 SMALL BROWNIES

3 large eggs plus 3 large yolks, at room temperature

1 cup [200 g] granulated sugar

1/2 cup [100 g] packed brown sugar

3/4 teaspoon salt

2 teaspoons pure vanilla extract

9 oz [255 g] bittersweet chocolate, chopped into small pieces

8 tablespoons [1 stick or 113 g] cold unsalted butter

1/2 cup [50 g] Dutch-process cocoa powder

1/2 cup [71 g] all-purpose flour

1) Adjust an oven rack to the middle of the oven. Preheat the oven to 350°F [180°C]. Grease a 8 by 8 in [20 by 20 cm] baking pan and line with a parchment sling. **2)** In the bowl of a stand mixer fitted with a paddle, beat the eggs, yolks, granulated and brown sugars, and salt on medium-high speed until the mixture is light in color and has doubled in volume, 5 to 6 minutes. Turn the mixer to low speed and mix in the vanilla until just combined. **3)**

While the egg mixture is beating, melt the chocolate and butter. Place the chocolate and butter in a small, heavy-bottom saucepan set over low heat and melt together, stirring frequently to prevent the chocolate from scorching. Continue cooking until the mixture is smooth. Off the heat, add the cocoa powder to the chocolate and whisk until completely combined.

4) Add the warm chocolate-butter mixture to the egg mixture and mix on low speed until combined. Add the flour and use a spatula to gently combine. 5) Pour the batter into the prepared pan and bake for 22 to 27 minutes, until the sides of the brownies have set, the top is starting to crackle and look glossy, and a wooden skewer or toothpick inserted into the center comes out with crumbs. The batter on the toothpick should not be wet but should have a good amount of crumbs clinging to it. 6) Transfer the pan to a wire rack and let cool completely. Use the parchment sling to gently lift the brownies from the pan. Cut them into bars and serve. Store brownies in an airtight container at room temperature for up to 2 days.

21

Cakey Brownies

Brownie purists may give some side eye at the mention of cakey brownies; by their definition, brownies should be rich with chocolate and fudgy in texture, and anything else is sacrilege. However, I have heard whispers that, in fact, there are many who do love a good cakey brownie, and so I set out to create this variation to satisfy those that needed one. I prefer these plain, but if you need frosting on yours, I've included that for you, too.

MAKES 12 LARGE OR 24 SMALL BROWNIES

1 1/2 cups [213 g] all-purpose flour

1 teaspoon baking powder

3/4 teaspoon salt

4 large eggs, at room temperature

1 1/2 cups [300 g] granulated sugar

1/2 cup [100 g] packed brown sugar

1/2 cup [112 g] canola oil

2 teaspoons pure vanilla extract

6 oz [170 g] bittersweet chocolate, chopped

8 tablespoons [1 stick or 113 g] unsalted butter

1/4 cup [25 g] Dutch-process cocoa powder

FROSTING (OPTIONAL)

4 oz [113 g] semisweet chocolate

8 tablespoons [1 stick or 113 g] unsalted butter, at room temperature

2 tablespoons corn syrup

1 teaspoon pure vanilla extract

Pinch salt

1 cup [120 g] confectioners' sugar

Sprinkles for decorating (optional)

1) Adjust an oven rack to the middle of the oven. Preheat the oven to 350°F [180°C]. Grease a 9 by 13 in [23 by 33 cm] baking pan and line with a parchment sling. 2) In a small bowl, whisk together the flour, baking powder, and salt. 3) In a large bowl, whisk together the eggs, granulated and brown sugars, oil, and vanilla. 4) Place the chocolate and butter in a small, heavy-bottom saucepan set over low heat and melt together, stirring frequently to prevent the chocolate from scorching. Continue cooking until the mixture is smooth. Off the heat, add the cocoa powder to the chocolate and whisk until completely combined. 5) Add the chocolate mixture to the sugar-egg mixture and whisk until smooth. Add the flour mixture and stir with a spatula until just combined. 6) Pour the batter into the prepared pan and bake for 20 to 22 minutes, until the sides of the brownies have set, the top is starting to crackle and look glossy, and a wooden skewer or toothpick inserted into the center comes out with crumbs. The batter on the toothpick should not be wet but should have a good amount of crumbs clinging to it. 7) Transfer the pan to a wire rack and let cool completely. Frost the brownies and add sprinkles, if desired. Use the parchment sling to gently lift the brownies from the pan. Cut them into bars and serve. Store brownies in an airtight container at room temperature for up to 2 days.

FOR THE FROSTING

1) Melt the chocolate in a heatproof bowl set over a pan of boiling water, being careful not to let the water touch the bottom of the bowl, and stir constantly until just melted. Remove from the heat and stir until smooth. 2) In the bowl of a stand mixer fitted with a paddle, beat the butter on medium speed until creamy, 2 to 3 minutes. Add the corn syrup, vanilla, and salt, and mix again on medium speed until light and creamy, 2 to 3 minutes. Scrape down the sides, add the confectioners' sugar, and mix again on medium speed until light, 2 to 3

minutes. Add the chocolate, and mix on low speed until combined. Finish mixing with a spatula, making sure the chocolate is evenly incorporated.

Cream Cheese Brownies

If twirling cream cheese filling into brownie batter is wrong, then I don't want to be right.

MAKES 12 LARGE OR 24 SMALL BROWNIES

8 oz [226 g] cream cheese, at room temperature

1/3 cup [65 g] granulated sugar

2 tablespoons unsalted butter, at room temperature

2 tablespoons all-purpose flour

1/2 teaspoon pure vanilla extract

Pinch salt

1 large egg

1 recipe My Favorite Brownies (page 68)

1) Adjust an oven rack to the middle of the oven. Preheat the oven to 350°F [180°C]. Grease a 9 by 13 in [23 by 33 cm] baking pan and line with a parchment sling. 2) In a medium bowl, mix together the cream cheese, sugar, butter, flour, vanilla, and salt until no lumps remain. Add the egg and mix again until combined. 3) Make the brownie batter as directed. Put two-thirds of the brownie batter in the prepared pan. Dollop the cream cheese and remaining brownie batter over the top, alternating the two. Drag the tip of a butter knife through the batter, creating swirls.

4) Bake until the sides of the brownies have set, the top is starting to crackle and look glossy, and a wooden skewer or toothpick inserted into the center comes out with crumbs, 28 to 34 minutes. The batter on the toothpick should not be wet but should have a good amount of crumbs clinging to it. 5) Transfer the pan to a wire rack and let cool completely. Use the parchment sling to gently lift the brownies from the pan. Cut them into bars and serve. Store brownies in an airtight container at room temperature for up to 2 days.

23

Turtle Brownies

Each Christmas throughout my childhood, my grandma would buy a box of fancy turtle candies and give them to my mom, who would immediately hide them from the rest of the family, sneaking bites here and there around the house while we begged her to share. They seemed like such a delicacy to my little eyes: caramel covered in chocolate and topped with a fancy pecan. When I recently gave my mom a small bag filled with these turtle brownies to try, I watched her tuck them away in her purse and then sneak nibbles, her eyes blinking their approval. Some things never change.

MAKES 12 LARGE OR 24 SMALL BROWNIES

CARAMEL

1 1/2 cups [300 g] granulated sugar

1/4 cup [60 g] water

3 tablespoons corn syrup

1/4 teaspoon salt

7 tablespoons [105 g] heavy cream

2 tablespoons unsalted butter

1 teaspoon pure vanilla extract

1 recipe My Favorite Brownies (page 68), Cakey Brownies (page 71), or White Chocolate Brownies (page 88), baked and fully cooled

3/4 cup [90 g] pecans, toasted and chopped into small pieces

FOR THE CARAMEL

In a large, heavy-bottom saucepan (the caramel will bubble up quite a bit once it starts cooking, so it's important to have a pan that is deep), combine the sugar, water, corn syrup, and salt, stirring very gently to combine while trying to avoid getting any sugar crystals on the sides of the pan. Cover the pot, and bring to a boil over medium-high heat, until the sugar has melted and the mixture is clear, 3 to 5 minutes. Uncover, and then cook until the sugar has turned a pale golden color, 4 to 5 minutes more, and registers about 300°F [150°C] on a candy thermometer. Turn the heat down slightly, and cook for a few minutes more until the sugar is golden and registers 350°F [180°C]. Remove the pot immediately from the heat and add the heavy cream. The cream will foam considerably, so be careful pouring it in. Add the butter next, followed by the vanilla, and stir to combine. Set aside to cool for 5 to 10 minutes. Pour the caramel over the cooled brownies, using an offset spatula to smooth it evenly. Sprinkle the chopped pecans over the caramel, and then refrigerate for 2 hours. When ready to serve, cut into bars. Brownies can be stored in an airtight container at room temperature for up to 3 days.

NOTES Keeping the lid on the pot during the first few minutes of boiling creates condensation, which helps melt sugar hanging out on the sides of the pan. If the caramel is too hard to cut through after chilling, let it sit out for 15 to 20 minutes.

Rocky Road Brownies

Brownies of their own accord are divine, elegant, and classic. Adding piles of mini marshmallows and chocolate chips may seem on first appearance to be rather lowbrow, but on second thought, one will lay aside any pretentiousness and just go for it. There is no shame in devouring any of these extra ingredients in my house.

MAKES 12 LARGE OR 24 SMALL BROWNIES

1 cup plus 2 tablespoons [160 g] all-purpose flour

3/4 teaspoon salt

1/2 teaspoon baking powder

1 cup [170 g] semisweet chocolate chips

1 cup [120 g] toasted pecans, chopped into small pieces

1 cup [50 g] mini marshmallows

4 large eggs, at room temperature

1 1/2 cups [300 g] granulated sugar

1/2 cup [100 g] packed brown sugar

1/2 cup [112 g] canola oil

2 teaspoons pure vanilla extract

8 oz [226 g] bittersweet chocolate, chopped

8 tablespoons [1 stick or 113 g] unsalted butter

1/4 cup [25 g] Dutch-process cocoa powder

1) Adjust an oven rack to the middle of the oven. Preheat the oven to 350°F [180°C]. Grease a 9 by 13 in [23 by 33 cm] baking pan and line with a parchment sling. 2) In a small bowl, whisk together the flour, salt, and baking powder. 3) In another small bowl, mix together the chocolate chips, pecan pieces, and mini marshmallows. 4) In a large bowl, whisk together the eggs, granulated and brown sugars, oil, and vanilla. 5) Place the chocolate and butter in a small, heavy-bottom saucepan set over low heat and melt together, stirring frequently to prevent the chocolate from scorching. Continue cooking until the mixture is smooth. Off the heat, add the cocoa powder to the chocolate and whisk until completely combined.

6) Add the chocolate mixture to the sugar-egg mixture and whisk until smooth. Add the flour mixture and stir with a spatula until just combined. Add half of the pecan pieces, mini marshmallows, and chocolate chips, and finish stirring. Pour the batter evenly into the prepared pan, then sprinkle the remaining half of the pecan pieces, mini marshmallows, and

chocolate chips over the top. 7) Bake for 25 to 29 minutes, until the sides of the brownies have set, the top is starting to crackle and look glossy, and a wooden skewer or toothpick inserted into the center comes out with crumbs. The batter on the toothpick should not be wet but should have a good amount of crumbs clinging to it. 8) Transfer the pan to a wire rack and let cool completely. Use the parchment sling to gently lift the brownies from the pan. Cut them into bars and serve. Store brownies in an airtight container at room temperature for 2 to 3 days.

25

Swirl Brownies, Two Ways

Sweetened condensed milk swirled into chocolate makes a delicious addition to my brownie base. I've added coconut cream and milk chocolate to make two decadent versions.

MAKES 12 LARGE OR 24 SMALL BROWNIES

COCONUT CREAM SWIRL BROWNIES

3/4 cup [50 g] sweetened shredded coconut

1/2 cup [120 g] sweetened condensed milk

1/2 teaspoon coconut extract

Pinch salt

1 recipe My Favorite Brownies (page 68) or Cakey Brownies (page 71)

1) Adjust an oven rack to the middle of the oven. Preheat the oven to 350°F [180°C]. Grease a 9 by 13 in [23 by 33 cm] baking pan and line with a parchment sling. 2) In a medium bowl, mix together the

shredded coconut, sweetened condensed milk, coconut extract, and salt until combined. 3) Make the brownie batter as directed. Pour the brownie batter into the prepared pan, and use an offset spatula to spread evenly. Dollop the coconut mixture over the top of the brownies, then drag the tip of a butter knife through the batter, creating swirls.

4) Bake until the sides of the brownies have set and a wooden skewer or toothpick inserted into the center comes out with crumbs, 28 to 34 minutes. The batter on the toothpick should not be wet but should have a good amount of crumbs clinging to it. 5) Transfer the pan to a wire rack and let cool completely. Use the parchment sling to gently lift the brownies from the pan. Cut them into bars and serve. Store brownies in an airtight container at room temperature for up to 2 days.

MILK CHOCOLATE SWIRL BROWNIES

½ cup [120 g] sweetened condensed milk

4 oz [113 g] milk chocolate, melted and cooled

Pinch salt

1 recipe My Favorite Brownies (page 68) or Cakey Brownies (page 71)

1) Adjust an oven rack to the middle of the oven. Preheat the oven to 350°F [180°C]. Grease a 9 by 13 in [23 by 33 cm] baking pan and line with a parchment sling. 2) In a medium bowl, mix together the sweetened condensed milk, melted milk chocolate, and salt until combined. 3) Make the brownie batter as directed. Pour the brownie batter into the prepared pan, and use an offset spatula to spread evenly. Dollop the chocolate mixture over the top of the brownies, then drag the tip of a butter knife through the batter, creating swirls.

4) Bake until the sides of the brownies have set and a wooden skewer or toothpick inserted into the center comes out with crumbs, 28 to 34 minutes. The batter on the toothpick should not be wet but should have a good amount of crumbs clinging to it. **5)** Transfer the pan to a wire rack and let cool completely. Use the parchment sling to gently lift the brownies from the pan. Cut them into bars and serve. Store brownies in an airtight container at room temperature for up to 2 days.

VARIATIONS

• *Milk Chocolate Cacao Nib Crunch Swirl Brownies*—Add ¾ cup [105 g] Candied Cacao Nibs (page 291) to the brownie batter, and swirl in the milk chocolate mixture as directed.

• *Milk Chocolate Candied Nut Swirl Brownies*—Add ¾ cup [105 g] Candied Nuts, Peanuts variation (page 291) to the brownie batter, and swirl in the milk chocolate mixture as directed.

Marshmallow Peanut Butter Brownies

I have a recipe for peanut butter cups on my website that I love to make. I realized recently the filling would probably also taste incredible swirled into chocolate brownies. It did. I then decided to take things one step further and also twirl in some marshmallow cream, which naturally made them even better.

MAKES 12 LARGE OR 24 SMALL BROWNIES

1/2 cup [107 g] creamy peanut butter

1/4 cup [30 g] confectioners' sugar

2 tablespoons [29 g] unsalted butter, at room temperature

3/4 teaspoon pure vanilla extract

Pinch salt

1 recipe My Favorite Brownies (page 68) or Cakey Brownies (page 71)

1/2 cup [70 g] store-bought marshmallow fluff

1) Adjust an oven rack to the middle of the oven. Preheat the oven to 350°F [180°C]. Grease a 9 by 13 in [23 by 33 cm] baking pan and line with a parchment sling. 2) In a medium bowl, mix together the peanut butter, sugar, butter, vanilla, and salt until combined and completely smooth. 3) Make the brownie batter as directed. Pour the brownie batter into the prepared pan. Dollop the peanut butter filling and the marshmallow cream over the top, alternating the two. Drag the tip of a butter knife through the batter, creating swirls. 4) Bake until the sides of the brownies have set, the top is starting to crackle and look glossy, and a wooden skewer or toothpick inserted into the center comes out with crumbs, 26 to 32 minutes. The batter on the toothpick should not be wet but should have a good amount of crumbs clinging to it. 5) Transfer the pan to a wire rack and let cool completely. Use the parchment sling to gently lift the brownies from the pan. Cut them into bars and serve. Store brownies in an airtight container at room temperature for up to 2 days.

NOTE I actually prefer these brownies on the second day; the marshmallow fluff softens and the chocolate flavor intensifies.

27

Peanut Butter Crunch Brownies

Peanut butter and chocolate go together like eggs and bacon, macaroni and cheese, coffee and donuts, maybe even Romeo and Juliet. Cacao nibs add both a bitter note that offsets the sweetness and richness of the chocolate and peanut butter, and a much-needed crunch.

MAKES 12 LARGE OR 24 SMALL BROWNIES

PEANUT BUTTER FILLING

1 1/2 cups [323 g] creamy peanut butter

1/2 cup [60 g] confectioners' sugar

4 tablespoons [57 g] unsalted butter, at room temperature

1/2 teaspoon pure vanilla extract

Pinch salt

CHOCOLATE GANACHE

10 oz [283 g] semisweet or bittersweet chocolate, finely chopped

1 cup [240 g] heavy cream

1 recipe My Favorite Brownies (page 68) or Cakey Brownies (page 71), baked and cooled

1/2 cup [60 g] cacao nibs

FOR THE FILLING

In a medium bowl, combine the peanut butter, sugar, butter, vanilla, and salt, and stir until completely smooth.

FOR THE GANACHE

Place the chocolate in a small bowl. Heat the heavy cream in a small saucepan until it is simmering and just about to boil. Pour the cream over the chocolate, cover the bowl with plastic wrap, and let sit for 5 minutes. Remove the plastic and whisk until completely smooth. Let cool to room temperature.

TO ASSEMBLE

When the brownies have cooled, place the peanut butter filling on top and use an offset spatula to smooth the peanut butter. Sprinkle the cacao nibs evenly over the peanut butter. Chill in the freezer for 15 minutes. Remove the pan from the freezer, and pour the room-temperature ganache over the top of the peanut butter. Use an offset spatula to carefully smooth it over the top of the bars. Let the bars sit until the chocolate is set. Carefully remove the bars from the pan (you may need to run a knife around the edges to loosen them a bit) and move to a countertop. Cut the brownies into pieces. Store brownies in an airtight container in the refrigerator for up to 3 days.

28

Chocolate Basil Brownies

I have loved the pairing of chocolate and basil together ever since my first encounter with it eighteen years ago at the now-defunct Lucia's restaurant. There it was basil ice cream paired with chocolate cake; here it is chocolate brownies topped with basil-infused buttercream. If basil isn't your thing, you can substitute mint leaves instead.

MAKES 12 LARGE OR 24 SMALL BROWNIES

BASIL BUTTERCREAM

1 cup [20 g] basil leaves

1/2 cup [120 g] whole milk

1/2 cup [120 g] half-and-half

3/4 cup [150 g] granulated sugar

1/4 cup [36 g] all-purpose flour

1/4 teaspoon salt

1 cup [2 sticks or 227 g] unsalted butter, at room temperature

1 teaspoon pure vanilla extract

Green food coloring (optional)

CHOCOLATE GANACHE

10 oz [283 g] semisweet or bittersweet chocolate, finely chopped

1 cup [240 g] heavy cream

1 recipe My Favorite Brownies (page 68) or Cakey Brownies (page 71), baked, cooled completely, and refrigerated in the pan for 1 hour

FOR THE BASIL BUTTERCREAM

1) Combine the basil leaves, milk, and half-and-half in a medium saucepan. Heat gently over medium heat until just simmering, then remove from the heat. Let cool and then refrigerate for at least 2 hours and up to overnight. Remove the basil leaves from the cream,

and then squeeze the leaves over the cream. Discard the leaves. **2)** In a medium bowl, whisk together the sugar, flour, and salt really well (the sugar will help keep the flour from lumping when it boils, so spend a good minute really whisking it together). Place the mixture in a medium, heavy-bottom saucepan. Slowly pour the basil cream into the flour, whisking to combine as you pour. Cook over medium heat, stirring constantly with a whisk, until the mixture comes to a gentle boil (periodically run a spatula round the edges of the saucepan to remove any flour lurking there). Reduce the heat slightly, and continue to whisk and occasionally stir until the mixture has thickened considerably, 2 to 3 minutes. Remove from the heat and continue stirring for 30 seconds. **3)** Transfer the mixture to a bowl and cover with plastic wrap, making sure the plastic sits directly on the surface (this will help keep it from forming a skin). Let cool to room temperature. **4)** When the mixture has cooled, place the butter in the bowl of a stand mixer fitted with a paddle, and beat on medium speed until smooth and creamy, scraping down the sides as needed. Start adding the flour mixture a few spoonfuls at a time, mixing on low speed after each addition, until it is all incorporated. Scrape down the sides and mix on medium speed until the buttercream is light and fluffy, 2 to 3 minutes. Add the vanilla and food coloring, if using, and mix on low speed until combined.

FOR THE GANACHE

Place the chocolate in a small bowl. Heat the heavy cream in a small saucepan until it is simmering and just about to boil. Pour the cream over the chocolate, cover the bowl with plastic wrap, and let sit for 5 minutes. Remove the plastic and whisk until completely smooth. Let cool to room temperature.

TO ASSEMBLE

1) Spread the basil buttercream evenly on top of the chilled brownies. Return the pan to the refrigerator and chill for 1 hour. Pour the cooled ganache over the top of the chilled buttercream and, using an offset spatula, spread it in an even layer. Return the pan to the refrigerator for 1 hour. **2)** Remove the pan from the refrigerator and let sit for 10 minutes before cutting, to allow the glaze to soften slightly. Cut into bars and serve. Store brownies in an airtight container in the refrigerator for up to 3 days.

White Chocolate Brownies

When I set out to make a white chocolate version of the beloved brownie, I didn't expect to like it as much as I do. Using a good white chocolate is the key to success here (see Note). I recommend using Guittard's white chocolate baking wafers or Valrhona Blond Dulcey feves.

MAKES 12 LARGE OR 24 SMALL BROWNIES

2 cups [284 g] all-purpose flour

¾ teaspoon salt

½ teaspoon baking powder

5 large eggs, at room temperature

1½ cups [300 g] granulated sugar

½ cup [100 g] brown sugar

¼ cup [56 g] canola oil

1 tablespoon pure vanilla extract

8 oz [226 g] white chocolate

8 tablespoons [1 stick or 113 g] unsalted butter, at room temperature

1) Adjust an oven rack to the middle of the oven. Preheat the oven to 350°F [180°C]. Grease a 9 by 13 in [23 by 33 cm] baking pan and line with a parchment sling. 2) In a small bowl, whisk together the flour, salt, and baking powder. 3) In a large bowl, whisk together the eggs, granulated and brown sugars, oil, and vanilla. 4) Place the chocolate and butter in a small, heavy-bottom saucepan set over low heat and melt together, stirring frequently to prevent the chocolate from scorching. Continue cooking until the mixture is smooth. 5) Add the white chocolate mixture to the sugar-egg mixture and whisk until smooth. Add the flour mixture and stir with a spatula until just combined. 6) Pour the batter into the prepared pan and bake for 28 to 32 minutes, until the sides of the brownies have set, the top is starting to crackle and look glossy, and a wooden skewer or toothpick inserted into the center comes out with crumbs. The batter on the toothpick should not be wet but should have a good amount of crumbs clinging to it. 7) Transfer the pan to a wire rack and let cool completely. Use the parchment sling to gently lift the brownies from the pan. Cut them into bars and serve. Store brownies in an airtight container at room temperature for up to 2 days.

NOTE Not all white chocolate is created equal. This recipe works best with a white chocolate that has at least 30 percent cocoa butter. These can be made with a store-brand baking white chocolate bar (such as Ghirardelli), but please note that the papery top on the brownies will separate more as it bakes with lower percentage cocoa butter chocolate and will seem hard out of the oven. They will still taste good, and the top will soften as they cool.

White Chocolate Swirl Brownies, Two Ways

White chocolate also tastes delicious swirled with sweetened condensed milk. I have two different variations here: Dark Chocolate and Raspberry.

MAKES 12 LARGE OR 24 SMALL BROWNIES

DARK CHOCOLATE SWIRL WHITE CHOCOLATE BROWNIES

1/2 cup [120 g] sweetened condensed milk

4 oz [113 g] bittersweet chocolate, melted and cooled

Pinch salt

1 recipe White Chocolate Brownies (page 88)

1) Adjust an oven rack to the middle of the oven. Preheat the oven to 350°F [180°C]. Grease a 9 by 13 in [23 by 33 cm] baking pan and line with a parchment sling. 2) In a medium bowl, mix together the sweetened condensed milk, melted chocolate, and salt until combined. 3) Make the brownie batter as directed. Pour the brownie batter into the prepared pan, and use an offset spatula to spread evenly. Dollop the chocolate mixture over the top of the brownies, then drag the tip of a butter knife through the batter, creating swirls.

4) Bake until the sides of the brownies have set and a wooden skewer or toothpick inserted into the center comes out with crumbs, 28 to 34 minutes. The batter on the toothpick should not be wet but should have a good amount of crumbs clinging to it. 5) Transfer the pan to a wire rack and let cool completely. Use the parchment sling to gently lift the brownies from the pan. Cut them into bars and serve. Store brownies in an airtight container at room temperature for up to 2 days.

RASPBERRY SWIRL WHITE CHOCOLATE BROWNIES

6 oz [170 g] raspberries

1/2 cup [120 g] sweetened condensed milk

1 teaspoon pure vanilla extract

Pinch salt

1 recipe White Chocolate Brownies (page 88)

1) Adjust an oven rack to the middle of the oven. Preheat the oven to 350°F [180°C]. Grease a 9 by 13 in [23 by 33 cm] baking pan and line with a parchment sling. **2)** Process the raspberries in a food processor until they have released their juices and have turned into a smooth purée, 1 to 2 minutes. Strain the mixture through a fine-mesh sieve into a medium bowl, pressing as much juice through as possible. Discard the leftover seeds. Add the sweetened condensed milk, vanilla, and salt to the bowl, and stir to combine. Chill the mixture while making the brownie batter. **3)** Make the brownie batter as directed. Pour the brownie batter into the prepared pan, and use an offset spatula to spread evenly. Dollop the raspberry mixture over the top of the brownies, then drag a knife through the batter, creating swirls. **4)** Bake until the sides of the brownies have set and a wooden skewer or toothpick inserted into the center comes out with crumbs, 28 to 34 minutes. The batter on the toothpick should not be wet but should have a good amount of crumbs clinging to it. **5)** Transfer the pan to a wire rack and let cool completely. Use the parchment sling to gently lift the brownies from the pan. Cut them into bars and serve. Store brownies in an airtight container at room temperature for up to 2 days.

31

White Chocolate Red Velvet Brownies

I've always been a fan of red velvet in cakes and cupcakes but discovered I might actually prefer it in brownies. The red color is dark and deep, the brownies are moist and full of white chocolate flavor, and, of course, cream cheese frosting is always a winner. Use a white chocolate with at least 30 percent cocoa butter for best results.

MAKES 12 LARGE OR 24 SMALL BROWNIES

1 1/2 cups [213 g] all-purpose flour

1/2 teaspoon baking powder

5 large eggs, at room temperature

1 1/2 cups [300 g] granulated sugar

1/2 cup [100 g] packed brown sugar

3/4 teaspoon salt

1/2 cup [112 g] canola oil

1 tablespoon Red Velvet Bakery Emulsion or red food coloring

1 tablespoon pure vanilla extract

8 oz [226 g] white chocolate, chopped into small pieces

8 tablespoons [1 stick or 113 g] unsalted butter

3 tablespoons Dutch-process cocoa powder

CREAM CHEESE FROSTING

8 tablespoons [113 g] unsalted butter, at room temperature

4 oz [113 g] cream cheese, at room temperature

1 teaspoon pure vanilla extract

Pinch salt

2 cups [230 g] confectioners' sugar

2 tablespoons heavy cream

1) Adjust an oven rack to the middle of the oven. Preheat the oven to 350°F [180°C]. Grease a 9 by 13 in [23 by 33 cm] baking pan and line with a parchment sling. 2) In a small bowl, whisk together the flour and baking powder. 3) In the bowl of a stand mixer fitted with a paddle, beat the eggs, granulated and brown sugars, and salt on medium-high speed until the mixture is light in color and has doubled in volume, 5 to 6 minutes. Turn the mixer to low speed and mix in the oil, red velvet emulsion, and vanilla until just combined. 4) While the egg mixture is beating, melt the chocolate and butter. Place the chocolate and butter in a small, heavy-bottom saucepan set over low heat and melt together, stirring frequently to prevent the chocolate from scorching. Continue cooking until the mixture is smooth. Off the heat, add the cocoa powder to the chocolate and whisk until completely combined.

5) Add the warm chocolate-butter mixture to the egg mixture and mix on low speed until combined. Add the flour mixture and use a spatula to gently combine. 6) Pour the batter into the prepared pan and bake for 20 to 23 minutes, until the sides of the brownies have set and a wooden skewer or toothpick inserted into the center comes out with crumbs. The batter on the toothpick should not be wet but should have a good amount of crumbs clinging to it. The top will be slightly firm and bumpy, and will not have its usual glossy sheen. It will soften as it cools. 7) Transfer the pan to a wire rack and let cool completely.

FOR THE CREAM CHEESE FROSTING

In the bowl of a stand mixer fitted with a paddle, beat the butter on medium speed until creamy, about 1 minute. Add the cream cheese and beat again on medium speed until smooth and creamy, 2 to 3 minutes. Add the vanilla and salt, and beat again on low speed until combined. Add the confectioners' sugar and beat on medium speed until light and creamy, scraping down the sides of the bowl as needed, 3 to 4 minutes. Add the heavy cream and mix on low speed until combined, 1 to 2 minutes.

TO ASSEMBLE

Use an offset spatula to spread the frosting evenly over the top of the cooled brownies. Refrigerate the brownies for 1 hour, until the frosting has set. Remove the pan from the refrigerator, then use the parchment sling to gently lift the brownies from the pan. Cut them into bars and serve. Store brownies in an airtight container at room temperature for up to 2 days.

32

White Chocolate Brownies with Toasted Sesame Caramel

Toasted sesame oil may be great in savory dishes, but personally I love it even more paired with sugar and chocolate. Here it is mixed into caramel, lending a nutty flavor that pairs well with the white chocolate in the brownies.

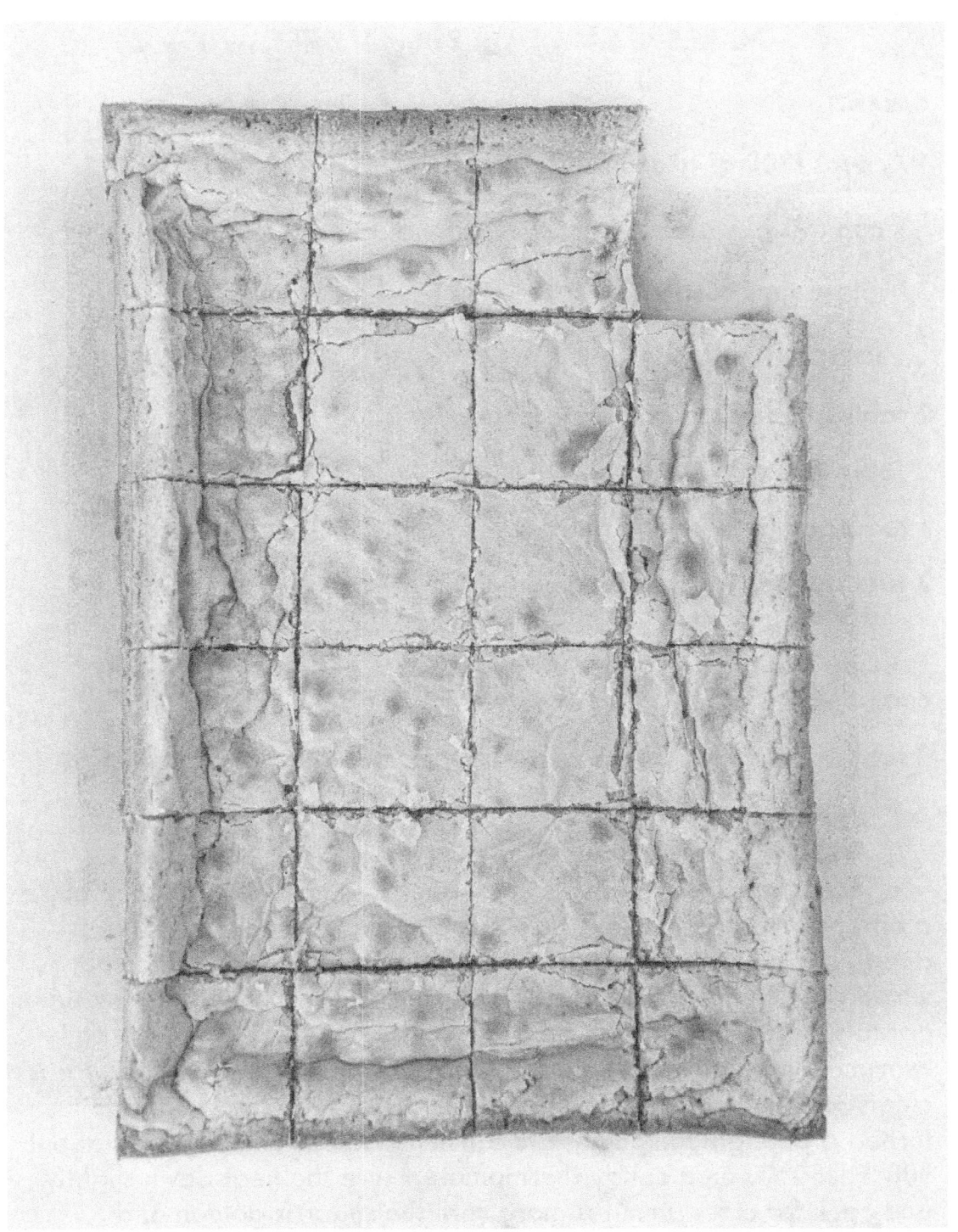

MAKES 12 LARGE OR 24 SMALL BROWNIES

CARAMEL

1½ cups [300 g] granulated sugar

¼ cup [60 g] water

3 tablespoons corn syrup

¼ teaspoon salt

7 tablespoons [105 g] heavy cream

2 tablespoons unsalted butter

1 teaspoon pure vanilla extract

2 tablespoons toasted sesame oil

1 recipe White Chocolate Brownies (page 88), baked and fully cooled

2 tablespoons each black and white sesame seeds, for sprinkling

FOR THE CARAMEL

In a large, heavy-bottom saucepan (the caramel will bubble up quite a bit once it starts cooking, so it's important to have a pan that is deep), combine the granulated sugar, water, corn syrup, and salt, stirring very gently to combine while trying to avoid getting any sugar crystals on the sides of the pan. Cover the pot, and bring to a boil over medium-high heat, until the sugar has melted and the mixture is clear, 3 to 5 minutes. Uncover, and then cook until the sugar has turned a pale golden color, 4 to 5 minutes more, and registers about 300°F [150°C] on a candy thermometer. Turn the heat down slightly, and cook for a few minutes more until the sugar is golden and registers 350°F [180°C]. Remove the pot immediately from the heat and add the heavy cream. The cream will foam considerably, so be careful pouring it in. Add the butter next, followed by the vanilla and toasted sesame oil, and stir to combine. Set aside to cool for 5 to 10 minutes. Pour the caramel over the cooled brownies, using an offset spatula to smooth it evenly. Sprinkle the sesame seeds over the caramel, and then refrigerate, uncovered, for 2 hours. When ready to serve, cut into bars. Serve at room temperature. Brownies can be stored in an airtight container at room temperature for up to 3 days.

NOTES Keeping the lid on during the first few minutes of boiling helps melt sugar on the sides of the pot. If the caramel is too hard to cut through after chilling, let it sit out for 15 to 20 minutes.

Blondies

This recipe appeared in my first book infused with coffee and remains one of my favorite treats to make for get-togethers, parties, holidays, and straight-up snacking. I made them (with the coffee) often at the Blue Heron Coffeehouse when I worked there, the original recipe snipped out of a local newspaper and then tweaked slightly. This is my "home" version, with plenty of vanilla and toasted pecans. If I'm not in the mood for white chocolate, I'll leave it out, replacing the chips with equal parts chocolate.

MAKES 12 LARGE OR 24 SMALL BLONDIES

1 1/2 cups [213 g] all-purpose flour

1 1/2 teaspoons baking powder

12 tablespoons [1 1/2 sticks or 170 g] unsalted butter

1 1/2 cups [300 g] brown sugar

3/4 teaspoon salt

1 1/2 tablespoons pure vanilla extract

1 large egg, at room temperature

3/4 cup [90 g] toasted pecans, chopped into bite-size pieces

3/4 cup [128 g] semisweet chocolate chips

1/2 cup [85 g] white chocolate chips

1) Adjust an oven rack to the middle of the oven. Preheat the oven to 350°F [180°C]. Grease a 9 by 13 in [23 by 33 cm] baking pan and line with a parchment sling. **2)** In a medium bowl, whisk together the flour and baking powder. **3)** In a medium saucepan over medium heat, melt the butter, brown sugar, and salt. Remove from the heat and stir in the vanilla. Let the mixture cool to room temperature. Add the egg and whisk until combined. Transfer the mixture to a large bowl. Add the flour mixture and stir until just combined. Add the pecans, chocolate chips, and white chocolate chips, and stir gently.

4) Transfer the batter to the prepared pan, and pat into an even layer. Bake for 18 to 24 minutes, until the blondies are set on the edges and the top is golden brown and just beginning to form cracks. A wooden skewer or toothpick inserted into the blondies should come out with just a couple of crumbs. **5)** Transfer the pan to a wire rack and let cool completely. Use the parchment sling to gently lift the blondies from the pan. Cut them into bars. Store blondies in an airtight container at room temperature for up to 2 days.

Brown Butter Blondies

This is a jazzed-up version of my blondies, full of brown butter, rich egg yolks, chocolate and more chocolate, and toasted pecans. While I love my original recipe, I find myself turning to this one on cool, almost-winter days when the leaves are just starting to turn, and we're all tucked in the house with good books and cozy slippers.

MAKES 12 LARGE OR 24 SMALL BLONDIES

2 cups [284 g] all-purpose flour

1 1/2 teaspoons baking powder

1 cup [2 sticks or 227 g] unsalted butter

1 cup [200 g] granulated sugar

1 cup [200 g] brown sugar

1 1/2 tablespoons pure vanilla extract

1 teaspoon salt

2 large eggs plus 4 large yolks, at room temperature

3/4 cup [90 g] toasted pecans, chopped into bite-size pieces

4 oz [113 g] bittersweet chocolate, chopped into bite-size pieces

1/2 cup [85 g] semisweet chocolate chips

1) Adjust an oven rack to the middle of the oven. Preheat the oven to 350°F [180°C]. Grease a 9 by 13 in [23 by 33 cm] baking pan and line with a parchment sling. **2)** In a medium bowl, whisk together the flour and baking powder. **3)** In a medium saucepan over medium heat, melt 12 tablespoons [170 g] of the butter. Brown the butter until it is dark golden brown and giving off a nutty aroma, 2 to 3 minutes (for tips on browning butter, see page 280). Remove from the heat and add the remaining 4 tablespoons [57 g] butter to the pot, swirling the pot until the butter stops foaming. Add the granulated and brown sugars, vanilla, and salt, and stir to combine. Let the mixture cool to room temperature. Add the eggs and yolks and whisk until combined. Transfer the mixture to a large bowl. Add the flour mixture and stir until just combined. Add the pecans, chopped chocolate, and chocolate chips, and stir gently. **4)** Transfer the batter to the prepared pan, and pat into an even layer. Bake for 16 to 22 minutes, until the blondies are set on the edges and the top is golden brown and just beginning to form cracks. A wooden skewer or toothpick inserted into the blondies should come out slightly wet with clinging crumbs for gooey blondies, and just a couple of crumbs for cakey blondies. **5)** Transfer the pan to a wire rack and let cool completely. Use the parchment sling to gently lift the blondies from the pan. Cut them into bars. Store blondies in an airtight container at room temperature for up to 2 days.

35

Espresso Caramel Blondies

One of my most beloved recipes from my first book was the Coffee Blondies, and while I adore that original recipe, I decided to elevate them in this book. Espresso and caramel is a favorite combination of mine, and a little drizzle of the caramel on top adds interesting cracks to the finished blondies, along with delicious caramel flavor. You could always omit the caramel drizzle, and serve it instead on the side with some No-Churn Ice Cream (page 289).

MAKES 12 LARGE OR 24 SMALL BLONDIES

2 cups [284 g] all-purpose flour

1½ teaspoons baking powder

1 cup [2 sticks or 227 g] unsalted butter

1 cup [200 g] granulated sugar

1 cup [200 g] brown sugar

¼ cup [60 g] brewed espresso or strong coffee

1½ tablespoons pure vanilla extract

1 teaspoon salt

1 teaspoon espresso grounds

2 large eggs plus 4 large yolks, at room temperature

4 oz [113 g] bittersweet chocolate, chopped into bite-size pieces

¼ cup Caramel (page 283), at room temperature

1) Adjust an oven rack to the middle of the oven. Preheat the oven to 350°F [180°C]. Grease a 9 by 13 in [23 by 33 cm] baking pan and line with a parchment sling. 2) In a medium bowl, whisk together the flour and baking powder. 3) In a medium saucepan over medium heat, melt 12 tablespoons [170 g] of the butter. Brown the butter until it is dark golden brown and giving off a nutty aroma, 2 to 3 minutes (for tips on browning butter, see page 280). Remove from the heat and add the remaining 4 tablespoons [57 g] of butter to the pot, swirling the pot until the butter stops foaming. Add the granulated and brown sugars, brewed espresso, vanilla, salt, and espresso grounds, and stir to combine. Let the mixture cool to room temperature. Add the eggs and yolks and whisk until combined. Transfer the mixture to a large bowl. Add the flour mixture and stir until just combined. Add the chopped chocolate, and stir gently. 4) Transfer the batter to the prepared pan, and pat into an even layer. Drizzle the top of the blondies with the caramel. Bake for 16 to 22 minutes, until the blondies are set on the edges and the top is golden brown and just beginning to form cracks. A wooden skewer or toothpick inserted into the blondies should come out slightly wet with clinging crumbs for gooey blondies, and just a couple of crumbs for cakey blondies. 5) Transfer the pan to a wire rack and let cool completely. Use the parchment sling to gently lift the blondies from the pan. Cut them into bars. Store blondies in an airtight container at room temperature for up to 2 days.

36

Cinnamon Roll Blondies

I never understood Edmund's choice of Turkish delight when the Queen of Narnia offered whatever his heart desired on her reindeer-drawn sleigh. As a child, I often thought, *Oh hey, what about cinnamon rolls?* Because they are not only delicious in real time, but also perfect for snowy, otherworldly adventures—the spicy cinnamon sugar warming you right down to your toes, and the tangy icing alerting the senses in case you happened to be cozied up next to an evil witch. I've tried to mimic my Sunday morning indulgence here in bar form: Blondies make a perfect base, and cinnamon sugar and cream cheese are both swirled into the top to make each bite pure, deep magic.

MAKES 12 LARGE OR 24 SMALL BLONDIES

CREAM CHEESE FILLING

4 oz [113 g] cream cheese, at room temperature

1/4 cup [50 g] granulated sugar

1 teaspoon pure vanilla extract

Pinch salt

CINNAMON SUGAR SWIRL

1/4 cup [50 g] brown sugar

2 tablespoons unsalted butter, at room temperature

Pinch salt

1 tablespoon ground cinnamon

1 recipe Brown Butter Blondies (page 99), omitting the chocolate chips, chopped chocolate, and pecans

Adjust an oven rack to the middle of the oven. Preheat the oven to 350°F [180°C]. Grease a 9 by 13 in [23 by 33 cm] baking pan and line with a parchment sling.

FOR THE CREAM CHEESE FILLING

In the bowl of a stand mixer fitted with a paddle, beat the cream cheese on medium speed until smooth, about 2 minutes. Add the granulated sugar, vanilla, and salt, and mix on medium speed until well combined.

FOR THE CINNAMON SUGAR SWIRL

In a small saucepan, melt the brown sugar, butter, and salt together over low heat until the sugar is dissolved. Remove from the heat and stir in the cinnamon until combined.

TO ASSEMBLE

1) Make the blondie batter as directed. Transfer the batter to the prepared pan, and spread into an even layer. Dollop the cream cheese and cinnamon sugar over the top of the batter, alternating the two. Drag the tip of a butter knife through the batter, creating swirls. 2) Bake for 25 to 29 minutes. A wooden skewer or toothpick inserted into the blondies should come out with just a couple of

crumbs. 3) Transfer the pan to a wire rack and let cool completely. Use the parchment sling to gently lift the blondies from the pan. Cut them into bars. Store blondies in an airtight container at room temperature for up to 2 days.

NOTE Leave a small space unswirled in the center of the batter when assembling. This is the spot you want to insert your toothpick to check when the bars are done, as the cream cheese and cinnamon swirl will remain wet throughout baking.

37

Banana Crunch Blondies

Adding bananas, chocolate ganache, and candied walnuts takes the humble blondie to the next level. Also, once you take a nibble of candied walnuts, your life will forever be altered. You will keep little bowls of them on your countertops; you will hide bags of them in your secret candy stash.

MAKES 12 LARGE OR 24 SMALL BLONDIES

1½ cups [213 g] all-purpose flour

1½ teaspoons baking powder

12 tablespoons [1½ sticks or 170 g] unsalted butter

1½ cups [300 g] brown sugar

1 cup [227 g] mashed bananas (about 2 bananas)

¾ teaspoon salt

1½ tablespoons pure vanilla extract

1 large egg

½ cup [60 g] toasted walnuts, chopped into bite-size pieces

¼ cup [30 g] cacao nibs

CHOCOLATE GANACHE

12 oz [340 g] bittersweet or semisweet chocolate, finely chopped

1 cup [240 g] heavy cream

2 cups [280 g] Candied Nuts, Walnuts variation (page 291)

1) Adjust an oven rack to the middle of the oven. Preheat the oven to 350°F [180°C]. Grease a 9 by 13 in [23 by 33 cm] baking pan and line with a parchment sling. 2) In a medium bowl, whisk together the flour and baking powder. 3) In a medium saucepan over medium heat, melt the butter, brown sugar, mashed bananas, and salt. Remove from the

heat and stir in the vanilla. Let the mixture cool to room temperature. Add the egg and whisk until combined. Transfer the mixture to a large bowl. Add the flour mixture and stir until just combined. Add the walnuts and cacao nibs and stir gently.

4) Spread the batter evenly in the prepared pan and bake for 18 to 24 minutes, until the blondies are set on the edges and the top is golden brown and just beginning to form cracks. A wooden skewer or toothpick inserted into the blondies should come out with just a couple of crumbs. 5) Transfer the pan to a wire rack and let cool completely.

FOR THE CHOCOLATE GANACHE

Place the chocolate in a small bowl. Heat the heavy cream in a small saucepan until it is simmering and just about to boil. Pour the cream over the chocolate, cover the bowl with plastic wrap, and let it sit for 5 minutes. Remove the plastic and whisk until completely smooth. Cool to room temperature. When the ganache is cool, whisk for 30 to 45 seconds, until the ganache thickens a little bit.

TO ASSEMBLE

Top the cooled blondies with the chocolate ganache, spreading it evenly over the top. Sprinkle the candied nuts over the ganache (I like to use the whole 2 cups [280 g] here, but you can sprinkle less if desired). Use the parchment sling to gently lift the blondies from the pan. Cut them into bars. Store the blondies in an airtight container at room temperature for 2 days.

38

S'mores Blondies

I won't lie to you, this recipe will take a bit of time to put together, but I promise the results are worth it. A simple blondie base coated in a layer of chocolate, then covered in a thick, homemade marshmallow slab will not disappoint. You can also toast each cut piece in front of your guests, which is always impressive.

MAKES 12 SMALL OR 24 LARGE BLONDIES

1½ cups [213 g] all-purpose flour

1½ teaspoon baking powder

12 tablespoons [1½ sticks or 170 g] unsalted butter

1½ cups [300 g] brown sugar

¾ teaspoon salt

1½ tablespoons pure vanilla extract

1 large egg

2 cups [360 g] milk chocolate or semisweet chocolate chips

MARSHMALLOW TOPPING

2 large egg whites

¼ teaspoon cream of tartar

½ cup [120 g] cold water, plus ½ cup [120 g] room-temperature water

5 teaspoons gelatin

2 cups [400 g] granulated sugar

¼ cup [85 g] corn syrup

¼ teaspoon salt

1 tablespoon pure vanilla extract

1) Adjust an oven rack to the middle of the oven. Preheat the oven to 350°F [180°C]. Grease a 9 by 13 in [23 by 33 cm] baking pan and line with a parchment sling. 2) In a medium bowl, whisk together the flour and baking powder. 3) In a medium saucepan over medium heat, melt the butter, brown sugar, and salt. Remove from the heat and stir in the vanilla. Let the mixture cool to room temperature. Add the egg and whisk until combined. Transfer the mixture to a large bowl. Add the flour mixture and stir until just combined.

4) Spread the batter evenly in the prepared pan and bake for 18 to 24 minutes, until the blondies are set on the edges and the top is golden brown and just beginning to form cracks. A wooden skewer or toothpick inserted into the blondies should come out with just a couple of crumbs. 5) Immediately spread the chocolate chips evenly over the top of the bars (careful, the pan is hot!) and return it to the oven until the chocolate chips are just starting to melt, 1 to 2 minutes. Remove the pan from the oven and use an offset spatula to smooth the chocolate evenly over the bars. Transfer the pan to a wire rack and let cool to room temperature.

FOR THE MARSHMALLOW TOPPING

1) In the bowl of a stand mixer fitted with a whisk, whip the egg whites and cream of tartar on medium-high speed until soft peaks form, 2 to 3 minutes. 2) In a small bowl, combine the cold water and the gelatin. 3) In a medium, heavy-bottom saucepan, combine the granulated sugar, corn syrup, salt, and the room-temperature water. Bring to a boil over medium-high heat, until the temperature reaches 240°F [115°C] on a candy thermometer; this will take a few minutes. Immediately remove the saucepan from the heat, and whisk in the bloomed gelatin. 4) Turn the stand mixer on low speed, and carefully pour the hot sugar syrup along the side of the mixing bowl, being careful not to hit the whisk as you pour. When all the syrup is in the bowl, turn up the speed to medium and continue whisking until the

mixture has doubled in volume, is quite thick and glossy, and the sides of the bowl have cooled, 10 to 12 minutes. Add the vanilla and mix on low speed to combine. 5) Scrape the marshmallow over the top of the chocolate-covered blondies. Use an offset spatula to smooth the top of the mixture. Cover the pan with greased plastic wrap (trying not to let the marshmallow topping touch the plastic) and let the marshmallows set at room temperature until firm; 8 hours or overnight. 6) Remove the plastic wrap from the pan and use the parchment sling to remove the bars from the pan. Slice the bar into pieces, and then use a kitchen torch to toast the tops and sides of the marshmallow topping until golden brown (being very careful not to toast the parchment paper if it is still underneath the bars). Serve the bars soon after toasting. Untoasted bars can be stored in an airtight container at room temperature for 2 days.

VARIATION
• *Bourbon S'mores Blondies—Add 3 tablespoons of bourbon to the blondie base.*

CHAPTER 3
Fruit-extravaganza

"Pine-apples,
blackberries,
apricots,
strawberries;—
All ripe
together
in summer
weather."

—Christina Rossetti, "Goblin Market"

39

Olive Oil Sugar Cookies with Blood Orange Glaze

I have a similar recipe with lemon and pistachios in my last book but recently fell in love with this adaptation: an olive oil cookie coated in blood orange glaze. The cookie is crisp and stands on its own, but the glaze makes a lovely accompaniment and also happens to be the prettiest shade of pink, thanks to the blood orange juice.

MAKES 24 COOKIES

2$^1/_3$ cups [332 g] all-purpose flour

$^1/_2$ teaspoon baking soda

$^1/_2$ teaspoon salt

4 tablespoons [57 g] unsalted butter, at room temperature

$^3/_4$ cup [150 g] granulated sugar

$^1/_4$ cup [30 g] confectioners' sugar

$^1/_2$ cup [112 g] extra-virgin olive oil

1 large egg

1 teaspoon pure vanilla extract

BLOOD ORANGE GLAZE

1 cup [120 g] confectioners' sugar

Zest of 1 blood orange

2 to 4 tablespoons [30 to 60 g] blood orange juice

1) In a medium bowl, whisk together the flour, baking soda, and salt.
2) In the bowl of a stand mixer fitted with a paddle, beat the butter on medium speed until creamy, about 1 minute. Add the granulated and confectioners' sugars and beat on medium speed until light and fluffy, 2 to 3 minutes. Add the olive oil and mix on low speed until combined. Scrape down the sides of the bowl and add the egg and vanilla, mixing on low speed until combined. Add the flour mixture

and mix on low speed until combined. 3) Wrap the dough in plastic wrap and chill in the refrigerator for at least 2 hours (and up to 2 days). 4) Adjust an oven rack to the middle of the oven. Preheat the oven to 350°F [180°C]. Line three sheet pans with parchment paper. 5) Lightly flour a work surface and roll the dough to $1/4$ in [6 mm] thick. Using a 2 in [5 cm] biscuit or cookie cutter, cut out circles (any dough scraps can be rewrapped and chilled while the cookies are baking). Gently slide a metal spatula underneath each round and transfer them to the prepared sheet pans. Place 8 cookies on each pan. Refrigerate the pans waiting to go into the oven while the cookies are baking. 6) Bake one pan at a time, rotating halfway through baking. Bake until the cookies are just beginning to brown on the edges, 10 to 12 minutes. Transfer the sheet pan to a wire rack and let the cookies cool completely on the pan.

FOR THE GLAZE

In a small bowl, whisk together the confectioners' sugar and orange zest. Add the blood orange juice, 1 tablespoon at a time, until you have a thin glaze. Spread each cooled cookie with glaze and let set before serving. Store cookies in an airtight container at room temperature for up to 3 days.

VARIATION
• *Lemon–Poppy Seed Glaze—Substitute lemon zest and juice for the blood orange. Sprinkle each cookie with a dusting of poppy seeds. Let the cookies set before serving.*

40

Lemon Sugar Cookies

I used to work at a coffeehouse that made the most perfect lemon sugar cookies: gigantic in size, with light lemon flavor and a dusting of sugar. However, when the baker left (along with a few other important recipes), this cookie was pronounced lost forever. On and off over the years, I have tried to re-create the magic of those cookies, and finally succeeded.

MAKES 14 COOKIES

2 cups [284 g] all-purpose flour

1 teaspoon baking powder

3/4 teaspoon salt

1/2 teaspoon baking soda

12 tablespoons [1 1/2 sticks or 170 g] unsalted butter, at room temperature

1 1/2 cups [300 g] granulated sugar

2 tablespoons lemon zest, from 2 or 3 lemons

1 large egg plus 1 large yolk

1 1/2 teaspoons lemon extract

1/2 teaspoon pure vanilla extract

COATING SUGAR

3/4 cup [150 g] granulated sugar

2 teaspoons lemon zest

1) Adjust an oven rack to the middle of the oven. Preheat the oven to 350°F [180°C]. Line three sheet pans with parchment paper. 2) In a medium bowl, combine the flour, baking powder, salt, and baking soda. 3) In the bowl of a stand mixer fitted with a paddle, beat the butter on medium speed until creamy, about 1 minute. Add the sugar and lemon zest and beat on medium speed until light and fluffy, 2 to 3 minutes. Scrape down the sides of the bowl and add the egg, yolk,

lemon extract, and vanilla extract, mixing on low speed until combined. Add the flour mixture and mix on low speed until combined. 4) In a small bowl, combine the coating sugar ingredients; use your fingers to gently work the lemon zest into the sugar. 5) Form the dough into 2 oz [57 g] balls (3 tablespoons), and roll each ball in the coating sugar. Use the back of a measuring cup or glass to flatten each ball of dough into a circle measuring about 2 in [5 cm] across. Place 6 cookies on each sheet pan. 6) Bake the cookies one pan at a time, rotating halfway through baking. Bake for 10 minutes, then give the pan a slight tap in the oven, and continue baking until the sides of the cookies are pale golden brown, 1 to 2 minutes more. 7) Transfer the pans to a wire rack and let the cookies cool to room temperature on the pan. Store cookies in an airtight container at room temperature for 2 to 3 days.

VARIATIONS
• *Lemon–Poppy Seed Sugar Cookies—Add 1 tablespoon of poppy seeds to the dough, and bake as directed.*

• *Lemon-Lime Sugar Cookies—Add 1 tablespoon of lime zest along with the lemon zest in the dough.*

Orange Almond Shortbread Cookies

I am convinced that triple sec is a magic ingredient. It may be lower-shelf fare, but whatever I add it to—Bundt cakes, layer cakes, lemonade, scones, and even cookies—its orange flavor always shines through. This is my Shortbread recipe (page 60) with almonds and orange zest, and a bump of flavor from the orange liqueur.

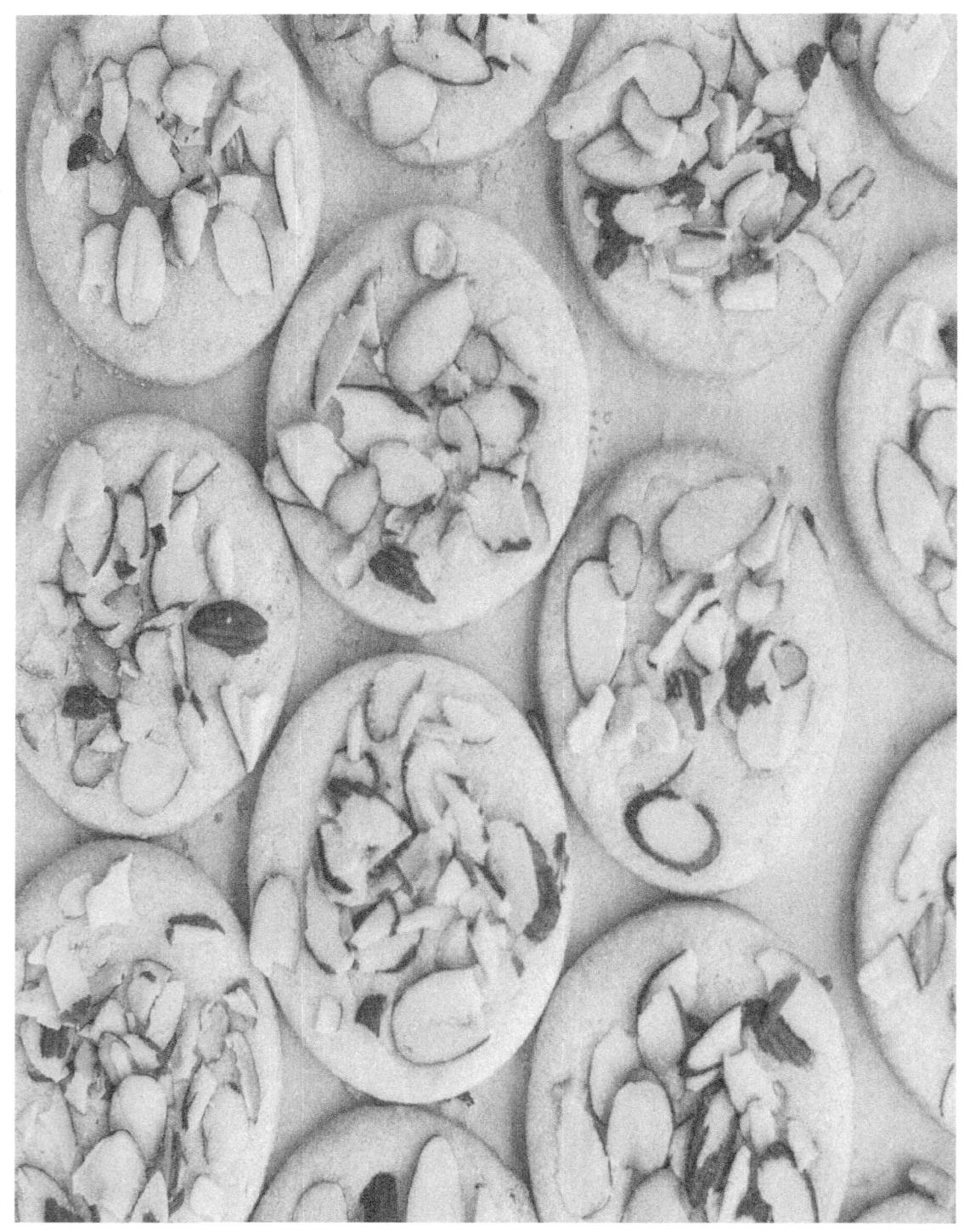

MAKES ABOUT 40 COOKIES

2 large egg yolks

2 tablespoons triple sec or other orange liqueur

1 teaspoon pure vanilla extract

2 cups [284 g] all-purpose flour, plus more for dusting

1/2 cup [100 g] granulated sugar

1/2 cup [60 g] confectioners' sugar

1 tablespoon orange zest

1/2 teaspoon salt

1 cup [2 sticks or 227 g] unsalted butter, at room temperature, cut into 1 in [2.5 cm] pieces

1 cup [100 g] sliced almonds

Sanding sugar, for sprinkling

1) Line several sheet pans with parchment paper. 2) In a small liquid measuring cup or bowl, use a fork to mix the egg yolks, triple sec, and vanilla together. 3) In the bowl of a food processor fitted with a blade, pulse the flour, granulated and confectioners' sugars, orange zest, and salt together. Scatter the butter over the top of the flour mixture, and pulse until the mixture looks like wet sand, 8 to 10 one-second pulses. Pour the egg yolk mixture over the top of the flour mixture, and pulse until the dough is smooth and starts to pull away from the sides of the processor, about 10 more one-second pulses.

4) Scrape the dough out of the processor and wrap it in plastic. Chill for 20 to 30 minutes in the refrigerator, just until it is cool to the touch, but not hard. 5) Flour a work surface, and roll the dough out somewhere between 1/8 in [4 mm] and 1/2 in [12 mm] thick (the thinner the dough, the crispier the shortbread, so this is a personal preference). Use a 1 1/2 in [4 cm] biscuit cutter to cut out circles, then place the cookies on the sheet pans, 12 to a pan. (If your shortbread circles stick to the counter at all, you can slide a spatula underneath to help move them to the baking pans.) Extra dough can be rerolled to make more cookies. 6) Adjust an oven rack to the middle of the oven. Preheat the oven to 325°F [165°C]. 7) Cover each cookie with sliced almonds and gently press them into the dough. Generously sprinkle sanding sugar over the top, then chill each pan in the refrigerator for 15 minutes before placing it in the oven. 8) Bake one pan at a time, rotating halfway through baking. Bake until the edges

are light golden brown, 13 to 14 minutes. **9)** Leave the cookies on the pans for 10 minutes, then transfer them to a wire rack to finish cooling and crisping up. Store cookies in an airtight container at room temperature for up to 4 days.

Raspberry Rye Cookies

Adding a little rye flour to these cookies lends a deep malty note, and freeze-dried raspberries contribute a strong underlying raspberry flavor that complements the berries gently mashed into the batter.

MAKES ABOUT 20 COOKIES

1/2 cup [16 g] freeze-dried raspberries

2 cups [284 g] all-purpose flour

1/2 cup [50 g] rye flour

3/4 teaspoon baking soda

3/4 teaspoon salt

1 cup [2 sticks or 227 g] unsalted butter, at room temperature

1 cup [200 g] brown sugar

3/4 cup [150 g] granulated sugar

1 large egg plus 1 large yolk

1 tablespoon pure vanilla extract

2 oz [57 g] raspberries

1) Adjust an oven rack to the middle of the oven. Preheat the oven to 350°F [180°C]. Line two sheet pans with parchment paper. 2) In the bowl of a food processor fitted with a blade, process the freeze-dried raspberries until they reduce to a powder. 3) In a medium bowl, whisk together the all-purpose and rye flours, baking soda, and salt. Place the raspberry powder on top, and whisk it into the flour. 4) In the bowl of a stand mixer fitted with a paddle, beat the butter on medium speed until creamy, about 1 minute. Add the brown and granulated sugars, and beat again on medium speed until light and fluffy, 2 to 3 minutes. Add the egg, yolk, and vanilla, and beat again on medium speed until combined, scraping down the sides of the bowl as needed. Add the flour mixture and mix on low speed until completely combined. 5) Form the dough into 1 1/2 oz [45 g] balls (2 tablespoons), rolling a raspberry or two into each cookie as you do so. Place 10 cookies on each sheet pan. 6) Bake one pan at a time, rotating halfway through baking. Bake until the sides are set and just starting to look light golden brown, 10 to 11 minutes. 7) Give the pan one tap on the oven rack before removing it from the oven, then let the cookies cool completely before removing them from the pan. Store cookies in an airtight container at room temperature for up to 3 days.

43

White Chocolate, Rosemary, and Apricot Cookies

At the core, this is a recipe for a simple oatmeal cookie. Adding white chocolate, apricot, and a hint of rosemary elevates it to something quite special. In the winter months, I like to substitute the apricots with dried cranberries.

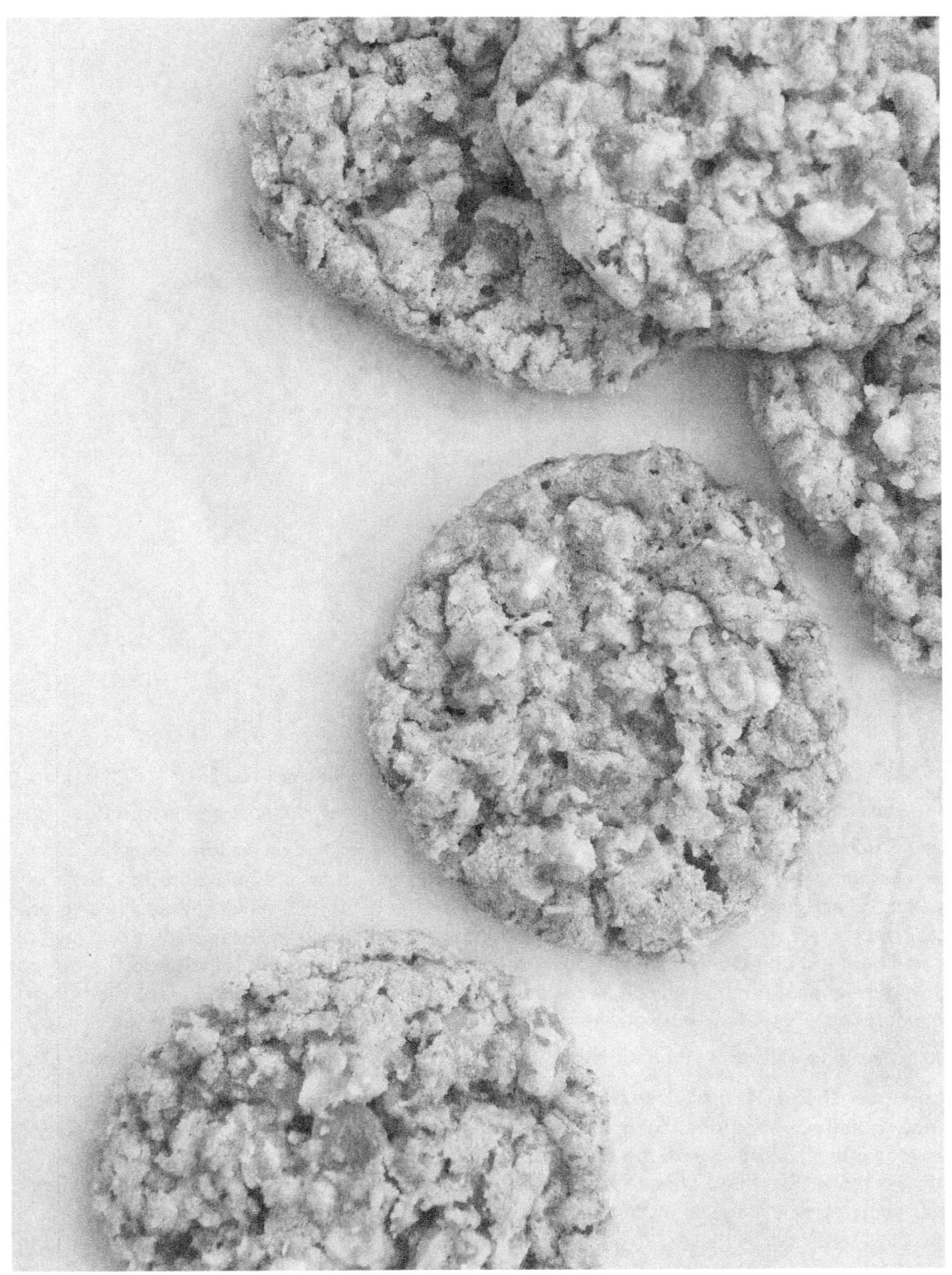

MAKES ABOUT 18 COOKIES

1 cup [142 g] all-purpose flour

¾ teaspoon baking soda

½ teaspoon salt

12 tablespoons [1½ sticks or 170 g] unsalted butter, at room temperature

¾ cup [150 g] brown sugar

⅓ cup [65 g] granulated sugar

1 teaspoon fresh rosemary, minced

1 large egg

2 teaspoons pure vanilla extract

2¼ cups [185 g] rolled oats

½ cup [55 g] dried apricots, chopped into small pieces

2 oz [57 g] white chocolate, finely chopped

1) Adjust an oven rack to the middle of the oven. Preheat the oven to 350°F [180°C]. Line three sheet pans with parchment paper. **2)** In a medium bowl, whisk together the flour, baking soda, and salt. **3)** In the bowl of a stand mixer fitted with a paddle, beat the butter on medium speed until creamy, about 1 minute. Add the brown and granulated sugars and rosemary, and beat on medium speed until light and fluffy, 2 to 3 minutes. Add the egg and vanilla, and mix on medium speed until combined. Add the flour mixture, and mix on low speed until just combined. Add the oats, mixing until almost combined, then add the apricots and white chocolate, and mix on low speed until combined. Using a spatula, stir the batter to incorporate any stray oats on the bottom of the mixing bowl and make sure the dried fruit and chocolate are evenly distributed. **4)** Form the dough into 1½ oz [45 g] balls (2 tablespoons) and put 6 cookies on each sheet pan. **5)** Bake the cookies one pan at a time, rotating halfway through baking. Bake for 11 minutes, give the pan a firm tap in the oven to set the sides, then bake until the edges are golden brown and the center is soft, 1 to 2 minutes more. Tap the pan once more, then remove from the oven and let the pan cool on a wire rack. Store cookies in an airtight container at room temperature for 2 days.

NOTE White chocolate doesn't melt the same as regular chocolate and stays firm longer. Chopping the white chocolate into smaller pieces helps the cookies spread evenly.

Banana Poppy Seed Cookies

I spent quite a bit of time working on a recipe for banana cookies. I had an ancient recipe that hadn't seen the light of day for over a decade, but, sadly, it just didn't hold up when I went to make it. The cookies turned out awkward and puffy when baked, with edges that tasted more gluey than chewy. After tinkering with it for days, I finally scrapped the recipe. Starting over with freeze-dried banana powder instead of mashed bananas, I realized I was onto something. The banana flavor sang, and the cookies had a crisp outer edge and a soft, tender center.

MAKES 15 COOKIES

1/2 cup [25 g] freeze-dried bananas

2 1/3 cups [332 g] all-purpose flour

1 tablespoon poppy seeds

3/4 teaspoon baking soda

3/4 teaspoon salt

1 cup [2 sticks or 227 g] unsalted butter, at room temperature

1 cup [200 g] brown sugar

3/4 cup [150 g] granulated sugar

1 large egg plus 1 large yolk

1 tablespoon pure vanilla extract

1) Adjust an oven rack to the middle of the oven. Preheat the oven to 350°F [180°C]. Line two sheet pans with parchment paper. 2) In the bowl of a food processor fitted with a blade, process the freeze-dried bananas until they reduce to a powder. 3) In a medium bowl, whisk together the flour, poppy seeds, baking soda, and salt. Place the banana powder on top, and whisk it into the flour. 4) In the bowl of a stand mixer fitted with a paddle, beat the butter on medium speed until creamy, about 1 minute. Add the brown and granulated sugars, and beat again on medium speed until light and fluffy, 2 to 3 minutes. Add the egg, yolk, and vanilla, and beat again on medium speed until combined, scraping down the sides of the bowl as needed. Add the flour mixture and mix on low speed until completely combined. 5) Form the dough into 1 1/2 oz [45 g] balls (2 tablespoons) and put 7 or 8 cookies on each sheet pan. 6) Bake one pan at a time, rotating halfway through baking. Bake until the sides are set and just starting to look light golden brown, 10 to 11 minutes. 7) Give the pan one tap on the oven rack before removing it from the oven, then let the cookies cool completely before removing them from the pan. Store cookies in an airtight container at room temperature for up to 3 days.

45

Banana Cream Pie Bars

Banana cream pie will never fail to remind me of my dad. I can see him on various father-themed holidays, laughing while opening up random books and crappy ties. There were always several boxes of pies stacked on the counter, and the top one was, without fail, his banana cream. It was my favorite kind of banana cream: bright yellow and absolutely silky smooth, with serious banana flavor. I've tried to re-create the magic of that pie below. My version is inspired by Milk Bar's banana cream pie, although I've changed things up a little bit: The bananas are roasted to bring out even more flavor, and I've added some heavy cream and blackstrap rum to the base.

MAKES 12 LARGE OR 24 SMALL BARS

BANANA FILLING

5 very ripe bananas

3 tablespoons cold water

¾ cup [150 g] plus 1 tablespoon granulated sugar

1 tablespoon blackstrap rum (optional)

1½ teaspoons gelatin

5 large egg yolks

1 cup [240 g] heavy cream

½ cup [120 g] whole milk

3 tablespoons cornstarch

½ teaspoon salt

4 tablespoons [57 g] unsalted butter

1 teaspoon pure vanilla extract

Yellow food coloring

1 recipe Pie Dough Base, (page 278), single, fully baked, and cooled

WHIPPED CREAM TOPPING

4 oz [113 g] cream cheese, at room temperature

2 tablespoons granulated sugar

1 teaspoon pure vanilla extract

Pinch salt

2 cups [480 g] heavy cream

FOR THE BANANA FILLING

1) Adjust an oven rack to the middle of the oven. Preheat the oven to 400°F [200°C]. 2) In an oven-safe baking dish, combine the bananas, 1 tablespoon of the water, 1 tablespoon of the sugar, and the rum, if desired. Bake the bananas for 15 to 20 minutes, until they are soft and leaking juices. 3) Pour the bananas and all their juices into a blender and purée until completely smooth. 4) In a small bowl, combine the gelatin with the remaining 2 tablespoons of water, stirring gently until all the gelatin is soaked (make sure there are no dry pockets). Let the gelatin sit and soften while the banana cream is cooking. 5) Add the remaining $3/4$ cup [150 g] of sugar, the egg yolks, $1/2$ cup [120 g] of the heavy cream, the milk, cornstarch, and salt to the banana mixture and blend again until smooth. Pour the mixture into a medium, heavy-bottom saucepan. 6) Cook the banana cream over medium heat, stirring constantly with a wooden spoon, until it becomes very thick and begins to boil, 5 to 7 minutes. Whisk the mixture until the banana cream thickens, similar to a pudding, and is glossy and smooth, 3 to 4 minutes (the banana cream will be a gray-brownish color at this point, but should have some gloss to it). Remove from the heat and strain the banana cream through a fine-mesh sieve into a medium bowl. 7) Stir the butter and vanilla into the warm banana cream, and then add the bloomed gelatin and mix it into the cream until dissolved (this may take a minute or two). Color the banana cream with food coloring until it is bright yellow (this will take almost $1/2$ teaspoon of food coloring; see Note). 8) Cover the banana cream with plastic wrap, making sure the wrap sits directly on top of the cream (this will keep it from forming a skin). Place the cream in the refrigerator until well chilled, 4 to 6 hours. 9) When the banana

cream has chilled, whip the remaining $1/2$ cup [120 ml] of heavy cream for the filling. In the bowl of a stand mixer fitted with a whisk, beat the heavy cream on low speed until small bubbles form, about 30 seconds. Increase the speed to high and continue beating until the cream is smooth, thick, and nearly doubled in volume, about 30 seconds. Using a spatula, gently fold the whipped cream into the banana cream. The banana cream will be a little stiff at first, but the cream will incorporate; just keep mixing until it is completely combined. 10) Scoop the chilled banana cream filling onto the prepared pie crust and use an offset spatula to even out the top. Chill the filling for 1 hour.

FOR THE WHIPPED CREAM TOPPING

In the bowl of a stand mixer fitted with a paddle, beat the cream cheese on medium speed until smooth. Add the sugar, vanilla, and salt. Beat on low speed until combined, then increase the speed to medium and beat until smooth. Scrape down the sides of the bowl and switch to the whisk. With the mixer running on low speed, slowly add the heavy cream and whisk until fully combined. Increase the speed to medium and beat until stiff peaks form, stopping to scrape down the sides of the bowl as needed, 2 to 3 minutes.

TO ASSEMBLE

Top the chilled pie with the whipped cream topping. Chill the whole pie for at least 1 hour before slicing, then use the parchment sling to lift them carefully out of the pan. Bars can be held unsliced in the refrigerator for 8 hours, and they will keep for up to 2 days, although the crust will not be as crisp as time goes on. Sliced bars are best eaten as soon as possible.

NOTE If you don't use a lot of yellow food coloring, your filling will be a grayish color. Remember that you will be folding whipped cream into the filling, which will also tame the yellow color, so make it a little brighter than you want it when adding the coloring.

Cream Cheese Pumpkin Pie Bars

I like pumpkin pie alright, but in all honesty I will always take a slice of anything else over it, especially if cheesecake is an option. But pumpkin pie swirled into cheesecake? I will never say no.

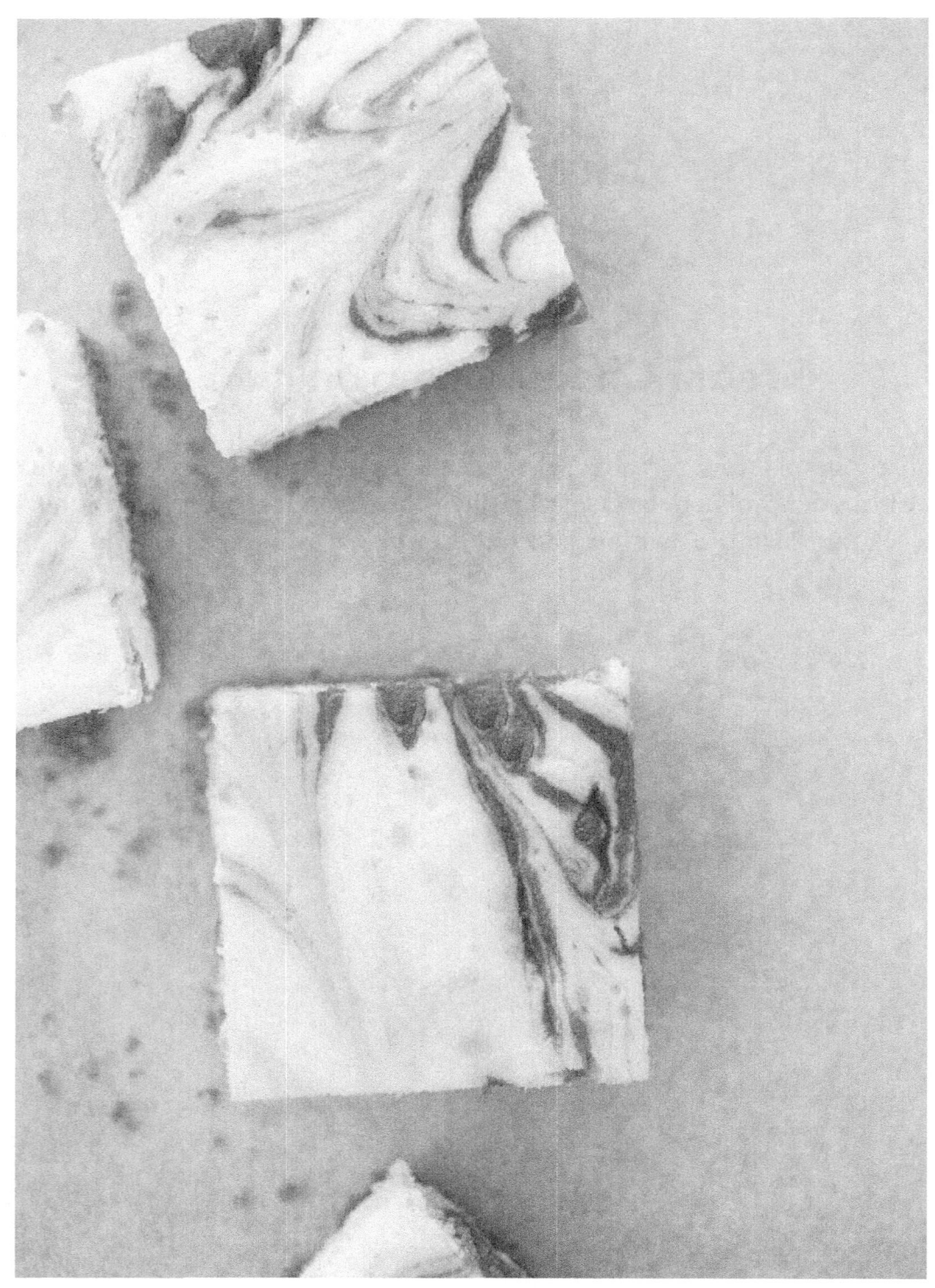

MAKES 12 LARGE OR 24 SMALL BARS

CRUST

1 1/2 cups [150 g] graham cracker crumbs

3 tablespoons granulated sugar

1/4 teaspoon ground cinnamon

1/4 teaspoon ground ginger

4 tablespoons [57 g] unsalted butter, melted and cooled

PUMPKIN PIE FILLING

1 cup [224 g] unsweetened pumpkin purée

1/2 cup [100 g] brown sugar

1 large egg, at room temperature

1 tablespoon maple syrup

1/2 teaspoon ground cinnamon

1/4 teaspoon ground ginger

1/4 teaspoon freshly grated nutmeg

1/4 teaspoon salt

CREAM CHEESE FILLING

24 oz [678 g] cream cheese, at room temperature

1 1/2 cups [300 g] granulated sugar

1 teaspoon pure vanilla extract

¼ teaspoon salt

3 large eggs, at room temperature

½ cup [120 g] heavy cream

FOR THE CRUST

1) Adjust an oven rack to the middle of the oven. Preheat the oven to 325°F [170°C]. Line a 9 by 13 in [23 by 33 cm] pan with a parchment sling. 2) Whisk together the graham cracker crumbs, granulated sugar, cinnamon, and ginger in a medium bowl. Add the melted butter and mix with a spatula until evenly incorporated. 3) Press the mixture onto the bottom of the prepared pan and bake for 10 minutes. Remove the pan from the oven and let cool. After the pan has cooled, wrap the outside sides of the pan in two layers of aluminum foil, with the shiny side facing out (this helps keep the sides of the cheesecake from browning).

FOR THE PUMPKIN PIE FILLING

In a medium bowl, combine the pumpkin, brown sugar, egg, maple syrup, cinnamon, ginger, nutmeg, and salt, and mix until completely combined.

FOR THE CREAM CHEESE FILLING

In the bowl of a stand mixer fitted with a paddle, beat the cream cheese on medium speed until light and completely smooth, 4 to 5 minutes. Scrape down the sides of the bowl often, making sure all the cream cheese has incorporated and is silky smooth. Add the granulated sugar and beat on medium speed until completely incorporated, stopping to scrape down the sides of the bowl as needed, 2 to 3 minutes. Add the vanilla and salt, and beat on medium speed for 2 to 3 minutes. Add the eggs one at a time, beating on low speed after each addition until just combined. Add the heavy cream, and mix on low speed until combined. Using a spatula, give the filling a couple of turns to make sure it is fully mixed.

TO ASSEMBLE

1) Pour the cream cheese filling over the cooled crust and use an offset spatula to smooth the top. Dollop the pumpkin pie filling over the top in 14 or 15 dollops. Use the tip of a butter knife to swirl the pumpkin into the cream cheese batter, being careful not to cut into the crust. Bang the bottom of the pan on the counter a few times to help get rid of any air bubbles. 2) Bake the cheesecake until the center of the cheesecake registers 150°F [65°C], 30 to 35 minutes. The outside 2 to 3 in [5 to 8 cm] of the cheesecake will be puffed and fairly firm and set, but the center will still be jiggly at this point. Turn off the heat, open the oven door just a crack, and let the cheesecake rest and cool in the warm oven for 30 minutes. 3) Transfer the pan to a wire rack and let cool. Once the cheesecake is completely cool, place a piece of parchment over the top of the pan (this helps keep condensation off the top of the cheesecake) and transfer it to the refrigerator. Let chill for at least 4 hours or overnight. Slice the bars and serve. The bars can be served cold or at room temperature but keep best in the refrigerator for up to 2 days.

47

Danish Pear-Apple Bars

Danish pie dough is different from regular pie dough in that it has milk and egg yolks added to the crust instead of icy cold water. The crust bakes up more tender but still has a slight flakiness to it. There are many versions of this bar in classic cookbooks and online; most of them are quite similar to one another. I've added pears along with the apples because I love the sweetness and flavor they lend.

MAKES 12 LARGE OR 24 SMALL BARS

CRUST

½ cup [120 g] whole milk, plus 1 or 2 tablespoons if needed

2 large egg yolks

2½ cups [355 g] all-purpose flour, plus more for dusting

2 tablespoons granulated sugar

1 teaspoon salt

1 cup [2 sticks or 227 g] cold unsalted butter, cut into 20 pieces

PEAR-APPLE FILLING

8 cups [1100 g] Bartlett pears, peeled, cored, and sliced into ¼ in [6 mm] pieces (4 to 5 pears)

1 cup [150 g] peeled and grated Gala apples (about 2 small apples)

⅓ cup [65 g] brown sugar

¼ cup [50 g] granulated sugar, plus 1 to 2 tablespoons for sprinkling

3 tablespoons cornstarch

1 teaspoon lemon juice

¾ teaspoon ground cinnamon

½ teaspoon ground ginger

¼ teaspoon freshly grated nutmeg

¼ teaspoon salt

2 tablespoons unsalted butter, melted

1 tablespoon brandy

1 teaspoon pure vanilla extract

Egg wash (see page 16)

ICING

2 oz [57 g] cream cheese, at room temperature

2 tablespoons milk

½ teaspoon pure vanilla extract

Pinch salt

1 to 1¼ cups [120 to 145 g] confectioners' sugar

FOR THE CRUST

1) In a small bowl or liquid measuring cup, combine the milk and egg yolks. **2)** In the bowl of a stand mixer fitted with a paddle, mix the flour, granulated sugar, and salt on low speed until combined. Add half of the chilled butter and mix on low speed until the butter is just starting to break down, about 1 minute. Add the rest of the butter and continue mixing until the butter is broken down in various sizes (some butter will be incorporated into the dough, some will be a bit large, but most should be about the size of small peas). Stop the mixer and use your hands to check for any dry patches of dough on the bottom of the bowl; incorporate the dry flour as best you can. With the mixer running on low speed, slowly add the milk-egg mixture, and mix until the dough starts to come together. If the dough is having trouble coming together, add 1 or 2 more tablespoons of milk.

3) Divide the dough in half, place each piece on a separate piece of plastic wrap, and flatten each slightly into a square. Cover and refrigerate until cool but still soft, about 45 minutes. **4)** Make sure your work surface is lightly floured and roll one square of the dough into a 9 by 13 in [22 by 33 cm] rectangle. Transfer the dough to a 9 by 13 in [22 by 33 cm] pan, and gently pat it into the bottom. Move the pan to the refrigerator and chill while making the filling. Roll out the second square of dough into a 9 by 13 in [22 by 33 cm] rectangle and place it on a sheet pan lined with parchment paper. Place this in the refrigerator as well.

FOR THE FILLING

1) Combine the pears, apples, brown sugar, $1/4$ cup [50 g] of the granulated sugar, cornstarch, lemon juice, cinnamon, ginger, nutmeg, and salt in a large bowl. **2)** In a small liquid measuring cup or bowl, combine the melted butter, brandy, and vanilla. Pour over the pear-apple mixture and toss to combine.

TO ASSEMBLE

1) Fill the prepared pie shell with the pear-apple mixture and smooth the top. Remove the rolled-out dough from the sheet pan and gently cut a few steam vents into the dough. Place the dough over the top of the pear-apple mixture (no need to press it down to seal the dough). Chill the pan in the freezer for 20 minutes while the oven preheats. **2)** Adjust an oven rack to the lowest position. Preheat the oven to 400°F [200°C]. Place a sheet pan on the oven rack (the preheated sheet pan helps crisp the bottom of the pie crust). **3)** When ready to bake, brush the top of the pie with the egg wash and sprinkle with the remaining 1 to 2 tablespoons of granulated sugar. Transfer the pie to the preheated sheet pan and bake for 45 to 60 minutes, until the crust is golden brown and the juices are bubbling. 4) Transfer the pan to a wire rack and let cool while you make the icing.

FOR THE ICING

1) In a small bowl, mix the cream cheese, milk, vanilla, and salt until smooth. Add 1 cup [120 g] of the confectioners' sugar and mix again until smooth. If the mixture is too thin, add more confectioners' sugar until the desired consistency is reached. 2) Once the bars are cool, top them with the icing and slice. Bars are best eaten the same day they are made but can be refrigerated in an airtight container for up to 2 days.

48

Mixed Berry Crumble Bars

Crumble bars are always a favorite; the crisp, flour-and-oat crust and buttery streusel top are the perfect container for the juicy berries. I sneak a grated apple into the filling to counter the tartness of the fruit, as the apple lends sweetness without having to add lots of extra sugar. I also love including a hit of cardamom to the filling, but cinnamon works just as well here, too.

MAKES 12 LARGE OR 24 SMALL BARS

CRUST

2 1/2 cups [355 g] all-purpose flour

1/2 cup [45 g] rolled oats

1/2 cup [100 g] granulated sugar

1/2 cup [100 g] brown sugar

1/2 teaspoon baking soda

1/2 teaspoon salt

1 cup [2 sticks | 227 g] unsalted butter, at room temperature, sliced into 1 in [2.5 cm] pieces

FILLING

1/4 cup [50 g] granulated sugar

1/4 cup [50 g] brown sugar

1/4 cup [28 g] cornstarch

1/2 teaspoon ground cardamom or cinnamon

1/4 teaspoon salt

16 oz [455 g] strawberries

8 oz [230 g] raspberries

8 oz [230 g] blueberries

½ cup [75 g] grated Gala apple (about 1 small apple)

2 teaspoons lemon juice

1 teaspoon pure vanilla extract

FOR THE CRUST

1) Adjust an oven rack to the middle of the oven. Preheat the oven to 350°F [180°C]. Grease a 9 by 13 in [22 by 33 cm] baking pan and line it with a parchment sling. 2) In the bowl of a stand mixer fitted with a paddle, mix the flour, oats, granulated and brown sugars, baking soda, and salt on low speed to combine. Add the butter and mix on low speed until the mixture resembles coarse sand. 3) Press half of the flour mixture into the bottom of the prepared pan. Bake for 10 minutes. Prepare the filling while the crust is baking.

FOR THE FILLING

1) In a small bowl, whisk together the granulated and brown sugars, cornstarch, cardamom, and salt. 2) In a large bowl, mix the berries, apple, lemon juice, and vanilla together. Pour the sugar mixture over the fruit and stir gently with a spatula to evenly combine.

TO ASSEMBLE

1) Remove the pan from the oven, spread the filling over the crust, and sprinkle the remaining crust mixture evenly over the top. Bake for 35 to 45 minutes, until the crumbly top is light golden brown and the fruit juices have started to bubble. 2) Transfer the pan to a wire rack to cool. Place the pan in the fridge and let the bars chill for 4 to 6 hours. Slice the bars and serve. Bars can be served cold or at room temperature and will keep in the fridge for up to 2 days.

Strawberry Crème Fraîche Bars

Strawberry-filled bars are just what every hot summer day needs. The creamy, smooth filling pairs perfectly with the crunchy streusel sandwich that surrounds it.

MAKES 12 LARGE OR 24 SMALL BARS

STRAWBERRY FILLING

¹/₄ cup [8 g] freeze-dried strawberries

1 lb [455 g] strawberries

2 tablespoons granulated sugar

2 tablespoons water

Two 14 oz [396 g] cans sweetened condensed milk

3 tablespoons crème fraîche

2 teaspoons lemon juice

1 teaspoon pure vanilla extract

1/4 teaspoon salt

4 or 5 drops red or pink food coloring (optional)

CRUST

2 cups [284 g] all-purpose flour

1 1/2 cups [150 g] almond flour or rolled oats

1/2 cup [100 g] brown sugar

1/4 cup [50 g] granulated sugar

1/2 teaspoon baking soda

1/2 teaspoon salt

1 cup [2 sticks or 227 g] unsalted butter, at room temperature

Adjust an oven rack to the middle of the oven. Preheat the oven to 350°F [180°C]. Grease a 9 by 13 in [22 by 33 cm] pan and line it with a parchment sling.

FOR THE FILLING

1) In the bowl of a food processor fitted with a blade, process the freeze-dried strawberries until they reduce to a powder. 2) In a medium saucepan, combine the fresh berries, sugar, and water. Cook, until the berries have broken down and released their juices,

15 to 20 minutes. Strain the berries through a fine-mesh sieve, pressing on the berries to release all their liquid. Discard the berries. 3) In a large bowl, whisk together the cooked berry juice, freeze-dried strawberry powder, sweetened condensed milk, crème fraîche, lemon juice, vanilla, salt, and food coloring, if using.

FOR THE CRUST

In the bowl of a stand mixer fitted with a paddle, mix the all-purpose flour, almond flour, brown and granulated sugars, baking soda, and salt on low speed to combine. Add the butter and mix on medium speed until the mixture is crumbly.

TO ASSEMBLE

1) Press half of the crust mixture into the bottom of the prepared pan. Bake for 10 minutes. 2) Remove the pan from the oven and carefully spread the filling over the crust. Sprinkle the remaining crust mixture evenly over the top. Bake for 15 to 20 minutes, until the filling is set and does not jiggle, and the crumbly top is light golden brown. 3) Transfer the pan to a wire rack and let cool. Place the pan in the refrigerator and chill for 4 to 6 hours. Slice the bars and serve. The bars can be served cold or at room temperature but keep best in an airtight container in the refrigerator for about 3 days.

50

Red Wine Cherry Cheesecake Swirl Bars

A good cheesecake often has a bright red cherry topping to go along with it. I decided on a whim to swirl the cherries inside the cheesecake instead, for a tasty, less messy treat, along with some red wine. One bite, and you'll hear the fairy piper call: *Merry, merry, / Take a cherry; / . . . / Mine are sweeter / For the eater / When the dews fall / And you'll be fairies all.* ("Cherry Time," Robert Graves)

MAKES 12 LARGE OR 24 SMALL BARS

CRUST

1 1/2 cups [150 g] graham cracker crumbs

3 tablespoons granulated sugar

4 tablespoons [57 g] unsalted butter, melted and cooled

CHERRY SWIRL

8 oz [226 g] pitted cherries, fresh or frozen and thawed

1/3 cup [65 g] granulated sugar

1/4 cup [60 g] red wine, such as Merlot

2 tablespoons cornstarch

1/4 teaspoon salt

1/8 teaspoon ground cinnamon

2 or 3 drops red food coloring (optional)

CREAM CHEESE FILLING

24 oz [678 g] cream cheese, at room temperature

1 1/2 cups [300 g] granulated sugar

1 tablespoon pure vanilla extract

1/4 teaspoon salt

3/4 cup [180 g] sour cream, at room temperature

3 large eggs, at room temperature

FOR THE CRUST

1) Adjust an oven rack to the middle of the oven. Preheat the oven to 325°F [165°C]. Line a 9 by 13 in [23 by 33 cm] pan with a parchment sling. 2) Whisk together the graham cracker crumbs and sugar in a medium bowl. Add the melted butter and mix with a spatula until evenly incorporated. Press the mixture onto the bottom of the prepared pan and bake for 10 minutes. 3) Remove the pan from the oven and let cool. After the pan has cooled, wrap the outside sides of the pan in two layers of aluminum foil, with the shiny side facing out (this helps keep the sides of the cheesecake from browning).

FOR THE CHERRY SWIRL

Purée the cherries in a blender or food processor until smooth. Place the puréed cherries, sugar, red wine, cornstarch, salt, cinnamon, and food coloring (if using) in a small saucepan. Heat over medium-high heat, stirring almost constantly until the mixture has thickened (when done, it should coat the back of a wooden spoon), 8 to 10 minutes. Remove from the heat, move the mixture to a small bowl, and let cool to room temperature. Cover the bowl and refrigerate until ready to use.

FOR THE CREAM CHEESE FILLING

1) In the bowl of a stand mixer fitted with a paddle, beat the cream cheese on medium speed until light and completely smooth, 4 to 5 minutes. Scrape down the sides of the bowl often, making sure all the cream cheese has incorporated and is silky smooth. Add the sugar and beat on medium speed until completely incorporated, stopping to scrape down the sides of the bowl as needed, 2 to 3 minutes. Add the vanilla and salt, and beat on medium speed for 2 to 3 minutes. Add the sour cream and mix on low speed until combined. Add the eggs one at a time, beating on low speed after each addition until just

combined. Using a spatula, give the filling a couple of turns to make sure it is fully mixed. **2)** Pour two-thirds of the cream cheese filling into the prepared crust. Dollop the cherry mixture on top of the cream cheese filling in the pan, and then dollop the remaining cream cheese filling next to the cherry. Use the tip of a butter knife to swirl the cherry filling into the cream cheese batter, being careful not to cut into the crust. Bang the bottom of the pan on the counter a few times to help get rid of any air bubbles. **3)** Bake the cheesecake until the center of the cheesecake registers 150°F [65°C], 30 to 35 minutes. The outside 2 to 3 in [5 to 8 cm] of the cheesecake will be puffed and fairly firm and set, but the center will still be jiggly at this point. Turn off the heat, open the oven door just a crack, and let the cheesecake rest and cool in the warm oven for 60 minutes. **4)** Transfer the pan to a wire rack and let cool. Once the cheesecake is completely cool, place a piece of parchment over the top of the pan (this helps keep condensation off the top of the cheesecake) and transfer it to the refrigerator. Let chill for at least 4 hours or overnight before slicing. Store bars in an airtight container in the refrigerator for up to 2 days.

NOTE The cherry filling will want to sink after it is dolloped, so make sure to really swirl it into the cheesecake. Any filling that does sink will leave a patch of cherry along the crustline, but this makes for a tasty bite.

VARIATION
• *Cherry Almond Cheesecake Swirl Bars—Add 1 teaspoon of almond extract to the cream cheese filling.*

51

Grapefruit Cake Bars

One of my all-time favorite Bundt cake recipes comes from Yossy Arefi's beautiful book, *Sweeter Off the Vine*. Each year, I make it several times over the winter months, gladly using up my lemons and grapefruit. I decided to see if I could make it into bar form, and happily, it worked. These bars are delicious cold, and I actually prefer them on the second day, which means you can make them ahead with no shame.

MAKES 12 LARGE OR 24 SMALL BARS

1 medium grapefruit

1 medium lemon

1½ cups [300 g] granulated sugar

1½ cups [213 g] all-purpose flour

½ teaspoon salt

¼ teaspoon plus ⅛ teaspoon baking soda

12 tablespoons [170 g] unsalted butter, at room temperature

3 large eggs, at room temperature

1 teaspoon pure vanilla extract

1 tablespoon grapefruit liqueur (optional, see Note)

½ cup [120 g] sour cream, at room temperature

GLAZE

1 medium grapefruit

2 cups [240 g] confectioners' sugar

Pinch salt

1 tablespoon grapefruit liqueur (optional)

1 teaspoon lemon juice

1) Adjust an oven rack to the middle of the oven. Preheat the oven to 350°F [180°C]. Grease a 9 by 13 in [23 by 33 cm] pan and line it with a parchment sling. 2) Scrub the grapefruit and lemon with warm, soapy water (this removes any excess wax), then dry the fruit. Put the granulated sugar into a medium bowl and zest the grapefruit and lemon directly over the sugar. Rub the zest into the sugar until combined and fragrant. 3) Cut the tops and bottoms off the grapefruit, then cut the peel and any white pith away from the outside. Over a bowl, carefully cut the wedges of the grapefruit away from the membrane, letting the fruit and juices fall into the bowl. Remove any seeds that have fallen in and break up the fruit into small pieces, about $1/2$ in [12 mm] wide.

4) In a medium bowl, whisk together the flour, salt, and baking soda. 5) In the bowl of a stand mixer fitted with the paddle, beat the butter on medium speed until creamy, about 1 minute. Add the sugar-zest mixture and mix on medium speed until light and fluffy, 2 to 3 minutes, making sure to scrape down the bottom and sides of the bowl as needed. Add the eggs one at a time, mixing for about 30 seconds on low speed after each addition. Add the vanilla and the liqueur, if using, and mix on low speed to combine. On low speed, add the sour cream, followed by the flour mixture, and mix until just combined. Remove the bowl from the mixer and gently fold in the fruit segments and their juices. 6) Pour the batter into the prepared pan and tap the pan lightly on the counter to remove any large air bubbles. Bake until a cake tester inserted into the center comes out clean, 18 to 22 minutes.

FOR THE GLAZE

Zest and juice the grapefruit. Add the zest, confectioners' sugar, and salt to a bowl. Whisk in about 3 tablespoons of the grapefruit juice, the liqueur, if using, and the lemon juice. The glaze should be thick but pourable. If the glaze seems too thick to pour, add a few more drops of grapefruit juice.

TO ASSEMBLE

1) When the cake has finished baking, move the pan to a wire rack and let cool for 5 minutes. Use a wooden skewer or toothpick to poke holes over the entire surface of the cake, about 1/2 in [12 mm] apart. Pour half of the glaze over the bars, and use an offset spatula to spread it evenly. Let the glaze soak into the cake and set (about 20 minutes), then whisk the remaining glaze and pour it over the set glaze, using an offset spatula to spread it evenly across. 2) Let the cake cool, then carefully cover and move it to the refrigerator for 2 hours or overnight before slicing. Bars can be served cold or at room temperature. Store leftover bars in an airtight container in the refrigerator for up to 3 days.

NOTE The grapefruit liqueur adds a nice underlying note in the bars, but isn't necessary. I used Tattersall's Grapefruit Crema.

Lemon Oat Bars

We made a version of these bars at a café I worked at in South Minneapolis, and they always sold out quickly. Over the years, I tinkered with the recipe by adding more sweetened condensed milk, a little salt, and some crème fraîche. They are great make-ahead bars and perfect for holidays, events, or just afternoon snacking. (I also have a Chocolate Hazelnut version, see page 173.)

MAKES 12 LARGE OR 24 SMALL BARS

LEMON FILLING

Two 14 oz [396 g] cans sweetened condensed milk

1/2 cup [120 g] lemon juice

3 tablespoons heavy cream

1 tablespoon lemon zest

1/2 teaspoon pure vanilla extract

Pinch salt

CRUST

2 cups [284 g] all-purpose flour

1 1/2 cups [120 g] rolled oats

1/2 cup [100 g] brown sugar

1/4 cup [50 g] granulated sugar

1/2 teaspoon baking soda

1/2 teaspoon salt

1 cup [2 sticks or 227 g] unsalted butter, at room temperature

Adjust an oven rack to the middle of the oven. Preheat the oven to 350°F [180°C]. Grease a 9 by 13 in [22 by 33 cm] pan and line it with a parchment sling.

FOR THE FILLING

In a large bowl, whisk together the sweetened condensed milk, lemon juice, heavy cream, zest, vanilla, and salt.

FOR THE CRUST

In the bowl of a stand mixer fitted with a paddle, mix the flour, oats, brown and granulated sugars, baking soda, and salt on low speed to combine. Add the butter and mix on medium speed until the mixture is crumbly.

TO ASSEMBLE

1) Press half of the oat mixture into the bottom of the prepared pan. Bake for 10 minutes. Remove the pan from the oven and carefully spread the filling over the crust. Sprinkle the remaining oat mixture evenly over the top. Bake for 15 to 20 minutes, until the filling is set and does not jiggle and the crumbly top is light golden brown. 2) Transfer the pan to a wire rack and let cool. Place the pan in the refrigerator and chill for 4 to 6 hours. Slice the bars and serve. The bars can be served cold or at room temperature but keep best in an airtight container in the refrigerator for about 3 days.

Citrus Pie Bars

The base for this recipe is one I use for key lime pie. I prefer it in small bars over triangles. I've found orange, blood orange, and lemon make great variations on the traditional classic, so I've given you those options here as well.

MAKES 12 LARGE BARS

CRUST

1 1/2 cups [150 g] graham cracker crumbs

3 tablespoons granulated sugar

4 tablespoons [57 g] unsalted butter, melted and cooled

FILLING

4 large egg yolks

½ cup [120 g] lime, orange, or lemon juice

2 tablespoons heavy cream

1 tablespoon lime, orange, or lemon zest

1 teaspoon pure vanilla extract

¼ teaspoon salt

One 14 oz [396 g] can sweetened condensed milk

1 or 2 drops food coloring (optional)

WHIPPED CREAM

4 oz [113 g] cream cheese, at room temperature

2 tablespoons granulated sugar

½ teaspoon pure vanilla extract

Pinch salt

1½ cups [360 g] heavy cream

FOR THE CRUST

1) Adjust an oven rack to the middle of the oven. Preheat the oven to 325°F [170°C]. Line a 9 by 9 in [23 by 23 cm] square baking pan with a parchment sling. 2) In a medium bowl, mix the graham cracker crumbs and sugar. Add the butter to the crumbs and stir until all the crumbs are coated. Use a measuring cup or spoon to press the crumbs evenly onto the bottom of the prepared pan. 3) Bake for 12 to 15 minutes, until lightly browned and fragrant. Transfer the pan to a wire rack and let cool slightly.

FOR THE FILLING

In a large bowl, whisk together the egg yolks, citrus juice, heavy cream, citrus zest, vanilla, and salt until combined. Pour in the sweetened condensed milk and whisk again until smooth and fully combined. Add the food coloring, if desired, and stir to evenly distribute. Pour the filling over the warm crust. Bake for 14 to 17 minutes, until the center is set but still a bit wiggly when jiggled.

FOR THE WHIPPED CREAM

In the bowl of a stand mixer fitted with a paddle, beat the cream cheese on medium speed until smooth. Add the sugar, vanilla, and salt. Beat on low speed until combined, then increase the speed to medium and beat until smooth. Scrape down the sides of the bowl and switch to the whisk. With the mixer running on low speed, slowly add the heavy cream and whisk until fully combined. Increase the speed to medium and beat until stiff peaks form, stopping to scrape down the sides of the bowl as needed, 2 to 3 minutes.

TO ASSEMBLE

When the pie has finished baking, transfer the pan to a wire rack and let cool completely. Place the pan in the refrigerator and chill for at least 4 hours or overnight. Top the chilled pie with the whipped cream, slice, and serve. Pie is best eaten immediately but can be stored covered in the refrigerator for 1 day.

VARIATIONS
- *Lime-Mint Pie Bars*—Add 2 tablespoons of crème de menthe and $1/2$ teaspoon of mint extract to the whipped cream along with the vanilla and make the filling with lime juice and zest.

- *Orange Dreamsicle Pie Bars*—Add the seeds of one vanilla bean to the pie filling mixture, using orange juice and zest in the filling. Bump up the vanilla in the whipped cream to 1 tablespoon.

CHAPTER 4
The Next Level

"In all ages there are beings who are perceived to be **extraordinary** . . . because they make one think of a more **beautiful**, a **freer**, a more winged life than the one we lead."

—Herman Hesse, *Pictor's Metamorphoses and Other Fantasies*

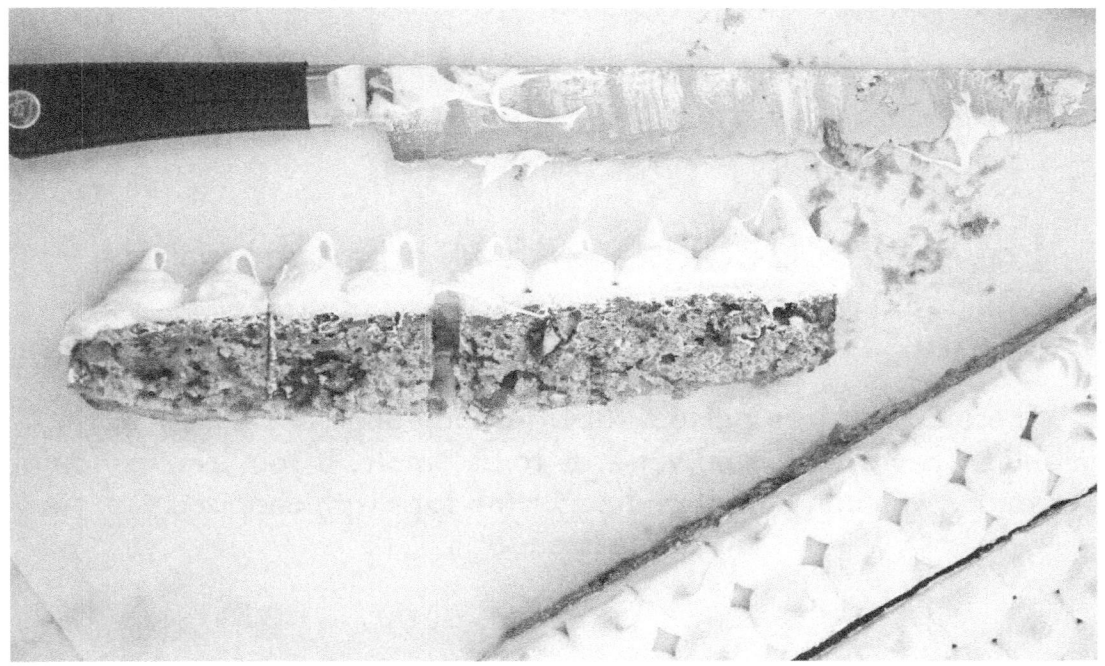

54

Lavender Cookies with White Chocolate–Crème Fraîche Glaze

These cookies are perfect for afternoon guests or dinner party nibbles. They are elegant yet easy to assemble. If you aren't a fan of lavender, you can omit it and cover the tops with chopped Candied Cacao Nibs (page 291).

MAKES ABOUT 25 COOKIES

LAVENDER COOKIES

1 cup [200 g] granulated sugar

½ teaspoon culinary lavender, plus more for sprinkling (optional)

1 cup [2 sticks or 227 g] unsalted butter, at room temperature

½ teaspoon salt

1 large egg yolk

1 teaspoon pure vanilla extract

2 cups [284 g] all-purpose flour

WHITE CHOCOLATE–CRÈME FRAÎCHE GLAZE

10 oz [283 g] white chocolate

½ cup [120 g] heavy cream

¼ cup [60 g] crème fraîche

FOR THE COOKIES

1) In the bowl of a food processor, process the granulated sugar and lavender together until the lavender buds are broken down. **2)** In the bowl of a stand mixer fitted with a paddle, beat the butter on medium speed until creamy, about 1 minute. Add the lavender-sugar and salt, and beat again on medium speed until light and fluffy, 2 to 3 minutes. Scrape down the bowl and add the egg yolk and vanilla, and mix on low speed until incorporated. Add the flour and mix on low speed until just combined. **3)** Transfer the dough to a workspace and form the dough into a 12 in [30.5 cm] long log. Place the log on a large piece of plastic, a few inches longer than the log. Wrap the log in plastic wrap and refrigerate until firm, about 2 hours. 4) Adjust an oven rack to the middle of the oven. Preheat the oven to 350°F [180°C]. Line three sheet pans with parchment paper. 5) Slice the chilled log into $1/4$ in [6 mm] thick rounds. Space the rounds about 2 in [5 cm] apart on the sheet pans. Bake one pan at a time, rotating halfway through baking. Bake until the edges are very light golden brown but the centers are still pale, 14 to 16 minutes. 6) Transfer the pan to a wire rack and let the cookies cool completely on the pan.

FOR THE GLAZE

Place the white chocolate in a medium bowl. Place the heavy cream and crème fraîche in a medium saucepan over medium heat and heat until almost boiling. Pour the cream mixture over the chocolate in the bowl. Let sit, undisturbed, for 30 seconds, then mix until smooth. Let the glaze cool for 15 to 20 minutes before using. When the cookies are cool, dip the tops of the cookies into the glaze to coat them. Sprinkle more lavender over the tops of the cookies, if desired. Let the glaze set before serving. Store cookies in an airtight container at room temperature for up to 2 days.

Smoky Butterscotch Cookies

Zoë François is known around Minneapolis for a butterscotch pot de crème she created for the restaurant Tilia. In her genius recipe, the butter and brown sugar are cooked together until deep amber and smoking, giving it a unique flavor. I came up with this cookie to mimic the taste but take the cheater's route by adding a few drops of liquid smoke to this crisp, sweet-and-salty cookie.

MAKES ABOUT 24 COOKIES

2¼ cups [320 g] all-purpose flour, plus more for dusting

½ teaspoon baking soda

12 tablespoons [1½ sticks or 170 g] unsalted butter

1¼ cups [250 g] brown sugar

½ teaspoon salt

1 teaspoon pure vanilla extract

¼ teaspoon liquid smoke

1 large egg

Granulated sugar, for sprinkling

Smoked salt or fleur de sel, for sprinkling (see Note)

1) In a small bowl, whisk together the flour and baking soda. 2) In a medium saucepan over medium heat, melt the butter, brown sugar, and salt. Remove from the heat and stir in the vanilla and liquid smoke. Let the mixture cool to room temperature. Add the egg and whisk until combined. Transfer the mixture to a large bowl. Add the flour mixture and stir until just combined. 3) Wrap the dough in plastic and chill the dough in the refrigerator for at least 4 hours (the dough will be very soft after it is mixed together and will need to be chilled well). 4) When ready to bake, adjust an oven rack to the middle of the oven. Preheat the oven to 350°F [180°C]. Line three sheet pans with parchment paper. Remove the dough from the refrigerator and let the dough warm up on the counter for 20 minutes. 5) Flour a work surface, and roll the dough out somewhere between $1/8$ in [4 mm] and $1/4$ in [6 mm] thick (the thinner the dough, the crispier the cookie, so this is a personal preference). Use a $1^1/_2$ in [4 cm] biscuit cutter to cut out circles, then place 8 cookies on each of the prepared pans. (If your cookie circles stick to the counter at all, you can slide a spatula underneath to help move them to the sheet pans.) Extra dough can be rerolled to make more cookies.

6) Sprinkle each cookie with a generous dusting of granulated sugar and a slight sprinkle of smoked salt, then chill each pan for 15 minutes before placing in the oven. 7) Bake cookies one pan at a time, rotating halfway through baking. Bake until the sides are light golden brown, 13 to 14 minutes. Leave the cookies on the pans for 10 minutes, then transfer them to a wire rack to finish cooling and crisping up. Store cookies in an airtight container at room temperature for up to 5 days.

NOTE I like to use San Francisco Salt Co.'s Alderwood Smoked Sea Salt on these cookies.

Palmiers with Apricot and Cardamom

Palmiers are a quick and easy way to make an elegant cookie. I prefer to assemble them with homemade puff pastry, but store-bought will also work well here. Make sure if you do use store-bought pastry to look for a brand that uses butter instead of oil.

MAKES 30 PALMIERS

½ cup [100 g] granulated sugar

½ recipe Rough Puff Pastry (page 279), or one 14 oz [397 g] puff pastry sheet, defrosted

1 teaspoon ground cardamom

¼ cup [80 g] apricot jam

1) Adjust an oven rack to the middle of the oven. Preheat the oven to 400°F [200°C]. Line two sheet pans with parchment paper. 2) On a clean work surface, sprinkle ¼ cup [50 g] of the sugar and lay the puff pastry on top of the sugar. Sprinkle another tablespoon or two of the sugar over the top of the puff pastry. Roll the dough out to a 20 by 12 in [50 by 30.5 cm] rectangle, about ¼ in [6 mm] thick, sprinkling more sugar as needed. Stir the cardamom into the jam, then use an offset spatula to spread the jam over the top of the puff pastry in a very thin layer. 3) Starting at the short edges, fold 2 in [5 cm] of dough toward the center. Gently fold the dough over two more times, so the two sides meet in the middle of the dough. Then fold one half over the other half, so they are stacked on top of each other. 4) Slice the dough into ⅜ in [1 cm] slices, then place them cut-side up on the prepared sheet pans 2 to 3 in [5 to 8 cm] apart (they will puff up quite a bit in the oven). You should be able to fit 15 cookies per sheet pan. Chill the cookies for 15 minutes in the freezer. 5) Bake the cookies one pan at a time, for 7 to 8 minutes, until the cookies are caramelized and cooked through. Carefully flip each cookie with a spatula and bake again for 3 to 4 minutes, until caramelized on the other side. Repeat for the second sheet pan. 6) Transfer the pan to a wire rack and let the cookies cool completely before serving. These are best eaten the day they're made.

57

French Meringues

Making kisses out of meringues is a sweet, elegant touch. While other meringues have a soft inside and firm outside, these are baked until they shatter upon first bite.

MAKES ABOUT 50 MERINGUES

2 cups [400 g] granulated sugar

1 cup [225 g] large egg whites (from 6 or 7 eggs)

¼ teaspoon salt

⅛ teaspoon cream of tartar

2 teaspoons pure vanilla extract

1) Adjust the oven racks to the upper and lower middle positions of the oven, and preheat the oven to 200°F [95°C]. Line two sheet pans with parchment paper. 2) Pour 1 in [2.5 cm] of water into a medium saucepan and bring it to a gentle boil. 3) In the bowl of a stand mixer, gently stir the sugar, egg whites, salt, and cream of tartar with a rubber spatula. Place the bowl over the saucepan, being careful not to let the water touch the bottom of the bowl. Stir with the spatula until the sugar is completely melted and reaches a temperature of 160°F [70°C], 4 to 5 minutes. As you stir the mixture, scrape down the sides of the bowl with the spatula (this will ensure no sugar crystals are lurking on the sides of the bowl and will help prevent the egg whites from cooking). 4) Remove the bowl from the heat and place it in the stand mixer fitted with a whisk. Whisk on low speed for a minute, then slowly increase the speed to medium-high. Beat until stiff, glossy peaks form, 8 to 10 minutes. The bowl should feel cool to the touch at this point. Add the vanilla and beat on medium-low speed until incorporated. 5) Working quickly, place the mixture into a pastry bag fitted with a ½ in [12 mm] plain tip. Pipe 1½ in [4 cm] mounds about 1 in [2.5 cm] apart on the prepared sheet pans, 5 rows of 5 meringues on each sheet. Bake the meringues for 1 hour. Turn off the

oven and let the meringues sit in the oven for 1 more hour. 6) Transfer the sheets to a wire rack and let the meringues cool completely. Store meringues in an airtight container at room temperature for 1 week.

VARIATION
• *Espresso Meringues—Add 2 teaspoons of ground espresso along with the vanilla.*

Meringues with Cacao Nibs and Caramel Swirl

Meringues always look so impressive, with their swoops and swirls and pure-white exterior. I've stirred in some cacao nibs for crunch and swirled in some caramel for extra extravagance.

MAKES 24 MERINGUES

2 cups [400 g] granulated sugar

1 cup [225 g] large egg whites (from 6 or 7 eggs)

1/4 teaspoon salt

1/8 teaspoon cream of tartar

1/3 cup [40 g] cacao nibs, finely chopped

2 teaspoons pure vanilla extract

1/2 cup [180 g] Caramel (page 283)

1) Adjust the oven racks to the upper and lower middle positions of the oven, and preheat the oven to 200°F [95°C]. Line two sheet pans with parchment paper. **2)** Pour 1 in [2.5 cm] of water into a medium saucepan and bring it to a gentle boil. **3)** In the bowl of a stand mixer, gently stir the sugar, egg whites, salt, and cream of tartar with a rubber spatula to combine. Place the bowl over the saucepan, being careful not to let the water touch the bottom of the bowl. Stir with the spatula until the sugar is completely melted and reaches a temperature of 160°F [70°C], 4 to 5 minutes. As you stir the mixture, scrape down the sides of the bowl with the spatula (this will ensure no sugar crystals are lurking on the sides of the bowl and will help prevent the egg whites from cooking). **4)** Remove the bowl from the heat and place it in the stand mixer fitted with a whisk. Whisk on low speed for 1 minute, then slowly increase the speed to medium-high. Beat until stiff, glossy peaks form, 8 to 10 minutes. The bowl should feel cool to the touch at this point. Add the cacao nibs and vanilla and beat on medium-low speed until incorporated. **5)** Use a spoon to mound the mixture onto the prepared sheet pans, making 12 meringues on each pan. Wet a spoon, and use the back to even the top of each meringue. Place 1 teaspoon of the caramel on top of each meringue, and use the tip of a butter knife to swirl it into the top of each meringue. **6)** Bake the meringues for 1 hour. Turn the heat off and allow the meringues to sit in the oven with the door closed for 30 minutes. **7)** Transfer the pans to wire racks and let the meringues cool completely. Store meringues in an airtight container at room temperature for up to 2 days.

59

Double Chocolate Espresso Cookies

This is riff on my Brown Butter Chocolate Chip Cookies (page 30); I've added espresso and cacao powder for a rich, decadent cookie. These chocolate treats would also pair well with Chocolate No-Churn Ice Cream (page 289) to make an intense ice cream sandwich.

MAKES ABOUT 20 COOKIES

1 1/2 cups [213 g] all-purpose flour

1/2 cup [50 g] Dutch-process cocoa powder

2 teaspoons ground espresso

1 teaspoon baking powder

1/2 teaspoon baking soda

14 tablespoons [198 g] unsalted butter, at room temperature

3/4 cup [150 g] granulated sugar

3/4 cup [150 g] brown sugar

1 tablespoon pure vanilla extract

3/4 teaspoon salt

1 large egg plus 1 large yolk

5 oz [142 g] semisweet or bittersweet chocolate, chopped into bite-size pieces

2 tablespoons cacao nibs (optional)

1) Adjust an oven rack to the middle of the oven. Preheat the oven to 350°F [180°C]. Line three sheet pans with parchment paper. **2)** In a small bowl, whisk together the flour, cocoa powder, ground espresso, baking powder, and baking soda. **3)** Slice 4 tablespoons [57 g] of the butter into four pieces, and place them in a large bowl. Melt the remaining 10 tablespoons [142 g] of butter in a medium skillet over medium-high heat. Brown the butter until it is dark golden brown and giving off a nutty aroma, 2 to 3 minutes (for tips on browning butter, see page 280). Pour the browned butter (and any bits of browned butter stuck to the bottom of the skillet) into the bowl with the room-temperature butter, and stir until all the butter is melted and combined. Stir in the granulated and brown sugars, vanilla, and salt with a rubber spatula, mixing until combined.

4) Whisk in the egg and the yolk until fully combined and the batter is smooth and glossy, about 45 seconds. Let the batter sit for 2 to 3 minutes, and then whisk again for another 45 seconds. Pour the flour mixture into the bowl and use a rubber spatula to combine (it may take a minute to incorporate all the dry ingredients). Place the chopped chocolate and cacao nibs, if using, over the dough and use your hands to knead it in until it is evenly distributed (you can use the spatula here, too, but I've found my hands make for quick work). The dough will be very shiny, slick, and dense, and it will take a minute to incorporate the chocolate. **5)**

Form the dough into $1^1/_2$ oz [45 g] balls (2 tablespoons). Place 7 cookies on each sheet pan.

6) Bake the cookies one pan at a time, rotating halfway through baking. For soft cookies with a gooey center, bake the cookies until the sides are set, the centers are very puffed, and the dough is still light, 8 to 9 minutes. For cookies with a crispy edge and tender center, bake until the cookies are light golden brown around the edges and the centers are still slightly puffed, 9 minutes. For cookies with a crisp edge and firm center, bake until the cookies are golden brown around the edges and the centers have begun to collapse, 10 minutes. **7)** Transfer the pan to a wire rack and let the cookies cool for 10 minutes, then move the cookies to the wire rack to cool completely. Store cookies in an airtight container at room temperature for up to 3 days.

NOTE For a more developed flavor, the dough can be rested for up to 48 hours in the refrigerator. Place balls of formed dough on a sheet pan lined with parchment paper, and cover with plastic wrap. Bake the next morning as directed, adding a little baking time (about 1 minute) to the chilled cookies. These cookies will be more plump and won't spread as much.

60

Espresso Cheesecake Bars

Cheesecake bars are a little less finicky than their cake counterparts, and while they are not quite as tall and grandiose, they still make for a very elegant dessert. I've made so many different flavors over the years at various places I've worked, but the adaptation I always come back to is espresso.

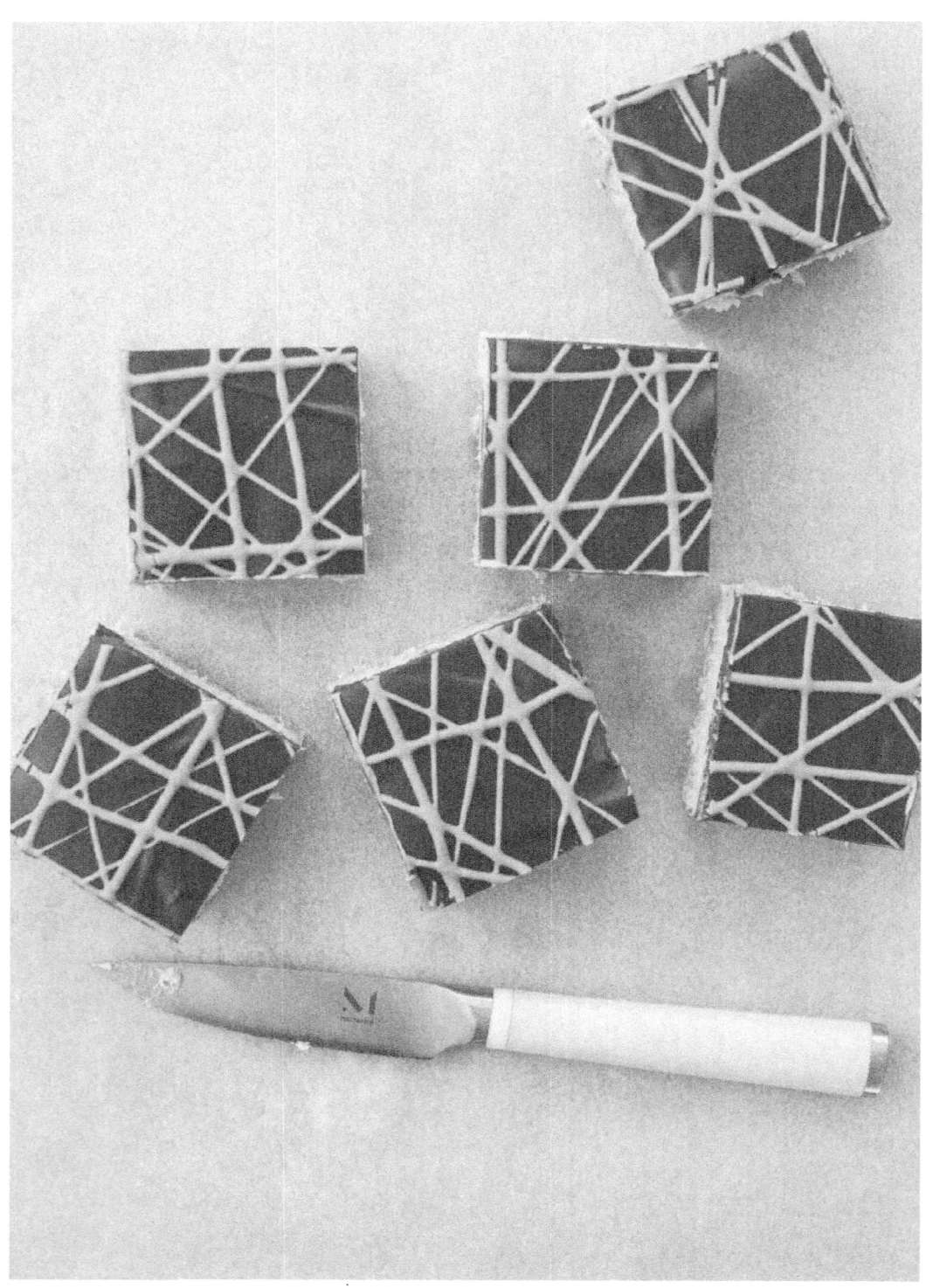

MAKES 12 LARGE OR 24 SMALL BARS

CRUST

1 1/2 cups [120 g] rolled oats

1 cup [142 g] all-purpose flour

1/2 cup [100 g] brown sugar

Pinch salt

8 tablespoons [1 stick or 113 g] unsalted butter, melted

FILLING

24 oz [678 g] cream cheese, at room temperature

1 1/2 cups [300 g] granulated sugar

1/4 teaspoon salt

1/4 cup [60 g] brewed espresso or strong coffee, at room temperature

1 tablespoon ground espresso

2 teaspoons pure vanilla extract

3 large eggs, at room temperature

1/4 cup [60 g] heavy cream

CHOCOLATE GANACHE

8 oz [226 g] semisweet or bittersweet chocolate

1 cup [240 g] heavy cream

2 oz [57 g] caramelized white chocolate, for decorating (optional)

FOR THE CRUST

1) Adjust an oven rack to the middle of the oven. Preheat the oven to 325°F [165°C]. Line a 9 by 13 in [23 by 33 cm] pan with a parchment sling. 2) Whisk together the oats, flour, brown sugar, and salt in a medium bowl. Add the melted butter and mix with a spatula until evenly incorporated. 3) Press the mixture onto the bottom of the prepared pan and bake for 10 minutes. Remove the pan from the oven and let cool. After the pan has cooled, wrap the outside sides in two layers of aluminum foil, with the shiny side facing out (this helps keep the sides of the cheesecake from browning).

FOR THE FILLING

1) In the bowl of a stand mixer fitted with a paddle, beat the cream cheese on medium speed until light and completely smooth, 4 to 5 minutes.
Scrape down the sides of the bowl often, making sure all the cream cheese has incorporated and is silky smooth. Add the granulated sugar and salt and beat on medium speed until completely incorporated, stopping to scrape down the sides of the bowl as needed, 2 to 3 minutes. Add the brewed espresso, ground espresso, and vanilla, and beat on medium speed for 2 to 3 minutes. Add the eggs, one at a time, beating on low speed after each addition until just combined. Add the heavy cream and mix on low speed until combined. Using a spatula, give the filling a couple of turns to make sure it is fully mixed. 2) Pour the filling over the cooled crust and use an offset spatula to smooth the top. Bang the bottom of the pan on the counter a few times to help get rid of any air bubbles. 3) Bake until the center of the cheesecake registers 150°F [65°C], 30 to 35 minutes. The outside 2 to 3 in [5 to 8 cm] of the cheesecake will be

puffed and fairly firm and set, but the center will still be somewhat jiggly at this point. Turn off the heat, open the oven door just a crack, and let the cheesecake rest and cool in the warm oven for 1 hour. 4) Transfer the pan to a wire rack and let the cheesecake cool. Once it is completely cool, place a piece of parchment over the top of the pan (this helps keep condensation off the top of the cheesecake) and transfer it to the refrigerator. Let chill for at least 6 hours or overnight.

FOR THE GANACHE

1) Place the chocolate in a small bowl. Heat the heavy cream in a small saucepan until it is simmering and just about to boil. Pour the cream over the chocolate, cover the bowl with plastic wrap, and let sit for 5 minutes. 2) Remove the plastic wrap and use a butter knife to stir the chocolate into the cream, until it is completely smooth. Let the mixture cool to almost room temperature. Once cool and ready to use, stir the ganache a few times before using.

TO ASSEMBLE

Pour the chocolate ganache over the top of the cheesecake, right in the center. Using an offset spatula, cover the whole top with the ganache, carefully smoothing it out as you move it to the edges. Let the ganache set before decorating.

TO DECORATE, IF DESIRED

When the ganache layer is completely set, melt the caramelized white chocolate in a small saucepan, stirring constantly, until smooth. Pour the chocolate into a disposable piping bag (or small zip-top bag) and snip the end to make a small opening (you want thin lines, so the smaller the hole, the better). The chocolate will immediately want to start pouring out, so tip the end up until you are ready to pipe, and be ready to pipe immediately. Quickly pipe the chocolate in straight lines across the cheesecake surface, making a crisscrossing pattern (or whatever pattern your heart desires). Let the white chocolate set before slicing. Use the parchment paper sling to gently lift the bars from the pan. Cut the bars into squares. The cheesecake slices easiest cold and can be eaten cold or at room temperature. Store bars in the refrigerator, covered, for up to 2 days.

61

Black and White Cheesecake Bars

This cheesecake bar will satisfy both chocolate and white chocolate fans alike. With a chocolate cookie crust, a creamy, white-chocolate filling, and a glossy chocolate ganache top, there is nothing not to love.

MAKES 12 LARGE OR 24 SMALL BARS

CRUST

2 cups [200 g] chocolate wafer cookies

5 tablespoons [70 g] unsalted butter

FILLING

24 oz [678 g] cream cheese, at room temperature

1½ cups [300 g] granulated sugar

¼ teaspoon salt

¾ cup [180 g] sour cream, at room temperature

2 teaspoons pure vanilla extract

3 large eggs, at room temperature

4 oz [113 g] white chocolate, melted and cooled to room temperature

CHOCOLATE GANACHE

8 oz [227 g] semisweet or bittersweet chocolate

1 cup [240 g] heavy cream

FOR THE CRUST

1) Adjust an oven rack to the middle of the oven. Preheat the oven to 350°F [180°C]. Grease a 9 by 13 in [23 to 33 cm] pan and line it with a parchment sling. 2) Place the cookies in the bowl of a food processor and process until broken down into fine crumbs. Move the crumbs to a medium bowl, and pour the melted butter over the top. Use a spatula to stir together until combined. 3) Press the mixture onto the bottom of the prepared pan and bake for 10 minutes. Remove the pan from the oven and let cool. After the pan has cooled, wrap the outside sides in two layers of aluminum foil, with the shiny side facing out (this helps keep the sides of the cheesecake from browning).

FOR THE FILLING

1) In the bowl of a stand mixer fitted with a paddle, beat the cream cheese on medium speed until light and completely smooth, 4 to 5 minutes. Scrape down the sides of the bowl often, making sure all the cream cheese has incorporated and is silky smooth. Add the sugar and salt and beat on medium speed until completely incorporated, stopping to scrape down the sides of the bowl as needed, 2 to 3 minutes. Add the sour cream and vanilla, and beat on medium speed until combined. Add the eggs, one at a time, beating on low speed

after each addition, until just combined. Add the white chocolate and mix on low speed until completely combined. Using a spatula, give the filling a couple of turns to make sure it is fully mixed. **2)** Pour the filling over the cooled crust and use an offset spatula to smooth the top. Bang the bottom of the pan on the counter a few times to help get rid of any air bubbles. Bake the cheesecake until the center of the cheesecake registers 150°F [65°C], 30 to 35 minutes. The outside 2 to 3 in [5 to 8 cm] of the cheesecake will be puffed and fairly firm and set, but the center will still be somewhat jiggly at this point. Turn off the heat, open the oven door just a crack, and let the cheesecake rest and cool in the warm oven for 1 hour. **3)** Transfer the pan to a wire rack and let the cheesecake cool. Once it is completely cool, place a piece of parchment over the top of the pan (this helps keep condensation off the top of the cheesecake) and transfer it to the refrigerator. Let chill for at least 6 hours or overnight.

FOR THE GANACHE

1) Place the chocolate in a small bowl. Heat the heavy cream in a small saucepan until it is simmering and just about to boil. Pour the cream over the chocolate, cover the bowl with plastic wrap, and let sit for 5 minutes. **2)** Remove the plastic wrap and use a butter knife to stir the chocolate into the cream, until it is completely smooth. Let the mixture cool to almost room temperature. Once cool and ready to use, stir the ganache a few times before using.

TO ASSEMBLE

1) Pour the chocolate ganache over the top of the cheesecake, right in the center. Using an offset spatula, cover the whole top with the ganache, carefully smoothing it out as you move it to the edges. Let the ganache set before slicing. **2)** When ready to serve, use the parchment paper sling to gently lift the cheesecake from the pan before cutting it into squares. Store bars in the refrigerator, covered, for up to 2 days.

Chocolate Hazelnut Bars

This is a chocolate take on my Lemon Oat Bars (page 146). The sweetened condensed milk and melted chocolate make a fudgy middle, and the hazelnut crust complements everything just right.

MAKES 12 LARGE OR 24 SMALL BARS

CHOCOLATE FILLING

Two 14 oz [396 g] cans sweetened condensed milk

7 oz [200 g] semisweet chocolate, melted

2 tablespoons [30 g] heavy cream

1 teaspoon pure vanilla extract

1/2 teaspoon salt

HAZELNUT CRUST

2 cups [284 g] all-purpose flour

1 1/2 cups [150 g] hazelnut flour (see page 19)

1/2 cup [100 g] brown sugar

1/4 cup [50 g] granulated sugar

1/2 teaspoon baking soda

1/2 teaspoon salt

1 cup [2 sticks or 227 g] unsalted butter, at room temperature, sliced into 1 in [2.5 cm] pieces

FOR THE FILLING

Adjust an oven rack to the middle of the oven. Preheat the oven to 350°F [180°C]. Grease a 9 by 13 in [23 to 33 cm] pan and line it with a parchment sling. In a large bowl, whisk together the sweetened condensed milk, chocolate, heavy cream, vanilla, and salt until smooth. Set aside.

FOR THE CRUST

In the bowl of a stand mixer fitted with a paddle, mix the all-purpose and hazelnut flours, brown and granulated sugars, baking soda, and salt on low speed to combine. Add the butter and mix on medium speed until the mixture is crumbly.

TO ASSEMBLE

1) Press half of the crust mixture into the bottom of the prepared pan and bake for 10 minutes. Remove the pan from the oven and carefully spread the chocolate filling over the crust. Sprinkle the remaining flour mixture evenly over the top. Bake for 15 to 20 minutes, until the chocolate has puffed up a bit and does not jiggle and the crumbly top is light golden brown. 2) Transfer the pan to a wire rack and let cool. Place the pan in the refrigerator and chill for 6 hours. Slice the bars and serve. The bars can be served cold or at room temperature but keep best in an airtight container in the refrigerator for up to 3 days.

63

French Silk Pie Bars

If my grandma were alive today, this is what I would make on her birthday each year, no questions asked. She was a chocolate fiend and always looked for an excuse to eat some. I spent many mornings bringing her iced mochas and chocolate-covered donuts when she was no longer able to get out and about herself; we would sit on lawn chairs in her front yard when the weather was nice, chatting and enjoying our sugar high. I know she would have appreciated the flaky crust, the creamy chocolate filling, and the mound of whipped cream gracing the top of these decadent bars.

MAKES 12 LARGE OR 24 SMALL BARS

CHOCOLATE FILLING

7 oz [200 g] bittersweet chocolate, melted and cooled

4 large eggs, at room temperature

¾ cup [150 g] granulated sugar

¼ cup [50 g] packed brown sugar

¼ teaspoon salt

3 tablespoons water, at room temperature

2 teaspoons pure vanilla extract

8 tablespoons [1 stick or 113 g] unsalted butter, at room temperature, cut into 8 pieces

½ cup [120 g] heavy cream

WHIPPED CREAM

4 oz [113 g] cream cheese, at room temperature

2 tablespoons granulated sugar

1 teaspoon pure vanilla extract

Pinch salt

2 cups [480 g] heavy cream

1 recipe Pie Dough Base (page 278), fully baked and cooled

Chocolate shavings, for decorating (optional)

FOR THE FILLING

1) Pour about 1 in [2.5 cm] of water into a medium saucepan and bring to a gentle boil. Melt the chocolate in a heatproof bowl set over the pan of boiling water, being careful not to let the water touch the bottom of the bowl. Stir almost constantly until just melted, and then set aside to cool. Add more water to the saucepan if needed, and bring to a boil again. **2)** In the bowl of a stand mixer, stir the eggs, granulated and brown sugars, salt, and water with a rubber spatula to combine. Place the bowl over the saucepan, being careful not to let the water touch the bottom of the bowl.

Stir with the spatula until the sugar is completely melted and reaches a temperature of 160°F [70°C], 4 to 5 minutes. While you are stirring, make sure to scrape down the sides of the bowl with the spatula, as this will ensure no sugar crystals are lurking on the sides and will help prevent the eggs from cooking. **3)** Remove the bowl from the heat and place it in the stand mixer fitted with a whisk. Whisk the mixture on high speed until light and fluffy, 8 to 10 minutes. The bowl should have cooled down to room temperature at this point. Switch to the paddle, add the melted chocolate and vanilla, and beat on low speed until combined. With the mixer running on medium speed, add a few pieces of the butter at a time, beating until completely incorporated (this will take a few minutes). Move the mixture to a large bowl. **4)** If not using immediately, cover the bowl with plastic wrap. Place the mixture in the refrigerator and hold for up to 24 hours. **5)** When ready to assemble, in the bowl of a stand mixer fitted with a whisk, beat the heavy cream on low speed until small bubbles form, about 30 seconds. Increase the speed to high and continue beating until the cream is smooth, thick, and nearly doubled in volume, about 30 seconds. Using a spatula, gently fold the chilled whipped cream into the chocolate mixture. The chocolate filling will be a little stiff at first, but the cream will incorporate; just keep mixing until it is completely combined.

FOR THE WHIPPED CREAM

In the bowl of a stand mixer fitted with a paddle, beat the cream cheese on medium speed until smooth. Add the sugar, vanilla, and salt. Beat on low speed until combined, then increase the speed to medium and beat until smooth. Scrape down the sides of the bowl and switch to the whisk. With the mixer running on low speed, slowly add the heavy cream and whisk until fully combined. Increase the speed to medium and beat until stiff peaks form, stopping to scrape down the sides of the bowl as needed, 2 to 3 minutes.

TO ASSEMBLE

Scoop the chocolate filling onto the prepared pie crust and use an offset spatula to even out the top. Top with the whipped cream and chocolate shavings, if desired. Chill the whole pie for at least 1 hour before slicing. The pie can be held unsliced in the refrigerator for 8 hours, and bars will keep for up to 2 days in an airtight container, although the crust will not be as crisp as time goes on.

64

Mud Pie Bars

After taking the first bite of these Mud Pie Bars, I declared very loudly to all who would listen that "when I order a chocolate dessert, this is exactly how I want it to taste." The only person in shouting distance was my husband, but he concurred, and we had to give the pan away before we ate the whole thing. These bars are inspired by Matt Lewis's Mud Pie Bars from his cookbook *Baked Explorations*, although I've swapped out chocolate pudding for mousse.

CRUST

2 cups [200 g] chocolate wafer cookies

5 tablespoons [70 g] unsalted butter

CAKE

8 oz [226 g] semisweet or bittersweet chocolate

12 tablespoons [1½ sticks or 170 g] unsalted butter

2 tablespoons Dutch-process cocoa powder

1¼ cups [250 g] granulated sugar

5 large eggs, at room temperature

1 teaspoon pure vanilla extract

¼ teaspoon salt

¼ cup [36 g] all-purpose flour

CHOCOLATE MOUSSE

2½ cups [600 g] heavy cream

5 large egg yolks, at room temperature

¼ cup [50 g] granulated sugar

¼ teaspoon salt

1 teaspoon pure vanilla extract

8 oz [226 g] semisweet or bittersweet chocolate, finely chopped

Whipped Cream (page 290)

Bittersweet or semisweet chocolate, for grating (optional)

FOR THE CRUST

1) Adjust an oven rack to the middle of the oven. Preheat the oven to 350°F [180°C]. Grease a 9 by 13 in [23 to 33 cm] pan and line it with a parchment sling. 2) Place the cookies in the bowl of a food processor and process until broken down into fine crumbs. Move the crumbs to a medium bowl, and pour the melted butter over the top. Use a spatula to stir together until combined. 3) Press the mixture onto the bottom of the prepared pan and bake for 10 minutes. Remove the pan from the oven and let cool.

FOR THE CAKE

1) In a small saucepan, melt the chocolate and butter together over low heat, stirring frequently, until smooth. Remove from the heat and stir in the cocoa powder. 2) In a large bowl, whisk together the sugar, eggs, vanilla, and salt until smooth. Add the flour and mix again until combined. Add the warm chocolate and whisk into the batter until combined. Let the mixture sit for 15 minutes. 3) Pour the cake batter over the cooled, baked crust and use an offset spatula to smooth the top. Bake until the edges are set and the center jiggles slightly, 15 to 18 minutes. Remove from the oven and let the cake cool completely on a wire rack. Cover the pan with plastic wrap and refrigerate for 4 hours, or over overnight.

FOR THE CHOCOLATE MOUSSE

1) Heat 1 cup [240 g] of the heavy cream in a small, heavy saucepan until hot. 2) In a medium saucepan off the heat, whisk the egg yolks. Whisking constantly, slowly add the sugar to the egg yolks, then the salt, and then slowly pour in the warmed heavy cream. Cook over medium heat, stirring constantly, until the mixture registers 160°F

[70°C]. Pour the mixture through a fine-mesh sieve into a large bowl and stir in the vanilla. **3)** In a small saucepan over low heat, melt the chocolate, stirring frequently until smooth. Whisk the chocolate into the custard until smooth, then let cool. **4)** In the bowl of a stand mixer fitted with a whisk, beat the remaining $1\frac{1}{2}$ cups [360 g] of heavy cream until stiff peaks form. Whisk one-third of the whipped cream into the chocolate custard to lighten it, then gently fold in the remaining whipped cream. Transfer the mousse to a large bowl and cover the bowl with plastic wrap. Refrigerate for 4 hours, or overnight.

TO ASSEMBLE

Pour the chocolate mousse on top of the baked, cooled cake. Use an offset spatula to even the top. Return the bars to the refrigerator and let chill for 1 hour. When ready to serve, cover the cake with the whipped cream. Coat the top with grated chocolate, if desired. Use the parchment sling to remove the cake from the pan, and cut into slices. Bars can be stored in the refrigerator in an airtight container for 2 days.

NOTE This recipe is time consuming but can be broken up over a couple of days. The crust and cake can be made the day before serving, and then the mousse and whipped cream topping can be made the next morning.

Crème Brûlée Cheesecake Bars

A crème brûlée coating on any dessert makes it seem very elegant and slightly pretentious, but I'm happy to report all you need is some granulated sugar and a kitchen torch to make it happen in your own kitchen. And, after making these cheesecake bars, I may have tried to crème brûlée everything, from cookies to pudding to the top of my chocolate malt.

MAKES 12 LARGE OR 24 SMALL BARS

CRUST

1 1/2 cups [150 g] graham cracker crumbs

3 tablespoons granulated sugar

4 tablespoons [57 g] unsalted butter, melted

CHEESECAKE

24 oz [678 g] cream cheese, at room temperature

1 1/2 cups [400 g] granulated sugar, plus 1/2 cup [100 g], for caramelizing

3/4 cup [180 g] sour cream, at room temperature

1 tablespoon pure vanilla extract

1/4 teaspoon salt

1 tablespoon unsalted butter, melted

3 large eggs, at room temperature

FOR THE CRUST

1) Adjust an oven rack to the middle of the oven. Preheat the oven to 325°F [165°C]. Line a 9 by 13 in [23 by 33 cm] pan with a parchment sling. 2) Whisk together the graham cracker crumbs and sugar in a medium bowl. Add the melted butter and mix with a spatula until evenly incorporated. 3) Press the mixture onto the bottom of the prepared pan and bake for 10 minutes. Remove the pan from the

oven and let cool. After the pan has cooled, wrap the outside sides in two layers of aluminum foil, with the shiny side facing out (this helps keep the sides of the cheesecake from browning).

FOR THE CHEESECAKE

In the bowl of a stand mixer fitted with a paddle, beat the cream cheese on medium speed until light and completely smooth, 4 to 5 minutes. Scrape down the sides of the bowl often, making sure all the cream cheese has incorporated and is silky smooth. Add $1^{1}/_{2}$ cups [300 g] of the sugar and beat on medium speed until completely incorporated, stopping to scrape down the sides of the bowl as needed, 2 to 3 minutes. Add the sour cream, vanilla, salt, and butter, and beat on medium speed for 2 to 3 minutes. Add the eggs one at a time, beating on low speed after each addition until just combined. Using a spatula, give the filling a couple of turns to make sure it is fully mixed.

TO ASSEMBLE

1) Pour the filling over the cooled crust and use an offset spatula to smooth the top. Bang the bottom of the pan on the counter a few times to help get rid of any air bubbles. 2) Bake the cheesecake until the center of the cheesecake registers 150°F [65°C], 30 to 35 minutes. The outside 2 to 3 in [5 to 8 cm] of the cheesecake will be puffed and fairly firm and set, but the center will still be jiggly at this point. Turn off the heat, open the oven door just a crack, and let the cheesecake rest and cool in the warm oven for 30 minutes. 3) Transfer the pan to a wire rack and let cool. Once the cheesecake is completely cool, place a piece of parchment over the top of the pan (this helps keep condensation off the top of the cheesecake) and transfer it to the refrigerator. Let chill for at least 6 hours or overnight. 4) Before serving, use the parchment paper sling to gently

lift the cheesecake from the pan. Sprinkle the remaining $1/2$ cup [100 g] of sugar evenly over the top of the cold cheesecake. Starting in one corner, use a kitchen torch to brown the sugar, moving it as soon as an area is browned, and rotating around the whole pan. When finished, the caramelized sugar top should be a firm, hard shell that is a deep amber color. Cut the cheesecake into squares. The sugar top will shatter a bit as you slice the bars, so you can slice the bars first and then caramelize each one individually instead. The crème brûlée topping tastes best the same day it's made.

Boston Cream Pie Bars

I'm a fan of anything smothered in pastry cream, and Boston cream pie fits that bill. The base here is a classic vanilla sponge cake, which is then layered with pastry cream and glossy chocolate ganache. I like to eat this in very small pieces, so I don't feel bad about going back for seconds and thirds.

MAKES 12 LARGE OR 24 SMALL BARS

1 recipe Pastry Cream (page 280)

VANILLA CAKE

2 large eggs, plus 2 large yolks, at room temperature

¼ cup [60 g] sour cream

¼ cup [60 g] whole milk

1 tablespoon pure vanilla extract

1¼ cups [179 g] all-purpose flour

¾ cup [150 g] granulated sugar

½ teaspoon baking powder

¼ teaspoon baking soda

½ teaspoon salt

8 tablespoons [1 stick or 113 g] unsalted butter, at room temperature, cut into 8 pieces

CHOCOLATE GANACHE

8 oz [226 g] semisweet or bittersweet chocolate, finely chopped

1 cup [240 g] heavy cream

2 tablespoons corn syrup

Make the pastry cream as directed on page 280, and refrigerate until completely cold, at least 4 hours.

FOR THE CAKE

1) Adjust an oven rack to the middle of the oven. Preheat the oven to 350°F [180°C]. Grease a 9 by 13 in [23 to 33 cm] pan and line it with a parchment sling. 2) In a medium bowl or liquid measuring cup, whisk together the eggs, yolks, sour cream, milk, and vanilla. 3) In the bowl of a stand mixer fitted with a paddle, mix the flour, sugar, baking powder, baking soda, and salt on low speed until combined. With the mixer running on low, add the butter one piece at a time, beating until the mixture resembles coarse sand.
Slowly add half the wet ingredients. Increase the speed to medium and beat until incorporated, about 30 seconds. Turn the mixer back to low speed, and add the rest of the wet ingredients, mixing until just combined. Increase the speed to medium and beat for 20 seconds. Scrape down the sides of the bowl, and use a rubber

spatula to mix the batter a few more times. **4)** Pour the mixture into the prepared pan and smooth the top with an offset spatula. Tap the pan gently on the counter a few times to get rid of any air bubbles. Bake for 11 to 14 minutes, until a wooden skewer or toothpick inserted in the center comes out clean. Move the pan to a wire rack and let cool completely.

FOR THE GANACHE

Place the chocolate in a medium bowl. In a small saucepan, heat the heavy cream and corn syrup together until simmering. Pour the cream over the chocolate, and cover with plastic wrap. Let it sit undisturbed for 5 minutes. Whisk together gently until smooth.

TO ASSEMBLE

Cover the cake in the pan with the chilled pastry cream, and use an offset spatula to smooth the top. Pour the chocolate ganache over the top of the pastry cream, and use a clean offset spatula to smooth it. Place the pan in the refrigerator and let it chill for 3 hours before slicing. Bars can be held in an airtight container in the refrigerator for 24 hours.

Carrot Cake Bars with Meringue

Carrot cake usually shows up around the holidays and winter months, but I always thought it should be the quintessential summer dessert, when carrots are bursting forth from the ground. This cake is festive regardless of when you make it; the meringue topping makes it quite the showstopper. If you are pressed for time, you could double the cream cheese frosting or cover the top with Ermine or Cardamom Buttercream (page 287).

MAKES 12 LARGE OR 24 SMALL BARS

CAKE

1 1/2 cups [213 g] all-purpose flour

1 teaspoon ground cinnamon

1/2 teaspoon baking soda

1/2 teaspoon baking powder

1/2 teaspoon salt

10 tablespoons [142 g] unsalted butter, at room temperature

3/4 cup [150 g] brown sugar

1/2 cup [100 g] granulated sugar

2 large eggs plus 2 large yolks

1 teaspoon pure vanilla extract

1/2 cup [120 g] sour cream

2 tablespoons whole milk

3 cups [300 g] peeled and grated carrots

3/4 cup [105 g] toasted pecans

CREAM CHEESE BUTTERCREAM

8 tablespoons [1 stick or 113 g] unsalted butter, at room temperature

4 oz [114 g] cream cheese, at room temperature

1 teaspoon pure vanilla extract

¼ teaspoon salt

1½ cups [180 g] confectioners' sugar

MERINGUE

2 cups [400 g] granulated sugar

1 cup [225 g] large egg whites (from 6 or 7 eggs)

¼ teaspoon salt

⅛ teaspoon cream of tartar

2 teaspoons pure vanilla extract

FOR THE CAKE

1) Adjust an oven rack to the middle position and preheat the oven to 350°F [180°C]. Grease a 9 by 13 in [23 by 33 cm] pan and line it with a parchment sling. 2) In a medium bowl, whisk together the flour, cinnamon, baking soda, baking powder, and salt. 3) Melt the butter in a medium skillet over medium-high heat. Brown the butter until it is dark golden brown and giving off a nutty aroma, 2 to 3 minutes (for tips on browning butter, see page 280). Pour the browned butter (and any bits of browned butter stuck to the bottom of the skillet) into a large bowl. Stir in the brown and granulated sugars, mixing until combined. Whisk in the eggs, yolks, and vanilla until fully combined. Add the sour cream and milk and whisk again until combined.

Pour the flour mixture into the bowl and use a rubber spatula to mix until combined. Add the grated carrots and mix until almost combined, then add the chopped pecans and mix until completely combined. 4) Pour the batter into the prepared pan and smooth the top. Tap the pan gently on the counter a few times to get rid of any air bubbles. Bake until a wooden skewer or toothpick comes out clean, 24 to 28 minutes. 5) Transfer the pan to a wire rack and let cool completely. Refrigerate for 1 hour before icing.

FOR THE CREAM CHEESE BUTTERCREAM

1) In the bowl of a stand mixer fitted with a paddle, beat the butter and cream cheese on medium speed until smooth and creamy, 2 to 3 minutes. Add the vanilla and salt and mix on low speed to combine. Add the confectioners' sugar and mix on low speed until combined. Scrape down the sides of the bowl and mix on medium speed until the buttercream is combined and smooth, 2 to 3 minutes. 2) Spread the buttercream over the cooled carrot cake. Chill the cake for 1 hour until the buttercream is firm.

FOR THE MERINGUE

1) Pour 1 in [2.5 cm] of water into a medium saucepan and bring it to a gentle boil. 2) In the bowl of a stand mixer, stir the granulated sugar, egg whites, salt, and cream of tartar with a rubber spatula to combine. Place the bowl over the saucepan, being careful not to let the water touch the bottom of the bowl. Stir with the spatula until the sugar is completely melted and reaches a temperature of 160°F [70°C], 4 to 5 minutes. As you stir the mixture, scrape down the sides of the bowl with a spatula (this will ensure no sugar crystals are lurking on the sides of the bowl and will help prevent the egg whites from cooking). 3) Remove the bowl from the heat and place it in the stand mixer fitted with a whisk. Whisk on low speed for 1 minute, then

slowly increase the speed to medium-high. Beat until stiff, glossy peaks form, 8 to 10 minutes. The bowl should feel cool to the touch at this point. Add the vanilla and beat on medium-low speed until incorporated.

TO ASSEMBLE

Working quickly, place the meringue mixture into a pastry bag fitted with a $1/2$ in [12 mm] plain tip. Pipe meringue kisses over the top of the buttercream. If desired, use a kitchen torch to carefully brown the meringue (however, I prefer them untoasted here). Slice the cake into bars and serve. Store the bars, covered, in the refrigerator for up to 2 days.

CHAPTER 5

Time to Play

"There's a point, around age twenty, when you have to choose whether to be like **everybody** else the rest of your life, or to **make a virtue of your peculiarities.**"

—Ursula K. Le Guin, *The Dispossessed*

Macarons

Macarons are not necessarily hard to make, but they can be quite a process, and each individual step of this process is essential to a perfect outcome. I don't write this to deter you from making them, but keep in mind if you are new to the macaron, there is a heavy learning curve. I wouldn't suggest, say, trying them for the first time the night before a big event where you promised to bring dessert, but I do encourage you to experiment with them when you have space to spend time figuring out how they work in your own kitchen.

I spent a lot of time over the years trying to make perfect macarons. After many, many trays of not-quite-right confections, I discovered that I have much more luck with Italian macarons over French. Italian meringues require a bit more work (a candy thermometer and boiling hot syrup), but I've found them to be more consistent for me (and Thomas Keller uses this method, too, so it must be legit). It's not a mistake that there are no cup measurements listed; the ingredients below need to be weighed precisely for best results.

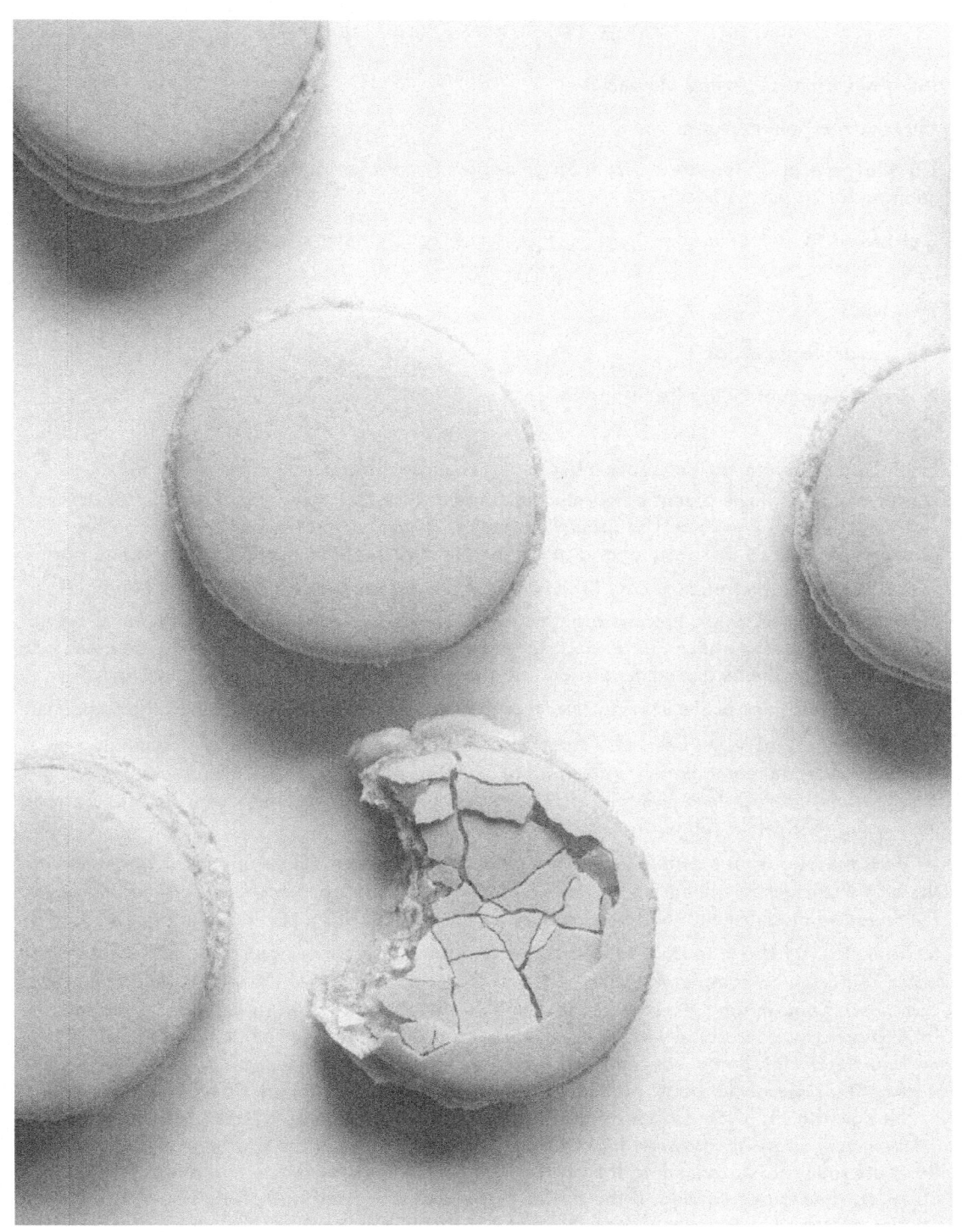

MAKES ABOUT 18 FILLED MACARONS

150 g blanched superfine almond flour

150 g confectioners' sugar

110 g large egg whites (from 3 or 4 large eggs) at room temperature and aged on the counter for at least 1 hour

Gel-based food coloring (optional, but not liquid food coloring, see Troubleshooting Tips, page 196)

90 g water

150 g granulated sugar

Rhubarb Caramel Filling (recipe follows)

1) Make a template for the cookies by tracing rounds with a pencil using a 1½ in [4 cm] biscuit cutter on three pieces of parchment paper. Make four rows with three circles across each row, leaving 2 in [5 cm] of space between each circle. Flip the papers over (so the pencil marks are on the bottom) and place them in half-sheet pans. Fit a large piping bag with a ½ in [12 mm] plain tip. **2)** In the bowl of a food processor, combine the almond flour and confectioners' sugar. Process together until very fine. Sift the mixture into a large bowl. Add half of the egg whites (55 g), and stir to combine. The mixture will be thick, so make sure all the dry ingredients are incorporated into the egg whites. Add the food coloring, if desired, to this thick paste, stirring to completely combine. Set aside. **3)** Place the remaining 55 g of egg whites in the bowl of a stand mixer fitted with a whisk. **4)** In a medium heavy-bottom saucepan, combine the water and granulated sugar. Cook the mixture over medium-high heat until it registers 244°F [115°C] on a candy thermometer. Remove from the heat and let the sugar sit while you beat the egg whites.

5) Beat the egg whites on medium speed until soft peaks form. Slowly pour the hot syrup into the egg whites while still mixing on low speed. When all the syrup has been added, increase the speed to medium-high and beat until stiff, glossy peaks form and the meringue is cool, 5 to 7 minutes. **6)** Use a spatula to fold about one-third of the meringue into the thick almond paste mixture until completely combined, and then add the rest of the whites, folding until combined. Keep folding the ingredients together, rotating the bowl as you go. During the folding process, occasionally press the mixture up against the sides of the bowl to help deflate the batter. Some ways to know if your batter is ready: When you press the batter against the sides of the bowl, your batter will slump down and not stick or cling to the sides of the bowl (this is often described as having a "hot-lava consistency"). Or, hold your spatula a few inches above the bowl with batter clinging to it. You want the batter to "ribbon" as it flows off your spatula back into the bowl. If the batter holds its shape and doesn't slump at all, more strokes are needed. If the batter melts back into itself and doesn't hold its shape at all, the batter has been over-mixed. You want the ribbon to hold its shape for a few seconds, and then slowly fade back into the batter. (This is the trickiest part of the process. It's better to undermix than overmix, so check your batter frequently.) **7)** Fill the prepared piping bag with the macaron batter. Hold the bag upright and pipe the macarons, filling each circle on the parchment paper. Continue to pipe all the circles. Lift up the sheet pan and tap the bottom on your work space a few times (this helps remove air bubbles and smooth any peaks). If there are any large air bubbles on the cookies after tapping, use a toothpick to gently pop the bubbles. Let the cookies rest for 20 to 40 minutes, until a "skin" forms over the tops and the tops are dry to the touch. (How much humidity is in the air will play a factor in how long it takes for the tops to dry.) **8)** While the macarons are drying, adjust an oven rack to the middle of the oven and preheat the oven to 325°F [160°C]. **9)** Bake the macarons one pan at a time, until the tops are secure (prod one of the shells and make sure it doesn't wiggle), 10 to 12 minutes. Remove from the oven and let the shells cool completely. **10)** Carefully remove the completely cooled shells from the parchment paper. Match up shells according to their size, and then turn one shell of each pair over. Pipe a small amount of rhubarb filling over each flipped shell (about 1 tablespoon). Sprinkle generously with caramel shards. Top with the matching macaron shell, and gently press them together. Store the filled macarons in an airtight container and refrigerate overnight and for up to 2 days. Macarons taste best when aged for at least a day in the refrigerator but can be served immediately if you just can't help yourself.

Rhubarb Caramel Filling

This rhubarb buttercream made an appearance on my website quite a few years ago, and while I love it on cakes, it tastes especially good in macarons along with Caramel Shards (page 292).

MAKES ABOUT 3 CUPS [720 G]

2 cups [200 g] rhubarb, cut into 1 in [2.5 cm] pieces (frozen rhubarb will work well here, too)

½ cup [120 g] water

Red food coloring (optional)

4 egg whites [140 g], at room temperature

1¼ cups [250 g] granulated sugar

¼ teaspoon cream of tartar

¼ teaspoon salt

1½ cups [3 sticks or 339 g] unsalted butter, at room temperature, cut into tablespoon-size pieces

1 teaspoon pure vanilla extract

½ cup [55 g] Caramel Shards (page 292), finely crushed, for sprinkling over the filling

1) Place the rhubarb and the water in a medium saucepan. Bring it to a boil, and then let simmer for 15 to 18 minutes, until the rhubarb is tender and most of the water has evaporated. Place the rhubarb in a food processor, and process into a smooth purée. If you'd like to add food coloring to brighten the color of the purée, add a few drops now, and then pulse the rhubarb a bit more, until the food coloring is evenly distributed. Set the purée aside to cool. **2)** Pour about 1 in [2.5 cm] of water into a medium saucepan and bring it to a gentle boil. **3)** In the bowl of a stand mixer, stir the egg whites, sugar, cream of tartar, and salt with a rubber spatula until combined. Place the bowl over the saucepan, being careful not to let the water touch the bottom of the bowl. Stir with the spatula until the sugar is completely melted and reaches a temperature of 160°F [70°C] on a candy thermometer, 4 to 5 minutes. **4)** Remove the bowl from the heat, and place it in the stand mixer fitted with a whisk. Whisk on medium-high speed until stiff, glossy peaks form, 8 to 10 minutes. The bowl should have cooled down to room temperature at this point. Reduce the speed to low, and, with the mixer running, add 1 to 2 tablespoons of butter at a time, beating well after each addition. When the butter has been completely incorporated, switch to the paddle. With the mixer running on low speed, add the vanilla, and then the cooled rhubarb purée, and beat until smooth, 1 to 2 minutes. Use immediately or cover and refrigerate for up to 1 week.

TROUBLESHOOTING TIPS

Oven Temperature

Make sure your oven is at the correct tempature! An oven thermometer comes in handy here.

"Aging" the Egg Whites

This is important for a few reasons. While the egg whites sit, some of their moisture is reduced and they begin to relax and lose their elasticity. That helps the egg whites beat into a meringue that is much stiffer and provides better overall structure for the macaron. Some recipes call for aging the egg whites up to 5 days, but I've found bringing them to a short rest at room temperature works just fine.

Food Coloring

Use gel-based food coloring over liquid (the liquid can add too much moisture to the batter and change the outcome). The color will fade some as the cookies bake, so make sure your batter is a little brighter than you want it to be.

Sugar Brands

Most confectioners' sugar brands contain cornstarch, and the amount of cornstarch included can affect the outcome of the macaron. Many bakers also claim that granulated sugar made with beet sugar can cause the macarons to turn out wonky, and insist on pure cane sugar. These things most likely won't affect the outcome, but if you are having trouble with your cookies, changing brands of sugar could help.

Feet

Italian macarons do have different "feet" than French macarons; they tend to be smaller and not as dramatic. (The "feet" of the macaron is the ruffled edge of the cookie that forms during baking.)

Mistakes

Having a notebook handy to jot down what went wrong or right can help you learn from your mistakes for the next batch.

Letting Go

Even not-quite-right macarons taste delicious. Fill and enjoy.

Chocolate Macarons

This chocolate version of the macaron is my favorite. It is terribly rich and indulgent but worth every bite. It's not a mistake that there are no cup measurements listed; the ingredients below need to be weighed precisely for best results.

MAKES ABOUT 18 FILLED MACARONS

125 g blanched superfine almond flour

25 g Dutch-process cocoa powder or black cocoa powder (for a darker color)

150 g confectioners' sugar

110 g egg whites (from 3 or 4 large eggs), at room temperature and aged on the counter for at least 1 hour

90 g water

150 g granulated sugar

Chocolate Ganache Crunch Filling or Coffee Cacao Nib Filling (recipes follow)

1) Make a template for the cookies by tracing rounds with a pencil using a 1 1/2 in [4 cm] biscuit cutter on three pieces of parchment paper. Make four rows with three circles across each row, leaving 2 in [5 cm] of space between each circle. Flip the papers over (so the pencil marks are on the bottom) and place them in half-sheet pans. Fit a large piping bag with a 1/2 in [12 mm] plain tip. 2) In the bowl of a food processor, combine the almond flour, cocoa powder, and confectioners' sugar. Process together until very fine. Sift the mixture into a large bowl. Add half of the egg whites [55 g], and stir to combine. The mixture will be thick, so make sure all the dry ingredients are incorporated into the egg whites. 3) Place the remaining 55 g of egg whites in the bowl of a stand mixer fitted with a

whisk. 4) In a medium heavy-bottom saucepan, combine the water and the granulated sugar. Cook the mixture over medium-high heat until it registers 244°F [115°C] on a candy thermometer. Remove from the heat and let the sugar sit while you beat the egg whites.

5) Beat the egg whites on medium speed until soft peaks form. Slowly pour the hot syrup into the egg whites while still mixing on low speed. When all the syrup has been added, increase the speed to medium-high and beat until stiff, glossy peaks form and the meringue is cool, 5 to 7 minutes. 6) Fold about one-third of the meringue into the thick almond paste mixture until completely combined, and then add the rest of the whites, folding until combined. Keep folding the ingredients together, rotating the bowl as you go. During the folding process, occasionally press the mixture up against the sides of the bowl to help deflate the batter. Some ways to know if your batter is ready: When you press the batter against the sides of the bowl, your batter will slump down and not stick or cling to the sides of the bowl (this is often described as having a "hot-lava consistency"). Or, hold your spatula a few inches above the bowl with batter clinging to it. You want the batter to "ribbon" as it flows off your spatula back into the bowl. If the batter holds its shape and doesn't slump at all, more strokes are needed. If the batter melts back into itself and doesn't hold its shape at all, the batter has been overmixed. (This is the trickiest part of the process. It's better to undermix than overmix, so check your batter frequently.) 7) Fill the prepared piping bag with the macaron batter. Hold the bag upright and pipe the macarons, filling each circle on the parchment paper. Continue to pipe all the circles. Lift up the sheet pan and tap the bottom on your work space a few times (this helps remove air bubbles and smooth any peaks). If there are any large air bubbles on the cookies after tapping, use a toothpick to gently pop the bubbles. Let the cookies rest for 30 to 40 minutes, until a "skin" forms over the tops and the tops are dry to the touch. 8) While the macarons are drying, adjust an oven rack to the middle of the oven and preheat the oven to 300°F [150°C]. 9) Bake the macarons one pan at a time, until the tops are secure (prod one of the shells and make sure it doesn't wiggle), 10 to 12 minutes. Remove from the oven and let the shells cool completely.

10) Carefully remove the completely cooled shells from the parchment paper. Match up shells according to their size, and then turn one shell of each pair over. Pipe a small amount of filling over each flipped shell (about 1 tablespoon). Top with the matching macaron shell, and gently press them together. Store the filled macarons in an airtight container and refrigerate overnight and for up to 2 days. Macarons taste best when aged for at least a day in the refrigerator but can be served immediately if you just can't help yourself.

Chocolate Ganache Crunch Filling

MAKES ABOUT 2 CUPS [480 G]

8 oz [226 g] semisweet or bittersweet chocolate

1 cup [240 g] heavy cream

Crunchy pearls, such as Valrhona Dark Chocolate Crunchy Pearls (optional)

1) Place the semisweet chocolate in a small bowl. Heat the heavy cream in a small saucepan until it is simmering and just about to boil. Pour the cream over the chocolate, cover the bowl with plastic wrap, and let sit for 5 minutes. **2)** Remove the plastic wrap and use a butter knife to stir the chocolate into the cream, until it is completely smooth. Let the mixture cool to room temperature. Once cool and ready to use, stir the ganache a few times before using. Pipe the chocolate ganache over the macaron shell as instructed on the facing page. Sprinkle 4 or 5 crunchy pearls over the ganache.

Coffee Cacao Nib Filling

MAKES ABOUT 2 CUPS [480 G]

1 recipe Coffee Buttercream (page 289)

1 recipe Candied Cacao Nibs (page 291)

Pipe the coffee buttercream over the macaron shell as instructed on the facing page. Sprinkle lightly with the candied cacao nibs.

Neapolitan Cookies

This cookie was inspired by pastry chef Matthew Rice's Neapolitan cookie, which I stumbled upon while searching Pinterest for the color pink. This cookie popped up, and I was intrigued by the pretty colors all rolled together. I headed straight to the kitchen. I used my sugar cookie (page 38) as a base and came up with the version here. My children beg for this cookie, and it's worth the extra steps needed to create it.

MAKES ABOUT 20 COOKIES

2½ cups plus 1 tablespoon [364 g] all-purpose flour

¾ teaspoon baking soda

¾ teaspoon salt

½ cup [8 g] freeze-dried strawberries

1 cup [2 sticks or 227 g] unsalted butter, at room temperature

1¾ cups [350 g] granulated sugar

1 large egg plus 1 large yolk

2 teaspoons pure vanilla extract

2 or 3 drops red food coloring (optional)

2 tablespoons Dutch-process cocoa powder

White, pink, and brown sprinkles, for rolling (optional)

1) Adjust an oven rack to the middle of the oven. Preheat the oven to 350°F [180°C]. Line three sheet pans with parchment paper. 2) In a medium bowl, combine the flour, baking soda, and salt. 3) In the bowl of a food processor fitted with a blade, pulverize the strawberries into a powder. 4) In the bowl of a stand mixer fitted with a paddle, beat the butter on medium speed until creamy, about 1 minute. Add the sugar and beat on medium speed until light and fluffy, 2 to 3 minutes. Add the egg, yolk, and vanilla, and beat on medium speed until combined. Add the flour mixture and beat on low speed until just combined. 5) Dump the dough out onto a work surface and divide it into three equal portions. Put one-third of the dough back into the mixer and add the powdered strawberries and food coloring, if using. Mix on low speed until totally combined, then remove the dough and quickly wipe out the bowl of the mixer. 6) Add another third of dough to the mixer. Add the cocoa powder and mix on low speed until totally combined.

7) Pinch a small portion (about ½ oz [15 g]) of each of the three doughs, and press them gently together, so they adhere to each other, but keep their unique colors. Press the piece into a cookie scoop or roll it into a ball, then roll the ball into sprinkles (if using). Place 6 or 7 cookies on each sheet pan. Bake the cookies one pan at a time, rotating halfway through baking. Bake until the sides are set and the cookies are puffed, 10 to 11 minutes. 8) Transfer

the sheet pan to a wire rack and let the cookies cool for 5 to 10 minutes on the pan, then remove them and let them cool completely on the wire rack. Cookies can be stored in an airtight container at room temperature for up to 2 days.

NOTES Use black cocoa powder for a darker color. The powdered strawberries on their own won't give a bright pink hue, so I like to add a little food coloring. I also like to roll each individual color of dough into the same color of sprinkles, but you can mix and match however your heart desires.

71

Roll-Up Cookies, Two Ways

These cookies, also known as pinwheels, have been around for decades. Many variations have a faint cinnamon-sugar spiral, but I wanted it to be more distinct. I decided to approach it like my favorite swirled chocolate bread filling, which is made up of melted butter, sugar, salt, and cocoa powder.

MAKES 24 COOKIES

2¼ cups [320 g] all-purpose flour

¾ teaspoon salt

½ teaspoon baking powder

⅛ teaspoon baking soda

12 tablespoons [1½ sticks or 170 g] unsalted butter, at room temperature

2 tablespoons unrefined coconut oil, at room temperature

¾ cup [150 g] granulated sugar

1 large egg

2 teaspoons pure vanilla extract

CHOCOLATE FILLING

4 tablespoons [57 g] unsalted butter

2 oz [57 g] bittersweet or semisweet chocolate, chopped

⅓ cup [65 g] brown sugar

¼ cup [25 g] Dutch-process cocoa powder

3 tablespoons all-purpose flour

Pinch salt

CINNAMON ROLL FILLING

4 tablespoons [57 g] unsalted butter

⅓ cup [65 g] brown sugar

1 tablespoon ground cinnamon

Pinch salt

¼ cup [36 g] all-purpose flour

GLAZE (OPTIONAL)

1 tablespoon cream cheese, at room temperature

2 to 3 tablespoons water

1 tablespoon unsalted butter, melted

½ teaspoon pure vanilla extract

1 cup [120 g] confectioners' sugar

1) In a large bowl, whisk together the flour, salt, baking powder, and baking soda. 2) In the bowl of a stand mixer fitted with a paddle, mix the butter on medium speed until creamy, about 1 minute. Add the coconut oil and mix again until smooth. Add the granulated sugar and mix again on medium speed until light and fluffy, 2 to 3 minutes. Add the egg and vanilla and mix on low speed until combined. 3) Add the flour mixture and mix on low speed until completely combined. Use a spatula to fold in any dry pieces of dough that may be lingering on the bottom of the bowl. Wrap the dough in plastic and refrigerate until the dough is cool but not firm, about 30 minutes.

4) Dump the dough out onto a piece of parchment paper on the counter. Pat the dough out to a 12 by 10 in [30.5 by 25 cm] rectangle. Smooth the top of the dough with the bottom of a measuring cup, or

set a piece of plastic over the dough and run your hands over the plastic to smooth it out. Move the parchment paper to a sheet pan. **5)** Spread the filling of your choice over the dough, using an offset spatula to spread it evenly. Starting with a long end, roll up the dough into a tight cylinder. The dough is forgiving, so if it tears at all while you are rolling, you can gently patch it as you go. Wrap the roll with plastic wrap, and chill the dough for 4 hours or overnight. **6)** Adjust an oven rack to the middle of the oven. Preheat the oven to 350°F [180°C]. Line three sheet pans with parchment paper. **7)** Remove the dough cylinder from the refrigerator and slice it into $1/4$ in [6 mm] thick slices. Put the cookies on the prepared pans, spacing them 2 in [5 cm] apart. Bake the cookies one pan at a time, rotating halfway through baking. Bake until the edges are light golden brown, 10 to 12 minutes. **8)** Let the cookies cool on the pans for a few minutes, then transfer the cookies to a wire rack to finish cooling. Spread with the glaze, if desired. Store cookies in an airtight container at room temperature for up to 3 days.

FOR THE CHOCOLATE FILLING

Place the butter and chocolate in a small, heavy-bottom saucepan set over low heat and melt together, stirring frequently to prevent the chocolate from scorching. Continue cooking until the mixture is smooth. Add the brown sugar, cocoa powder, flour, and salt. Stir to form a smooth paste. Set aside to cool to room temperature.

FOR THE CINNAMON ROLL FILLING

In a small saucepan, melt the butter over low heat. Remove from the heat, then add the brown sugar, cinnamon, salt, and flour. Stir to form a smooth paste. Set aside to cool to room temperature.

FOR THE GLAZE

In a small bowl, combine the cream cheese, water, butter, and vanilla until smooth. Stir in the confectioners' sugar, and stir until completely combined. Add more water as needed to make a thin glaze. When the cookies have cooled, spread a coating of glaze over each one.

NOTE Roll-up cookies tend to lose their circle shape while chilling in the refrigerator. To keep them circular, turn the log of dough every 15 minutes in the refrigerator for the first hour of chilling. Also, after 1 hour of chilling, you can bring the log to the counter and gently roll it again to help push it back into a circular shape. The glaze will soften the cookies, so if you just want a crisp circle, you can omit it.

72

Half-and-Half Cookies, Two Ways

All my inspiration for double and tricolored cookies comes from Irvin Lin's fantastic book, *Marbled, Swirled, and Layered*. This two-toned cookie has a lot of flavor on its own, but the glaze adds even more, along with a pop of color. You can swap freeze-dried raspberries for the strawberries, if desired.

MAKES 14 COOKIES

STRAWBERRY LEMONADE COOKIES

1/2 cup [16 g] freeze-dried strawberries

2 cups [284 g] all-purpose flour

1 teaspoon baking powder

3/4 teaspoon salt

1/2 teaspoon baking soda

12 tablespoons [1 1/2 sticks or 170 g] unsalted butter, at room temperature

1 1/2 cups [300 g] granulated sugar

2 tablespoons lemon zest

1 large egg plus 1 large yolk

1 1/2 teaspoons lemon extract

1 teaspoon pure vanilla extract

Red food coloring (optional)

GLAZE

4 cups [480 g] confectioners' sugar

2 tablespoons corn syrup

2 to 4 tablespoons [30 to 60 g] lemon juice

1 teaspoon pure vanilla extract

Yellow food coloring (optional)

1) Adjust an oven rack to the middle of the oven. Preheat the oven to 350°F [180°C]. Line three sheet pans with parchment paper. 2) In the bowl of a food processor, pulverize the strawberries into a powder. 3) In a medium bowl, combine the flour, baking powder, salt, and baking soda. 4) In the bowl of a stand mixer fitted with a paddle, beat the butter on medium speed until creamy, about 1 minute. Add the granulated sugar and lemon zest, and beat on medium speed until light and fluffy, 2 to 3 minutes. Scrape down the sides of the bowl, and add the egg, yolk, lemon extract, and vanilla, then beat together on low speed until combined. Add the flour mixture and mix on low speed until combined. 5) Dump the dough out onto a work surface and divide it into two equal portions. Put half of the dough

back into the mixer, and add the powdered freeze-dried strawberries and food coloring, if using. Mix on low speed until totally combined. 6) Pinch a 1 oz portion [28 g] from each of the doughs and press them gently together so they adhere to each other but keep their unique color. Press the piece into a cookie scoop or roll it into a ball, place 4 or 5 dough balls on each sheet pan, then use the back of a measuring cup or glass to flatten each ball of dough into a circle measuring about 2 in [5 cm] across. Bake the cookies one pan at a time, rotating halfway through baking. Bake for 10 minutes, then give the pan a slight tap in the oven, and continue baking until the sides of the cookies are pale golden brown, 1 to 2 minutes more. Transfer the pans to a wire rack and let the cookies cool to room temperature.

FOR THE GLAZE

Place the confectioners' sugar in a medium bowl. Add the corn syrup, 2 tablespoons of lemon juice, and vanilla, and mix until combined. If the mixture is very thick, add more lemon juice as needed. Add a drop or two of yellow food coloring, if desired.

TO ASSEMBLE

Line three sheet pans with clean parchment paper. Spread 3 or 4 tablespoons of the glaze over the top of each cookie, and place the cookies on the prepared pans. Let the glaze set completely at room temperature (about 2 hours) before serving. Once the cookies are dry, they can be stored in an airtight container at room temperature for 2 to 3 days.

ORANGE DREAMSICLE COOKIES

2 cups [284 g] all-purpose flour

1 teaspoon baking powder

¾ teaspoon salt

½ teaspoon baking soda

12 tablespoons [1½ sticks or 170 g] unsalted butter, at room temperature

1½ cups [300 g] granulated sugar

2 tablespoons orange zest

1 large egg plus 1 large yolk

1½ teaspoons orange extract

1 teaspoon pure vanilla extract

GLAZES

4 cups [480 g] confectioners' sugar, divided

1 tablespoon plus 1 teaspoon pure vanilla extract

2 tablespoons corn syrup, divided

2 to 4 tablespoons [30 to 60 g] water

2 to 4 tablespoons [30 to 60 g] orange juice

Orange food coloring (optional)

1) Adjust an oven rack to the middle of the oven. Preheat the oven to 350°F [180°C]. Line three sheet pans with parchment paper. 2) In a medium bowl, combine the flour, baking powder, salt, and baking soda. 3) In the bowl of a stand mixer fitted with a paddle, beat the butter on medium speed until creamy, about 1 minute. Add the granulated sugar and orange zest, and beat on medium speed until

light and fluffy, 2 to 3 minutes. Scrape down the sides of the bowl, and add the egg, yolk, orange extract, and vanilla, then beat together on low speed until combined. Add the flour mixture and mix on low speed until combined. 4) Form the dough into 2 oz [57 g] balls (3 tablespoons). Place 4 or 5 dough balls on each sheet pan, then use the back of a measuring cup or glass to flatten each ball of dough into a circle measuring about 2 in [5 cm] across. Bake the cookies one pan at a time, rotating halfway through baking. Bake for 10 minutes, then give the pan a slight tap in the oven, and continue baking until the sides of the cookies are pale golden brown, 1 to 2 minutes more. Move the pans to a wire rack and let the cookies cool to room temperature.

FOR THE GLAZES

1) Divide the confectioners' sugar evenly into two separate medium bowls. Add 1 tablespoon of the vanilla extract to one bowl, and 1 teaspoon to another. Add 1 tablespoon of corn syrup to each bowl. Add 2 tablespoons of water to the bowl with the 1 tablespoon of vanilla, and mix until combined. If the mixture is very thick, add more water as needed. 2) Add 2 tablespoons of the orange juice to the second bowl. Add more as needed if the mixture is too thick. Add a drop or two of orange food coloring, if desired.

TO ASSEMBLE

Line three sheet pans with clean parchment paper. Spread about 1 tablespoon of the vanilla glaze over half of the top of each cookie, and place the cookies on the prepared pans. Transfer the pans to the refrigerator and let the cookies set for about 20 minutes, until they are dry enough to handle. Glaze the other half of each cookie with about 1 tablespoon of the orange glaze. Let the glaze set completely at room temperature (about 2 hours) before serving. Once the cookies are dry, they can be stored in an airtight container at room temperature for 2 to 3 days.

73

Kitchen Sink Cookies

We made a "monster" version of this cookie at several bakeries I worked at. The cookies were packed full with chocolate-coated candy, chocolate and butterscotch chips, and plenty of peanut butter. I kept the peanut butter–oat base but instead have included potato chips, pretzels, and mini marshmallows. The combination is crunchy and delicious.

MAKES ABOUT 35 COOKIES

8 tablespoons [1 stick or 113 g] unsalted butter, at room temperature

1 cup [200 g] granulated sugar

1 cup [200 g] brown sugar

2 tablespoons corn syrup

1 1/2 cups [323 g] creamy peanut butter

3 large eggs

1 teaspoon pure vanilla extract

3/4 teaspoon salt

2 teaspoons baking soda

4 1/2 cups [360 g] rolled oats

1 cup [35 g] kettle-cooked potato chips

1 cup [35 g] pretzels

1 cup [50 g] mini marshmallows

2/3 cup [113 g] chocolate chips

2/3 cup [113 g] butterscotch chips

1) Adjust the oven rack to the middle position of the oven. Preheat the oven to 350°F [180°C]. Line five sheet pans with parchment paper. 2) In the bowl of a stand mixer fitted with a paddle, beat the butter on medium speed until creamy, about 1 minute. Add the granulated and brown sugars and corn syrup, and beat on medium speed until light and fluffy, 2 to 3 minutes. Add the peanut butter and beat on medium speed until fully combined. Add the eggs and vanilla, and beat on medium speed until smooth. Add the salt and baking soda, and mix on low speed until combined. Add the oats and mix on medium speed until combined. Add the potato chips and pretzels, and mix on low speed until they are crushed into various-size pieces, about 1 minute. Add the mini marshmallows and chocolate and butterscotch chips, and mix on low speed until combined.

3) Form the dough into 1 1/2 oz [45 g] balls (2 tablespoons). Place 7 balls on each sheet pan. Using the back of a glass or measuring cup, flatten each ball of dough so it's roughly 2 in [5 cm] across. After flattening the dough, if there are marshmallows along the edges of the

cookies, gently remove them and place them on top of the cookie. (If the marshmallows are on the edges when baking, they will melt wonkily. However, if they are tucked inside the dough or are on top, they will retain their shape much better.)

4) Bake the cookies one pan at a time, rotating halfway through baking. Bake the cookies for 6 minutes, then give the pan a tap and then continue to bake for 2 to 3 minutes more, until the edges are light golden brown. **5)** Transfer the pan to a wire rack and let the cookies cool completely on the pan. Store cookies in an airtight container at room temperature for up to 3 days.

Chocolate Sandwich Cookies

Some may scoff about making your own Oreo cookies, but I would argue there is always a need. It is true that they are time consuming, but they are delicious and perfect for gift giving, and you can fill them however your little heart desires.

MAKES ABOUT 40 FILLED COOKIES

COOKIES

1 cup plus 2 tablespoons [160 g] all-purpose flour

1/2 cup [50 g] Dutch-process cocoa powder, plus more for dusting

1/2 teaspoon salt

1/2 teaspoon baking soda

8 tablespoons [1 stick or 113 g] unsalted butter, at room temperature

1/2 cup [100 g] granulated sugar

1/4 cup [50 g] brown sugar

1 teaspoon pure vanilla extract

3 tablespoons heavy cream

CREAM FILLING

1 1/2 cups [3 sticks or 339 g] unsalted butter, at room temperature

1 tablespoon pure vanilla extract

1/4 teaspoon salt

4 cups [480 g] confectioners' sugar

1/2 cup [56 g] cornstarch

FOR THE COOKIES

1) In a small bowl, combine the flour, cocoa powder, salt, and baking soda. 2) In the bowl of a stand mixer fitted with a paddle, beat the butter on medium speed until creamy, about 1 minute. Add the granulated and brown sugars and beat on medium speed until light and fluffy, 2 to 3 minutes. Add the vanilla and mix on medium speed until combined. Add the flour mixture and mix on low speed until just combined (the mixture will be crumbly), then add the heavy cream and mix until completely combined and the dough is coming together. Wrap the dough in plastic wrap and chill in the refrigerator until cool but not firm, about 30 minutes. 3) Adjust the oven rack to the middle position of the oven. Preheat the oven to 350°F [180°C]. Line four sheet pans with parchment paper.

4) Lightly dust a work surface with cocoa powder. Roll the dough $1/8$ in [4 mm] thick. Use a $1 1/2$ in [4 cm] biscuit cutter to cut out rounds. The dough scraps can be rerolled and cut out multiple times. (This dough is very forgiving, so if it cracks as you are rolling it out, you can gently press it back together.) Place the rounds on the prepared sheet pans, fitting about 20 cookies on each pan. 5) Bake the cookies one pan at a time, for 12 to 13 minutes. The cookies will puff up slightly while baking and then fall down when they are cooked through. 6) Transfer the pan to a wire rack and let the cookies cool completely (the cookies will crisp up as they cool). Store in an airtight container at room temperature for up to 1 week.

FOR THE FILLING

In the bowl of a stand mixer fitted with a paddle, beat the butter on medium speed until creamy, about 1 minute. Add the vanilla and salt, and mix again on low speed until combined. Scrape down the sides and add the confectioners' sugar and cornstarch, and mix until combined.

TO ASSEMBLE

Pipe or place a teaspoon of filling in the center of the bottoms of half of the cookies, then top the cookie bottoms with the remaining cookies. Squeeze gently and slightly twist the top of the cookie until the filling reaches the edges. Cookies can be stored in an airtight container at room temperature for 2 days.

VARIATIONS

- *Strawberry Sandwich Cookies—Process 1/2 cup [16 g] of freeze-dried strawberries in a food processor fitted with a blade, and add the fruit powder to the mixer along with the cornstarch in the fillings. Add 1 or 2 drops of red food coloring, if desired. (Freeze-dried bananas or raspberries will also work here.)*

- *Mint Sandwich Cookies—Add 1 teaspoon of pure mint extract along with the vanilla extract in the filling. Add 1 or 2 drops of green food coloring, if desired.*

- *Thin Mints—Instead of filling the cookies, coat each individual cookie with a layer of mint chocolate. Melt 6 oz [170 g] of semisweet or bittersweet chocolate in a heatproof bowl set over a pan of boiling water, being careful not to let the water touch the bottom of the bowl, and stir constantly until the chocolate is just melted. Remove from the heat and stir in 2 oz [57 g] more chocolate and 1/2 teaspoon of mint extract. Use a fork to dip the cookies into the chocolate, completely coating the cookie. Let any excess chocolate drip off, and move the cookies to a sheet pan lined with parchment paper. Let the cookies set at room temperature before serving.*

Scotcharoos

Scotcharoo bars are crispy cereal-based bars filled with peanut butter and butterscotch, then topped with chocolate. They show up at many a Minnesota potluck, and while there are many "right" ways to make them, this is my favorite right way.

MAKES 9 BARS

5 cups [170 g] crisped rice cereal

3/4 cup [336 g] corn syrup

3/4 cup [150 g] brown sugar

1/2 teaspoon salt

1 1/4 cups [270 g] creamy peanut butter

1 cup [170 g] butterscotch chips

1 teaspoon pure vanilla extract

1 cup [170 g] chocolate chips

1 tablespoon shortening or refined coconut oil

1) Line an 8 by 8 in [20 by 20 cm] baking pan with a parchment sling, and spray with a light coat of nonstick spray. Place the cereal in a large bowl. **2)** In a medium, heavy-bottom saucepan, bring the corn syrup, brown sugar, and salt to a boil. Remove from the heat, and stir in the peanut butter, butterscotch chips, and vanilla until smooth. Pour the hot mixture over the cereal and use a greased spatula to stir the mixture together (it will be hot!) until completely combined. Pour the mixture into the prepared pan, and press it until the top is smooth. Let the bars cool for 1 hour.

3) Place the chocolate chips and shortening in a small, heavy-bottom saucepan set over low heat. Melt together, stirring frequently to prevent the chocolate from scorching. Continue cooking until the mixture is smooth. Pour over the cooled bars and let the chocolate set at room temperature until firm. Remove the treats from the pan using the sling and cut into approximately 2 1/2 in [6 cm] squares. Store bars in an airtight container at room temperature for 2 days.

Caramel Bars with Candied Peanuts

This is my take on the famous Snickers bar. It's missing the nougat, but I don't think you'll notice when biting into a piece. Candied peanuts bring extra crunch and flavor, and I tend to cut the bars into small pieces because a little goes quite a long way.

MAKES 24 LARGE OR 48 SMALL BARS

SHORTBREAD

1 cup [2 sticks or 227 g] unsalted butter, at room temperature

1 cup [200 g] granulated sugar

½ teaspoon salt

1 large egg

1 teaspoon pure vanilla extract

2 cups [284 g] all-purpose flour

CARAMEL

1½ cups [300 g] granulated sugar

¼ cup [60 g] water

3 tablespoons corn syrup

¼ teaspoon salt

7 tablespoons [105 g] heavy cream

2 tablespoons unsalted butter

1 teaspoon pure vanilla extract

2 cups [280 g] Candied Nuts, Peanuts variation (page 291)

16 oz [455 g] semisweet or bittersweet chocolate

FOR THE SHORTBREAD

1) Adjust an oven rack to the middle of the oven. Preheat the oven to 350°F [180°C]. Grease a 9 by 13 in [23 by 33 cm] baking pan and line with a parchment sling. 2) In the bowl of a stand mixer fitted with a paddle, beat the butter on medium speed until creamy, about 1 minute. Add the sugar and salt, and mix on medium speed until light and creamy, 2 to 3 minutes. Add the egg and vanilla, and mix on low speed until combined. Add the flour and mix until combined. 3) Press the mixture into the prepared pan. Bake for 18 to 22 minutes, until the shortbread is golden brown. Set the pan on a wire rack and let cool.

FOR THE CARAMEL

In a large, heavy-bottom saucepan, combine the sugar, water, corn syrup, and salt, stirring very gently to combine while trying to avoid getting any sugar crystals on the side of the pan. Cover the pot and bring to a boil over medium-high heat, until the sugar has melted and the mixture is clear, 3 to 5 minutes. Uncover, and then cook until the sugar has turned a pale golden color and registers about 300°F [150°C] on a candy thermometer, 4 to 5 minutes. Turn the heat down slightly and cook for a few minutes more, until the sugar is golden and registers 350°F [180°C]. Remove the pan immediately from the heat and add the heavy cream. The cream will foam considerably, so be careful pouring it in. Add the butter next, followed by the vanilla, and stir to combine. Set aside to cool for 5 to 10 minutes.

TO ASSEMBLE

1) Pour the caramel over the cooled shortbread, using an offset spatula to smooth it evenly. Sprinkle the candied nuts over the caramel, and then let the caramel set at room temperature. 2) Melt 14 oz [400 g] of the chocolate in a heatproof bowl set over a pan of boiling water, being careful not to let the water touch the bottom of

the bowl, and stir constantly until just melted. Remove from the heat and add the remaining 2 oz [57 g] of chocolate, stirring until smooth.

3) Pour the chocolate over the set caramel. Let the chocolate set at room temperature before slicing. Bars can be stored in an airtight container at room temperature for up to 3 days.

Chocolate–Peanut Butter Pretzel Bark

There are so, so many ways to make and top chocolate bark. And while it's technically not a cookie, I have found myself on quite a number of occasions whipping up a tray of bark for last-minute guests, holiday parties, and the like. The most basic way to make it is to melt semisweet chocolate, spread chopped nuts, dried fruit, sprinkles, or other toppings over the top, let set, and cut into pieces. I personally like to add a layer of peanut butter–chocolate ganache and then top it with pretzels, which makes for a dreamy bite.

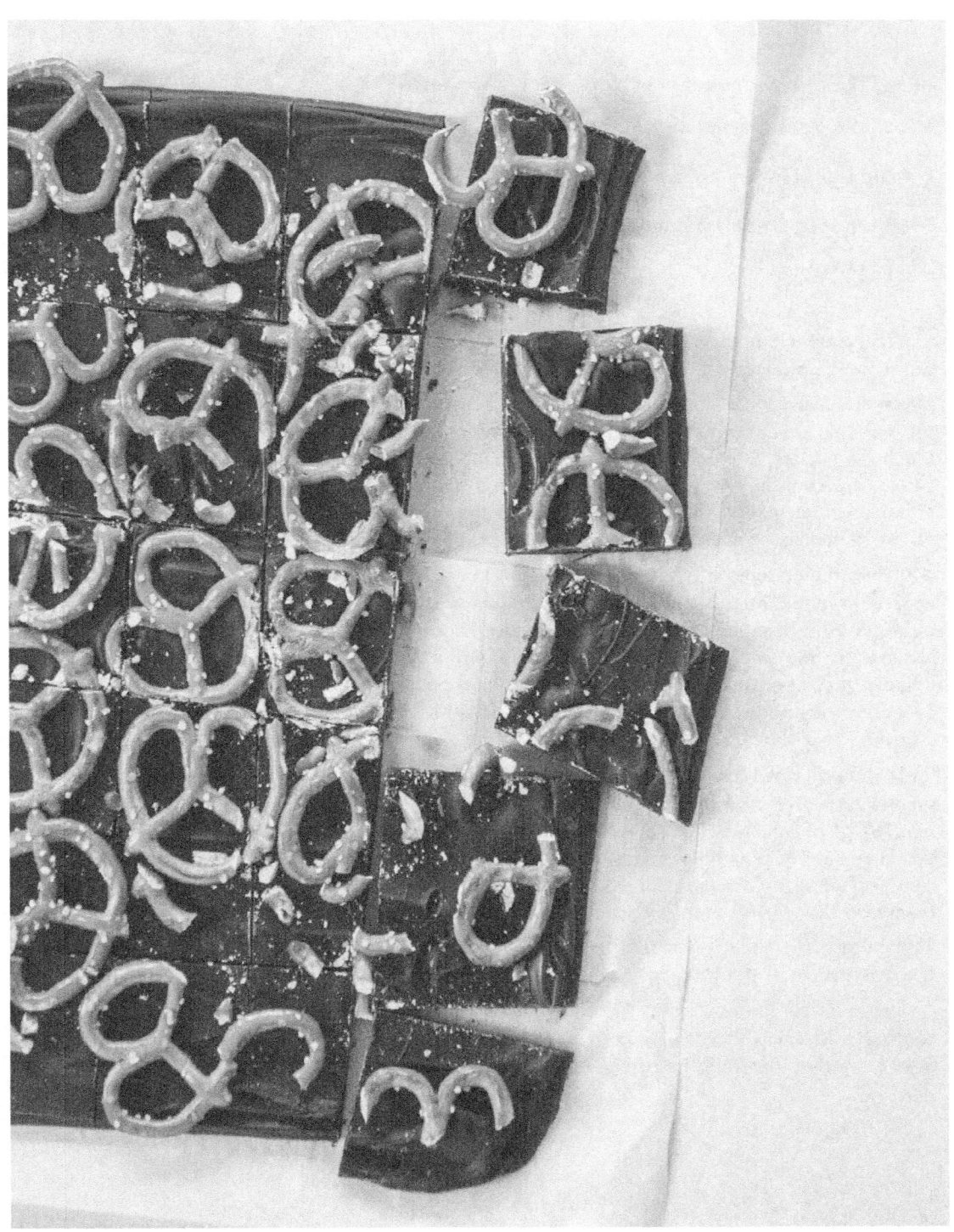

MAKES ABOUT 48 PIECES

10 oz [283 g] bittersweet chocolate, finely chopped

14 oz [396 g] semisweet chocolate, finely chopped

$1/3$ cup [80 g] heavy cream

3 tablespoons creamy peanut butter

2 cups [70 g] pretzels

1) With a pencil, measure out and mark a 9 by 13 in [23 by 33 in] rectangle on a piece of parchment paper. Flip the paper over (so the pencil marks are on the bottom), and then place the paper on a sheet pan. 2) Place the bittersweet chocolate in a heatproof bowl and set it over a saucepan of barely simmering water (do not allow the bottom of the bowl to touch the water). Stir occasionally until the chocolate is melted and smooth. Remove the chocolate from the heat, and then pour it onto the rectangle on the parchment. Using an offset spatula, spread the chocolate to fill in the rectangle. Chill in the refrigerator until set, about 15 minutes.

3) While the chocolate is setting, in the same bowl you used to melt the bittersweet chocolate, combine 6 oz [170 g] of the semisweet chocolate, the cream, and the peanut butter. Warm over the barely simmering water again, stirring frequently, until the mixture is just melted and smooth. Let the mixture cool until it is room temperature, about 15 minutes. Remove the sheet pan from the refrigerator and pour the chocolate–peanut butter mixture over the first chocolate rectangle. Using an offset spatula, spread the semisweet chocolate in an even layer. Chill in the refrigerator until very cold and firm, about 1 hour.

4) In a clean bowl, warm another 6 oz [170 g] of the semisweet chocolate over barely simmering water until the chocolate is smooth. Remove from the heat and add the remaining 2 oz [57 g] of semisweet chocolate to the warm chocolate, and stir until completely melted. Working quickly, pour the chocolate over the firm chocolate–peanut butter layer, using a clean offset spatula to spread it to cover. Cover the surface with pretzels, gently pressing them into the warm chocolate so they adhere. Chill in the refrigerator just until firm, about 20 minutes. 5) Carefully lift the parchment from the sheet pan onto a large cutting board. Trim the edges of the bark so they are straight and even. Cut the bark crosswise into 2 in [5 cm] wide strips, then cut the strips into squares or triangles. 6) Store the bark in an airtight container, layering sheets of wax or parchment paper between the layers so they don't stick to one another. Store in the refrigerator for up to 1 week.

78

Caramelized **White Chocolate Pistachio Bark**

This is a slightly easier way to make chocolate bark—no layering involved. I love the combination of the salty pistachios and the sweet, caramelized white chocolate, along with the orangy bits (find these from King Arthur). If you can't find the orange pieces, you can mix 1 to 2 teaspoons of grated orange zest in with the white chocolate after it is melted.

MAKES ABOUT 48 PIECES

16 oz [455 g] caramelized white chocolate (regular white chocolate will work, too)

1/2 cup [70 g] pistachios, shelled and chopped into small pieces

1/4 cup [35 g] orangy bits or candied orange peel

1) With a pencil, measure out and mark a 9 by 13 in [23 by 33 in] rectangle on a piece of parchment paper. Flip the parchment over (so the pencil marks are on the bottom), and then place the paper on a sheet pan. **2)** Place 14 oz [400 g] of the caramelized white chocolate in a heatproof bowl and set it over a saucepan of barely simmering water (do not allow the bottom of the bowl to touch the water). Stir occasionally until the chocolate is melted and smooth. Remove the chocolate from the heat, and then stir in the remaining 2 oz [57 g] of chocolate. Pour it onto the rectangle on the parchment. Using an offset spatula, spread the chocolate to fill the rectangle. Cover the surface with the pistachios and orangy bits, gently pressing them into the warm chocolate so they adhere. Let the chocolate set at room temperature before slicing. **3)** Carefully lift the parchment from the sheet pan onto a large cutting board. Trim the edges of the bark so they are straight and even. Cut the bark crosswise into 2 in [5 cm] wide strips, then cut the strips into squares or triangles. **4)** Store the bark in an airtight container, layering sheets of wax or parchment paper between the layers so they don't stick to one another. Store in the refrigerator for up to 1 week.

CHAPTER 6
Pan-Banging Cookies

"Everybody has their **taste** in noises as well as other matters; and **sounds** are quite innoxious, or most distressing, by their sort rather than their quantity."

–Jane Austen, *Persuasion*

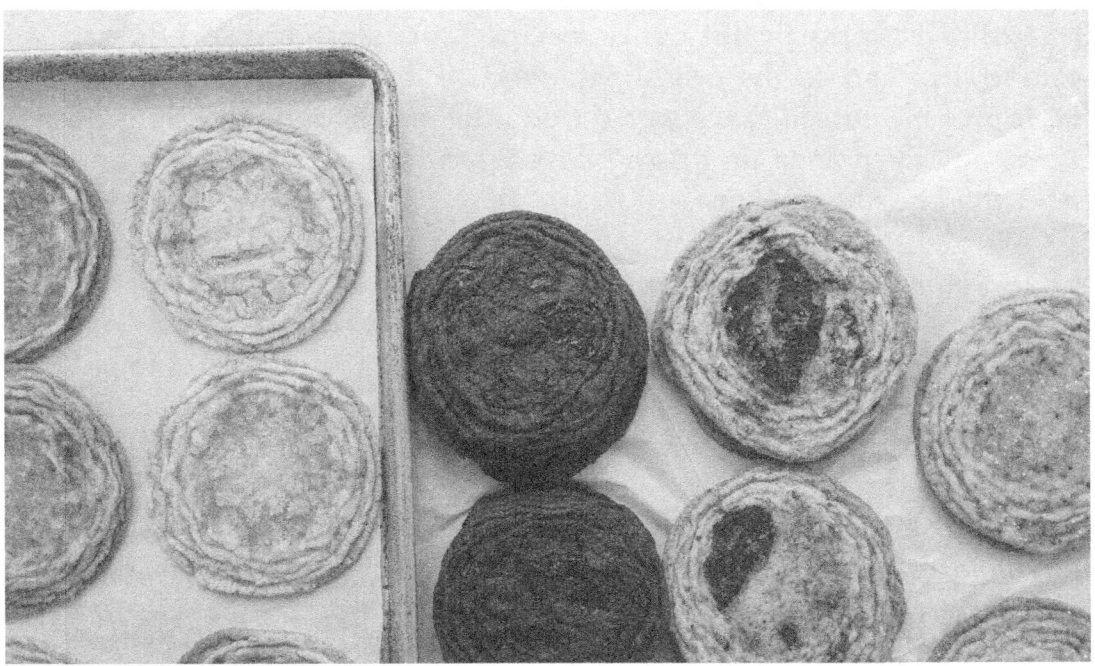

THE PAN-BANGING METHOD

When I first came up with the pan-banging chocolate chip cookie recipe, I had no idea that it would become its own hashtag. I get asked a lot of questions on the technique, how it evolved, and how to troubleshoot when problems arise, so here is some backstory and a few tips for you.

The Story

As I mentioned in the introduction, in ninth grade, I began a quest to make the perfect chocolate chip cookie. I spent hours after school determined to make one heads and tails above the rolls of cookie dough my mom brought home from the grocery store. One day, out of frustration at a particular cookie recipe that refused to spread as I wanted, I picked up the pan slightly and hit it on the oven rack. Across the top of my cookie there was a beautiful crack, and the edges of the cookie set. Ever since that day, I have been tapping my pan on the oven rack when baking cookies.

When writing the cookie chapter for my last book, I had been using this tapping method on my chocolate chip cookies, and was experimenting with a dough for thin and crispy cookies. While they baked, I found that the dough kept spreading, so I kept tapping. Each time I did so, a ripply edge appeared on my cookie. I was intrigued by how the cookies looked but more impressed with the final result: The cookie had the crisp outer edge that I had been searching for, while the center remained soft and full of melty chocolate. My husband declared them his favorite, and my kids said they were better than any cookie I had made in the past, so I added them to the cookie chapter and they soon became our house cookie.

Bakers tapping their cookie pans in the oven isn't new, of course, but the pan-banging technique I use here is unique in that the pan is tapped in the oven every few minutes, creating ripples on the edge of the cookie. This creates two textures in the cookie: a crisp outer edge, and a soft, gooey center. So, when I write about my "pan-banging" cookie technique, I am referring to this outer-edge ripple method. This technique did evolve out of the simple tap motion, but to my knowledge, it hasn't been used in this particular way before.

I wasn't sure how the people baking out of my cookbook would feel about the extra work that went into the cookies, but I started finding people were making them and loving them as much as I did. Soon #bangonapan and #panbanging hashtags were born, and the cookie went viral after the recipe was included in the *New York Times*. I am constantly overwhelmed by how many people make them throughout the week and share them with me. I'm excited to bring you a handful of new pan-banging cookies here.

Some Notes

- I've found that higher-protein flours (such as King Arthur Flour or Costco brand) do not get as many ripples as a lower-protein flour. I always use Gold Medal All-Purpose Flour when making these cookies.

- I find that aluminum foil helps the cookies spread a bit more and creates a slightly crisper bottom. But parchment paper will work well, too.

- These cookies have a higher granulated-sugar-to-brown-sugar ratio, and the baked bottoms are very buttery. The white sugar helps with the spreading and keeps the edges crisp (brown sugar is more acidic and reacts differently with the dough), which is why there is more of it in the recipe. I have played with different ratios, but have found these measurements to work best with both crispiness and rippling. The extra butter in the dough also helps with spreading. Please note that changing the amount of sugar and flour will affect how the cookie spreads; adding more brown sugar will make for a chewier cookie.

- In my original recipe, the dough is chilled before baking to help keep the cookies from spreading too quickly. I've found after making these cookies hundreds of times that the dough will still ripple without a trip to the freezer. I now make the cookies slightly smaller, which helps them not spread into each other on the tray. However, only put 3 or 4 cookies on a single baking tray to prevent them from baking into each other.

- European butter can be substituted for regular butter, and I've substituted Land O'Lakes Extra Creamy Butter and Plugrá with great success. Note that using European butter will make the bottom of these cookies even more buttery (but also note that they taste amazing).

- These cookies will ripple a little on their own (without the help of the banging), but if you don't bang the pan or don't bang the pan soon enough, it will affect the final result. The cookies should be level (the dough in the center has fallen and spread) and the sides should just barely be starting to set at the first bang. When the cookies puff up again (about 2 minutes later), the next pan-bang should take place. Banging too close together will cause the ripples to be not very defined, and waiting too long can cause the dough to not want to ripple dramatically anymore and makes for ripples that are harder in texture. This does make the process slightly tedious, but I think all the work is worth it.

- You can add extra ingredients to the dough, but note a few things: Too many add-ins (chocolate, toffee, nuts, etc.) will prevent the dough from spreading as it should. Chopped chocolate spreads much better than chocolate chips, and I highly recommend using it here.

- Cookie dough can be refrigerated overnight before using. Shape the dough into balls and cover with plastic wrap before chilling, and then bring it to room temperature before baking (when the cookies are chilled solid, they won't ripple as well).

- These cookies are delicious warm, but I've found I love them chilled even more. I usually store them in the refrigerator for a day or two and sneak pieces of them cold.

Chocolate Chip Cookies

The recipe that started it all. I've taken out the freezing step here and made the cookies slightly smaller. If you are partial to the old method, you can make your cookies into 3 1/2 oz [99 g] dough balls (a heaping 1/3 cup) and freeze the dough for 15 minutes before baking. I've also included the option of sprinkling on salt at the end, because many readers wrote to tell me it should be so.

MAKES 10 COOKIES

2 cups [284 g] all-purpose flour

3/4 teaspoon salt

1/2 teaspoon baking soda

1 cup [2 sticks or 227 g] unsalted butter, at room temperature

1 1/2 cups [300 g] granulated sugar

1/4 cup [50 g] brown sugar

1 large egg

2 tablespoons water

1 tablespoon pure vanilla extract

6 oz [170 g] semisweet or bittersweet chocolate, chopped into bite-size pieces (averaging 1/2 in [12 mm] with some smaller and some larger)

Fleur de sel for sprinkling (optional)

1) Adjust an oven rack to the middle of the oven. Preheat the oven to 350°F [180°C]. Line three sheet pans with aluminum foil, dull-side up. 2) In a small bowl, whisk together the flour, salt, and baking soda. 3) In the bowl of a stand mixer fitted with a paddle, beat the butter on medium speed until creamy, about 1 minute. Add the granulated and brown sugars and beat on medium speed until light and fluffy, 2 to 3 minutes. Add the egg, water, and vanilla, and mix on low speed to combine. Add the flour mixture and mix on low speed until combined. Add the chocolate and mix on low speed until incorporated into the batter. 4) Form the dough into 3 oz [85 g] balls (1/4 cup). Place 3 or 4 cookies an equal distance apart on the sheet pans. Bake the cookies one pan at a time. Bake until the dough balls have spread flat but are puffed slightly in the center, 9 minutes. Lift one side of the sheet pan up about 4 in [10 cm] and gently let it drop down against the oven rack, so the edges of the cookies set and the center falls back. After the cookies puff up again in 2 minutes, repeat lifting and dropping the pan. Repeat a few more times to create ridges around the edge of the cookie. Bake for 15 to 16 minutes total, until the cookies have spread out and the edges are golden brown but the centers are much lighter and not fully cooked. 5) Transfer the pan to a wire rack, and sprinkle the cookies with fleur de sel, if desired. Let the cookies cool for 10 minutes, then move them to a wire rack to finish cooling. Store cookies in an airtight container at room temperature for 2 days (or refrigerate for up to 3 days).

Oatmeal Chocolate Cookies

These oatmeal cookies don't get quite as many ripples as their chocolate counterparts, but the edges are crisp, and the centers are soft and gooey. They would also make a perfect ice cream sandwich along with some No-Churn Ice Cream (page 289).

MAKES 14 COOKIES

2 cups [160 g] rolled oats

1 cup [142 g] all-purpose flour

3/4 teaspoon baking soda

3/4 teaspoon salt

12 tablespoons [1 1/2 sticks or 170 g] unsalted butter, at room temperature

1 cup [200 g] granulated sugar

1/2 cup [100 g] brown sugar

1 large egg

1 tablespoon pure vanilla extract

4 oz [113 g] semisweet or bittersweet chocolate, chopped into bite-size pieces (averaging 1/2 in [12 mm] with some smaller and some larger)

1) Adjust an oven rack to the middle of the oven. Preheat the oven to 350°F [180°C]. Line three sheet pans with aluminum foil, dull-side up. 2) In a small bowl, whisk together the oats, flour, baking soda, and salt. 3) In the bowl of a stand mixer fitted with a paddle, beat the butter on medium speed until creamy, about 1 minute. Add the granulated and brown sugars and beat on medium speed until light and fluffy, 2 to 3 minutes. Add the egg and vanilla and mix on low speed to combine. Add the flour mixture and mix on low speed until combined. Add the chocolate and mix on low speed until combined. 4) Form the dough into 3 oz [85 g] balls (1/4 cup). Place 4 or 5 cookies an equal distance apart on the sheet pans. Bake the cookies one pan at a time. Bake until the dough balls have spread flat but are puffed slightly in the center, 9 minutes. Lift one side of the sheet pan up about 4 in [10 cm] and gently let it drop down against the oven rack, so the edges of the cookies set and the center falls back down. After the cookies puff up again in 2 minutes, repeat lifting and dropping the pan. Repeat a few more times to create ridges around the edge of the cookie. Bake for 15 to 16 minutes total, until the cookies have spread out and the edges are golden brown but the centers are much lighter and not fully cooked. 5) Transfer the pan to a wire rack. Let the cookies cool for 10 minutes, then move them to a wire rack to finish cooling. Store cookies in an airtight container at room temperature for 2 days (or refrigerate for up to 3 days).

Rum Raisin Cookies

"When you depart from me, sorrow abides and happiness takes his leave," Leonato banters with Don Pedro in William Shakespeare's *Much Ado About Nothing*, and I think the raisin often speaks this to the rolled oats, quietly tagging along into the cookie dough batter. The oats, initially, might prefer chocolate as a companion, or even some dried cherries, but after a gigantic splash of rum, I think she forgets what exactly it was that annoyed her about the wrinkly little raisin in the first place.

MAKES ABOUT 14 COOKIES

3/4 cup [96 g] raisins

1/2 cup [120 g] rum

2 cups [160 g] rolled oats

1 cup [142 g] all-purpose flour

3/4 teaspoon baking soda

3/4 teaspoon salt

1/2 teaspoon ground cinnamon

12 tablespoons [1 1/2 sticks or 170 g] unsalted butter, at room temperature

1 cup [200 g] granulated sugar

1/2 cup [100 g] brown sugar

1 teaspoon grated orange zest

1 large egg

1 teaspoon pure vanilla extract

1) In a medium bowl, combine the raisins and the rum. Let the raisins soak for 20 minutes and up to 1 hour. Drain the raisins and reserve the rum. **2)** Adjust an oven rack to the middle of the oven. Preheat the oven to 350°F [180°C]. Line three sheet pans with aluminum foil, dull-side up. **3)** In a small bowl, whisk together the oats, flour, baking soda, salt, and cinnamon. **4)** In the bowl of a stand mixer fitted with a paddle, beat the butter on medium speed until creamy, about 1 minute. Add the granulated and brown sugars and orange zest and beat on medium speed until light and fluffy, 2 to 3 minutes. Add the egg, vanilla, and 1 tablespoon of the reserved rum, and mix on low speed to combine. Add the flour mixture and mix on low speed until combined. Add the raisins and mix on low speed until combined. **5)** Form the dough into 3 oz [85 g] balls ($1/4$ cup). Place 4 or 5 cookies an equal distance apart on the sheet pans. Bake the cookies one pan at a time. Bake until the dough balls have spread flat but are puffed slightly in the center, 9 minutes. Lift one side of the sheet pan up about 4 in [10 cm] and gently let it drop down against the oven rack, so the edges of the cookies set and the center falls back down. After the cookies puff up again in 2 minutes, repeat lifting and dropping the pan. Repeat a few more times to create ridges around the edge of the cookie. Bake for 15 to 16 minutes total, until the cookies have spread out and the edges are golden brown but the centers are much lighter and not fully cooked. **6)** Transfer the pan to a wire rack. Let the cookies cool for 10 minutes, then move them to a wire rack to finish cooling. Store cookies in an airtight container at room temperature for 2 days (or refrigerate for up to 3 days).

NOTE If you really want a boozy cookie, you can soak the raisins longer, but I found a short soak was perfect for my taste buds.

Triple Chocolate Cookies

This cookie is a triple threat of chocolate, and will sing, dance, and act its way right into your belly.

MAKES ABOUT 12 COOKIES

1³/₄ cups [249 g] all-purpose flour

¹/₃ cup [33 g] Dutch-process cocoa powder

³/₄ teaspoon salt

¹/₂ teaspoon baking soda

1 cup [2 sticks or 227 g] unsalted butter

1¹/₂ cups [300 g] granulated sugar

¹/₄ cup [50 g] brown sugar

1 large egg

2 tablespoons water

1¹/₂ teaspoons pure vanilla extract

4 oz [113 g] milk chocolate, chopped into bite-size pieces (averaging ¹/₂ in [12 mm] with some smaller and some larger)

2 oz [57 g] bittersweet chocolate, chopped into bite-size pieces

1) Adjust an oven rack to the middle of the oven. Preheat the oven to 350°F [180°C]. Line three sheet pans with aluminum foil, dull-side up. 2) In a small bowl, whisk together the flour, cocoa powder, salt, and baking soda. 3) In the bowl of a stand mixer fitted with a paddle, beat the butter on medium speed until creamy, about 1 minute. Add the granulated and brown sugars and beat on medium speed until light and fluffy, 2 to 3 minutes. Add the egg, water, and vanilla, and mix on low speed to combine. Add the flour mixture and mix on low speed until combined. Add the milk and bittersweet chocolates and mix into the batter on low speed. 4) Form the dough into 3 oz [85 g] balls (¹/₄ cup). Place 4 cookies an equal distance apart on the sheet pans. Bake the cookies one pan at a time.

Bake until the dough balls have spread flat but are puffed slightly in the center, 9 minutes. Lift one side of the sheet pan up about 4 in [10 cm] and gently let it drop down against the oven rack, so the edges of the cookies set and the center falls back down. After the cookies puff up again in 2 minutes, repeat lifting and dropping the pan. Repeat this process a few more times to create ridges around the edge of the cookies. Bake for 15 to 16 minutes total, until the cookies have spread out and the edges are set and ripply but the center is still soft.

5) Transfer the pan to a wire rack. Let the cookies cool for 10 minutes, then move them to a wire rack to finish cooling. Store cookies in an airtight container at room temperature for 2 days (or refrigerate for up to 3 days).

Rocky Road Cookies

Growing up, our freezer never lacked a small pint of rocky road ice cream; it was an important staple in our house. I decided to re-create the magic in pan-banging form, turning my Triple Chocolate Cookie (page 234) into a mini-marshmallow wonderland.

MAKES ABOUT 12 COOKIES

1¾ cups [249 g] all-purpose flour

⅓ cup [33 g] Dutch-process cocoa powder

¾ teaspoon salt

½ teaspoon baking soda

1 cup [2 sticks or 227 g] unsalted butter

1½ cups [300 g] granulated sugar

¼ cup [50 g] brown sugar

1 large egg

2 tablespoons water

1½ teaspoons pure vanilla extract

3 oz [85 g] semisweet or bittersweet chocolate, chopped into bite-size pieces (averaging ½ in [12 mm] with some smaller and some larger)

½ cup [50 g] sliced almonds, toasted, plus ½ cup [50 g] for rolling

¾ cup [38 g] mini marshmallows

1) Adjust an oven rack to the middle of the oven. Preheat the oven to 350°F [180°C]. Line three sheet pans with aluminum foil, dull-side up. **2)** In a small bowl, whisk together the flour, cocoa powder, salt, and baking soda. **3)** In the bowl of a stand mixer fitted with a paddle, beat the butter on medium speed until creamy, about 1 minute. Add the granulated and brown sugars and beat on medium speed until light and fluffy, 2 to 3 minutes. Add the egg, water, and vanilla, and mix on low speed to combine. Add the flour mixture and mix on low speed until combined. Add the chocolate and ½ cup [50 g] of the toasted almonds and mix into the batter on low speed. **4)** Form the dough into 3 oz [85 g] balls (¼ cup). Roll each ball into the remaining ½ cup [50 g] of almonds, gently pressing them to adhere if needed. Place 4 cookies an equal distance apart on the sheet pans. Bake the cookies one pan at a time. Bake until the dough balls have spread flat but are puffed slightly in the center, 9 minutes. Lift one side of the sheet pan up about 4 in [10 cm] and gently let it drop down against the oven rack, so the edges of the cookies set and the center falls back down. Scatter

4 to 5 marshmallows over the center of each cookie, trying to avoid the edges. After the cookies puff up again in 2 minutes, repeat lifting and dropping the pan. Repeat this process a few more times to create ridges around the edge of the cookies. Bake for 15 to 16 minutes total, until the cookies have spread out and the edges are set and ripply but the center is still soft. **5)** Transfer the pan to a wire rack. Let the cookies cool for 10 minutes, then move them to a wire rack to finish cooling. Store cookies in an airtight container at room temperature for 2 days (or refrigerate for up to 3 days).

84

Toasted Sesame Cookies

In my first book, my chocolate chip cookie recipe had a variation that included toasted sesame oil. I've snuck it in again here, but this time around I've added white and black sesame seeds as well. Toasted sesame oil also tastes amazing with chocolate, and you can add up to 3 oz [85 g] of bittersweet or semisweet chocolate here if desired (I highly suggest it).

MAKES ABOUT 12 COOKIES

1 3/4 cups [249 g] all-purpose flour

3/4 teaspoon salt

1/2 teaspoon baking soda

12 tablespoons [1 1/2 sticks or 170 g] unsalted butter, at room temperature

1 cup [200 g] granulated sugar

1/2 cup [100 g] brown sugar

1 large egg

2 tablespoons toasted sesame oil

1 tablespoon water

1 1/2 teaspoons pure vanilla extract

3 oz [85 g] bittersweet or semisweet chocolate, chopped into bite-size pieces (averaging 1/2 in [12 mm] with some smaller and some larger, optional)

Black and white sesame seeds, for rolling

1) Adjust an oven rack to the middle of the oven. Preheat the oven to 350°F [180°C]. Line three sheet pans with aluminum foil, dull-side up. **2)** In a small bowl, whisk together the flour, salt, and baking soda. **3)** In the bowl of a stand mixer fitted with a paddle, beat the butter on medium speed until creamy, about 1 minute. Add the granulated and brown sugars and beat on medium speed until light and fluffy, 2 to 3 minutes. Add the egg, toasted sesame oil, water, and vanilla, and mix on low speed to combine. Add the flour mixture and mix on low speed until combined. Add the chocolate, if using, and mix until combined. **4)** Form the dough into 3 oz [85 g] balls (1/4 cup). Roll in the sesame seeds, and place 4 cookies an equal distance apart on each sheet pan. Bake the cookies one pan at a time.

Bake until the dough balls have spread flat but are puffed slightly in the center, 9 minutes. Lift one side of the sheet pan up about 4 in [10 cm] and gently let it drop down against the oven rack, so the edges of the cookies set and the center falls back down. After the cookies puff up again in 2 minutes, repeat lifting and dropping the pan. Repeat a few more times to create ridges around the edge of the cookie. Bake for 15 to 16 minutes total, until the cookies have spread out and the edges are golden brown but the centers are much lighter and not fully cooked. 5) Transfer the pan to a wire rack. Let the cookies cool for 10 minutes, then move them to a wire rack to finish cooling. Store cookies in an airtight container at room temperature for 2 days (or refrigerate for up to 3 days).

85

Peanut Butter Cookies

It took quite a while to get a solid, ripply version of these cookies, but after many (many) tests, I found the addition of almond flour helped the cookies spread and ripple like a dream. I love these plain, but if you are a chocolate-and-peanut-butter kind of person, you can add some bittersweet here.

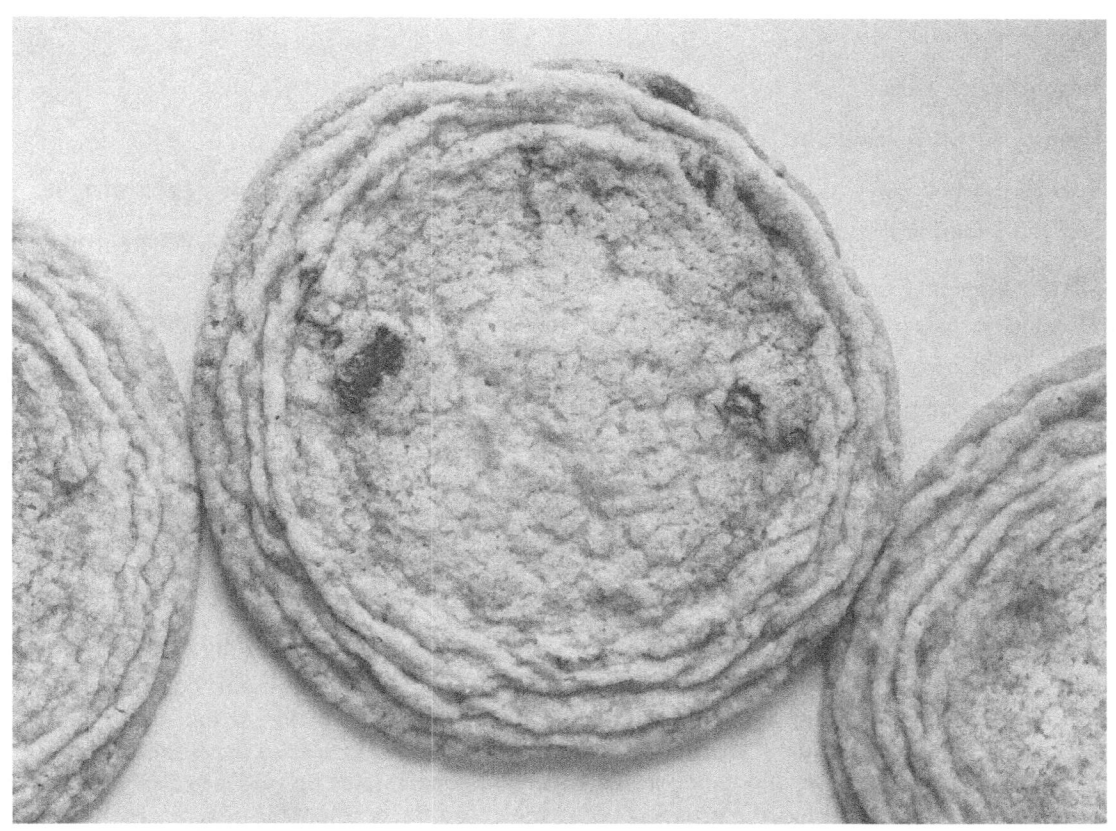

MAKES 12 COOKIES

1 cup [142 g] all-purpose flour

3/4 cup [75 g] almond flour

1/2 teaspoon baking soda

1/2 teaspoon salt

12 tablespoons [1 stick or 170 g] unsalted butter, at room temperature

1 1/4 cups [250 g] granulated sugar

1/4 cup [50 g] brown sugar

1/4 to 1/2 cup [54 to 107 g] creamy peanut butter (see Note)

1 large egg

1 tablespoon water

1 teaspoon pure vanilla extract

2 oz [57 g] semisweet or bittersweet chocolate, chopped into bite-size pieces (averaging $1/2$ in [12 mm] with some smaller and some larger, optional)

1) Adjust an oven rack to the middle of the oven. Preheat the oven to 350°F [180°C]. Line three sheet pans with aluminum foil, dull-side up. 2) In a small bowl, whisk together the all-purpose and almond flours, baking soda, and salt. 3) In the bowl of a stand mixer fitted with a paddle, beat the butter on medium speed until creamy, about 1 minute. Add the granulated and brown sugars and beat on medium speed until light and fluffy, 2 to 3 minutes. Add the peanut butter and mix again on medium speed until fully combined. Add the egg, water, and vanilla, and mix on low speed to combine. Add the flour mixture and mix on low speed until combined. Add the chocolate, if using, and mix on low speed until combined.

4) Form the dough into 3 oz [85 g] balls ($1/4$ cup). Place 4 cookies an equal distance apart on the sheet pans. Bake the cookies one pan at a time. Bake until the dough balls have spread flat but are puffed slightly in the center, 8 minutes. Lift one side of the sheet pan up about 4 in [10 cm] and gently let it drop down against the oven rack, so the edges of the cookies set and the center falls back down. After the cookies puff up again in 2 minutes, repeat lifting and dropping the pan. Repeat a few more times to create ridges around the edge of the cookie. Bake for 14 to 15 minutes total, until the cookies have spread out and the edges are golden brown but the centers are much lighter and not fully cooked. 5) Transfer the pan to a wire rack. Let the cookies cool for 10 minutes, then move them to a wire rack to finish cooling. Store cookies in an airtight container at room temperature for 2 days (or refrigerate for up to 3 days).

NOTE You can add up to $1/2$ cup [107 g] of peanut butter here, but the more that is added, the chewier the cookie will be. Just using $1/4$ cup [54 g] of peanut butter will help the cookie keep its crisp edges.

Ginger Molasses Cookies

I snuck in one cookie recipe from my website. The warm spices highlighted in this cookie are always welcome in the cool winter months, but I do find myself often making it in the heat of the summer. This cookie gets a lot of ripples, and has a nice crunch due to the sprinkle of sugar.

MAKES 10 COOKIES

1 3/4 cups [249 g] all-purpose flour

2 teaspoons ground ginger

3/4 teaspoon ground cinnamon

1/2 teaspoon plus 1/8 teaspoon salt

1/2 teaspoon baking soda

Pinch cloves

12 tablespoons [1 1/2 sticks or 170 g] unsalted butter, at room temperature

1 3/4 cups [350 g] granulated sugar

1 large egg

2 tablespoons mild molasses

1 teaspoon pure vanilla extract

1) Adjust an oven rack to the middle of the oven. Preheat the oven to 350°F [180°C]. Line three sheet pans with aluminum foil, dull-side up. **2)** In a small bowl, whisk together the flour, ginger, cinnamon, salt, baking soda, and cloves. **3)** In the bowl of a stand mixer fitted with a paddle, beat the butter on medium speed until creamy, about 1 minute. Add 1 1/2 cups [300 g] of the sugar and beat on medium speed until light and fluffy, 2 to 3 minutes. Add the egg, molasses, and vanilla, and mix on low speed to combine. Add the flour mixture and mix on low speed until combined. Remove the bowl from the stand mixer and, using a spatula, make sure the molasses is completely combined into the dough and that the dough is a uniform color. **4)** Form the dough into 3 oz [85 g] balls (1/4 cup), and roll them in the remaining 1/4 cup [50 g] of sugar. Place 3 or 4 cookies an equal distance apart on the sheet pans. Bake the cookies one pan at a time. Bake until the dough balls have spread flat but are puffed slightly in the center, 8 minutes. Lift one side of the sheet pan up about 4 in [10 cm] and gently let it drop down against the oven rack, so the edges of the cookies set and the inside falls back down. After the cookies puff up again in about 2 minutes, repeat lifting and dropping the pan. Repeat 3 or 4 more times to create ridges around the edge of the cookie. Bake for 14 to 15 minutes total, until the cookies have spread out and the edges are golden brown but the centers are much lighter and not fully cooked. **5)** Transfer the pan to a wire rack. Let the cookies cool for 10 minutes, then move them to a wire rack to finish cooling. Store cookies in an airtight container at room temperature for 2 days (or refrigerate for up to 3 days).

Snickerdoodles

I didn't realize how many people loved snickerdoodles until I posted a teaser picture on Instagram of these cookies. My comments and inbox were filled with people begging for the recipe. I was sorry to keep the recipe from everyone for almost two years, but the cookies are finally here, and I'm excited to share the recipe with you. I am certain they are worth the wait.

MAKES 12 COOKIES

2 cups [284 g] all-purpose flour

1 teaspoon baking soda

$3/4$ teaspoon salt

$1/2$ teaspoon cream of tartar

$1/4$ teaspoon freshly grated nutmeg

1 cup [2 sticks or 227 g] unsalted butter, at room temperature

$1^3/4$ cups [350 g] granulated sugar

1 large egg

1 teaspoon pure vanilla extract

1 tablespoon ground cinnamon

1) Adjust an oven rack to the middle of the oven. Preheat the oven to 350°F [180°C]. Line three sheet pans with aluminum foil, dull-side up. 2) In a small bowl, whisk together the flour, baking soda, salt, cream of tartar, and nutmeg. 3) In the bowl of a stand mixer fitted with a paddle, beat the butter on medium speed until creamy, about 1 minute. Add $1^1/2$ cups [300 g] of the sugar and beat on medium speed until light and fluffy, 2 to 3 minutes. Add the egg and vanilla and mix on low speed to combine. Add the flour mixture and mix on low speed until combined. 4) In a small bowl, combine the remaining $1/4$ cup [50 g] of sugar and the cinnamon. 5) Form the dough into 3 oz [85 g] balls ($1/4$ cup). Roll each ball in the cinnamon-sugar mixture. Place 3 or 4 cookies an equal distance apart on the sheet pans. Bake the cookies one pan at a time. Bake until the dough balls have flattened but are puffed slightly in the center, 8 minutes. Lift one side of the sheet pan up about 4 in [10 cm] and gently let it drop down against the oven rack, so the edges of the cookies set and the center falls back down. After the cookies puff up again in 2 minutes, repeat lifting and dropping the pan. Repeat a few more times to create ridges around the edge of the cookie. Bake for 14 to 15 minutes total, until the cookies have spread out and the edges are golden brown but the centers are much lighter and not fully cooked. 6) Transfer the pan to a wire rack. Let the cookies cool for 10 minutes, then move them to a wire rack to finish cooling. Store cookies in an airtight container at room temperature for 2 days (or refrigerate for up to 3 days).

Sugar Cookies

This is another recipe that makes quite a bit of ripples on the edges. I like the crunch the sugar on the outside brings, but if it is too sweet for your taste buds, you can always add a nice sprinkle of fleur de sel as the cookies emerge from the oven.

MAKES ABOUT 12 COOKIES

2 cups [284 g] all-purpose flour

1 teaspoon baking soda

3/4 teaspoon salt

1/2 teaspoon cream of tartar

1 cup [2 sticks or 227 g] unsalted butter, at room temperature

1 3/4 cups [350 g] granulated sugar

1 large egg

1 tablespoon pure vanilla extract

1) Adjust an oven rack to the middle of the oven. Preheat the oven to 350°F [180°C]. Line three sheet pans with aluminum foil, dull-side up. 2) In a small bowl, whisk together the flour, baking soda, salt, and cream of tartar. 3) In the bowl of a stand mixer fitted with a paddle, beat the butter on medium speed until creamy, about 1 minute. Add 1 1/2 cups [300 g] of the sugar and beat on medium speed until light and fluffy, 2 to 3 minutes. Add the egg and vanilla and mix on low speed to combine. Add the flour mixture and mix on low speed until combined.

4) Form the dough into 3 oz [85 g] balls (1/4 cup). Roll each ball in the remaining 1/4 cup [50 g] of sugar. Place 4 cookies an equal distance apart on the sheet pans. Bake the cookies one pan at a time. Bake until the dough balls have flattened but are puffed slightly in the center, 8 minutes. Lift one side of the sheet pan up about 4 in [10 cm] and gently let it drop down against the oven rack, so the edges of the cookies set and the center falls back down. After the cookies puff up

again in 2 minutes, repeat lifting and dropping the pan. Repeat a few more times to create ridges around the edge of the cookie. Bake for 14 to 15 minutes total, until the cookies have spread out and the edges are golden brown but the centers are much lighter and not fully cooked. **5)** Transfer the pan to a wire rack. Let the cookies cool for 10 minutes, then move them to a wire rack to finish cooling. Store cookies in an airtight container at room temperature for 2 days (or refrigerate for up to 3 days).

VARIATION
• *Sugar Cookies with Chocolate and Sprinkles—Add 2 oz [57 g] of semisweet chocolate, chopped into bite-size pieces, and $1/2$ cup [90 g] of sprinkles to the dough after mixing in the flour. Roll the dough in the sugar and more sprinkles.*

• *Red Velvet Cookies—Add 1 tablespoon of Red Velvet Bakery Emulsion to the batter along with the vanilla.*

Banana–Espresso–Cacao Nib Cookies

I try to sneak coffee and chocolate in wherever I can. The bitter notes of the espresso and cacao nibs round out the sweetness of the sugar and chocolate, and they both work well with the banana flavor. The almond flour helps these cookies spread and ripple, but does make them slightly more chewy than crisp.

MAKES ABOUT 12 COOKIES

1/4 cup [8 g] freeze-dried bananas

1 1/4 cups [179 g] all-purpose flour

1/2 cup [50 g] almond flour

1 1/2 teaspoons ground espresso

1/2 teaspoon baking soda

1/2 teaspoon salt

12 tablespoons [1 1/2 sticks or 170 g] unsalted butter, at room temperature

1 1/4 cups [250 g] granulated sugar

1/4 cup [50 g] brown sugar

1 large egg

1 tablespoon pure vanilla extract

1 tablespoon water

1/4 cup [30 g] cacao nibs, finely chopped

2 oz [57 g] semisweet or bittersweet chocolate, chopped into bite-size pieces (averaging 1/2 in [12 mm] with some smaller and some larger, optional)

1) Adjust an oven rack to the middle of the oven. Preheat the oven to 350°F [180°C]. Line three sheet pans with aluminum foil, dull-side up. 2) In the bowl of a food processor, process the freeze-dried bananas until reduced to a powder. 3) In a small bowl, whisk together the all-purpose and almond flours, ground espresso, baking soda, and salt. Add the banana powder on top and whisk it into the flour mixture. 4) In the bowl of a stand mixer fitted with a paddle, beat the butter on medium speed until creamy, about 1 minute. Add the granulated and brown sugars, and beat on medium speed until light and fluffy, 2 to 3 minutes. Add the egg, vanilla, and water, and mix on low speed to combine. Add the flour mixture and mix on low speed until combined. Add the cacao nibs and chocolate, if using, and mix on low speed until combined. 5) Form the dough into 3 oz [85 g] balls (1/4 cup).

Place 4 cookies an equal distance apart on the sheet pans. Bake the cookies one pan at a time. Bake until the dough balls have spread flat but are puffed slightly in the center, 8 minutes. Lift one side of the sheet pan up about 4 in [10 cm] and gently let it drop down against the oven rack, so the edges of the cookies set and the center falls back down. After the cookies puff up again in 2 minutes, repeat lifting and dropping the pan. Repeat a few more times to create ridges around the edge of the cookie. Bake for 14 to 15 minutes total, until the cookies have spread out and the edges are golden brown but the centers are much lighter and not fully cooked. **6)** Transfer the pan to a wire rack. Let the cookies cool for 10 minutes, then move them to a wire rack to finish cooling. Store cookies in an airtight container at room temperature for 2 days (or refrigerate for up to 3 days).

S'mores Cookies

Marshmallows baked on chocolate chip cookies, then toasted to perfection? This might be another recipe my kids requested. It's a bit more time consuming, but also a lot of fun. Homemade Marshmallows (page 284) will really make these cookies stand out.

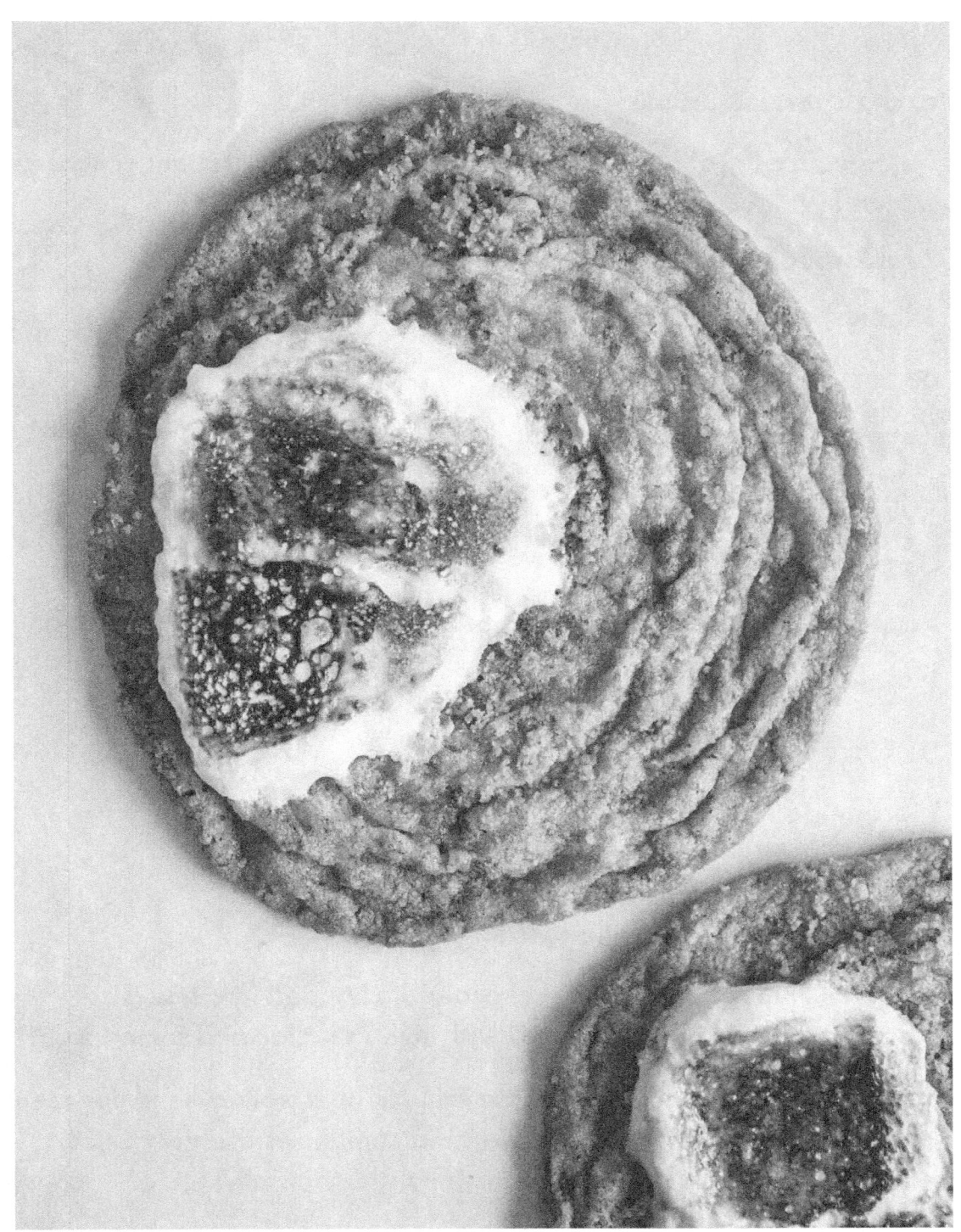

MAKES ABOUT 12 COOKIES

GRAHAM CRACKER CRUMBS

3/4 cup [75 g] graham cracker crumbs (or 6 whole graham crackers pulsed in a food processor)

2 tablespoons granulated sugar

2 tablespoons unsalted butter, melted and cooled

COOKIES

2 cups [284 g] all-purpose flour

3/4 teaspoon salt

1/2 teaspoon baking soda

1 cup [2 sticks or 227 g] unsalted butter, at room temperature

1 1/2 cups [300 g] granulated sugar

1/4 cup [50 g] packed brown sugar

1 large egg

2 tablespoons water

1 1/2 teaspoons pure vanilla extract

4 oz [113 g] milk or semisweet chocolate, chopped into bite-size pieces (averaging 1/2 in [12 mm] with some smaller and some larger)

Marshmallows (page 284), cut into thin squares, somewhere between 1/4 and 1/2 in [6 and 12 mm] (if your marshmallows are very thick, you will want to cut them in half or thirds horizontally)

FOR THE GRAHAM CRACKER CRUMBS

In a small bowl, combine the graham cracker crumbs, sugar, and melted butter, and mix until combined. The mixture should be coated in butter but not wet (you want the crumbs to cling evenly to the cookies).

FOR THE COOKIES

1) Adjust an oven rack to the middle of the oven. Preheat the oven to 350°F [180°C]. Line three sheet pans with aluminum foil, dull-side up. 2) In a small bowl, whisk together the flour, salt, and baking soda. 3) In the bowl of a stand mixer fitted with a paddle, beat the butter on medium speed until creamy, about 1 minute. Add the granulated and brown sugars and beat on medium speed until light and fluffy, 2 to 3 minutes. Add the egg, water, and vanilla, and mix on low speed to combine. Add the flour mixture and mix on low speed until combined. Add the chocolate and mix into the batter on low speed. 4) Form the dough into 3 oz (85 g) balls ($1/4$ cup). Roll each ball into the graham cracker crumbs until fully coated. Place 4 cookies an equal distance apart on the sheet pans. Bake the cookies one pan at a time. Bake until the dough balls have spread flat but are puffed slightly in the center, 9 minutes. Lift one side of the sheet pan up about 4 in [10 cm] and gently let it drop down against the oven rack, so the edges of the cookies set and the center falls back. After the cookies puff up again in 2 minutes, repeat lifting and dropping the pan.

Repeat a few more times to create ridges around the edge of the cookie. Bake for 15 to 16 minutes total, until the cookies have spread out and the edges are golden brown but the centers are much lighter and not fully cooked. 5) Remove the pan from the oven and place two or three thin square pieces of marshmallow on top of each cookie. Place the pan back in the oven for 45 seconds to 1 minute, just until the marshmallows start to melt. Remove the pan. Use a kitchen torch or broiler to gently toast the top of each marshmallow until golden. You can use a knife to very gently slide the marshmallow slightly across the cookie if you want more of the cookie covered, or leave as is. **6)** Let the cookies cool for 10 minutes on the sheet pan, then transfer them to a wire rack to finish cooling. Store cookies in an airtight container at room temperature for 2 days (or refrigerate for up to 3 days).

CHAPTER 7
Mix + Match

"I said the twelve pack, not the twenty-four pack. You're just gonna have to mix and match."

—Uncle Rico, *Napoleon Dynamite*

Brownie Cookies with Cardamom Buttercream Filling

The Brownie Cookies (page 45) in "The Classics" chapter makes a perfect base for all kinds of sandwich cookies. I personally like them filled with Coffee Buttercream (page 289), but some No-Churn Ice Cream (page 289) would also work on a hot summer day.

MAKES ABOUT 8 SANDWICH COOKIES

1 recipe Ermine Buttercream, Cardamom variation (page 287)

1 recipe Brownie Cookies (page 45)

¾ cup [105 g] Candied Cacao Nibs (page 291)

TO ASSEMBLE

Spread or pipe 2 tablespoons of the buttercream over the bottom of half the cookies. Sprinkle generously with the candied cacao nibs. Top with the remaining cookies, pressing gently to adhere them together. Cookies can be stored in an airtight container at room temperature for 2 days.

Peanut Butter Cookies with Peanut Butter Filling

I was a Girl Scout for three years of my childhood, and to me, the best part of that adventure was the peanut butter sandwich cookies filled with even more peanut butter. I've tried to mimic the flavor memory here while making a few subtle changes: The cookie base is softer, there is a (much-needed) layer of chocolate, and the filling spills out instead of barely covering the cookies. I think it's a step in the right direction.

MAKES 12 SANDWICH COOKIES

PEANUT BUTTER FILLING

1 cup [2 sticks or 227 g] unsalted butter, at room temperature

1/2 cup [107 g] peanut butter

2 tablespoons heavy cream

1 teaspoon pure vanilla extract

1/4 teaspoon salt

2 cups [240 g] confectioners' sugar

4 oz [113 g] semisweet or bittersweet chocolate, melted

1 recipe Peanut Butter Cookies (page 37)

FOR THE FILLING

In the bowl of a stand mixer fitted with a paddle, beat the butter on medium speed until creamy, about 1 minute. Add the peanut butter and mix again on medium speed, until combined and creamy. Scrape down the sides of the bowl and add the heavy cream, vanilla, and salt, and mix on low speed until combined. Add the confectioners' sugar and mix on low speed until combined, then increase the mixer speed to medium and mix until light and creamy, 3 to 4 minutes, scraping down the sides as necessary.

TO ASSEMBLE

Spread a thin layer of the melted chocolate over the bottom of half of the cookies, and let the chocolate set at room temperature. Once set, spread or pipe 2 tablespoons of filling over the chocolate. Top with the remaining cookies, pressing gently to adhere them together. Cookies can be stored in an airtight container at room temperature for 2 days.

Snickerdoodle Cookies with Pumpkin Buttercream

These little sandwich cookies would be delicious around the holidays, with their sugar-and-spice-and-everything-nice outsides and creamy-pumpkin insides. I think any and all kids' tables on Thanksgiving Day would cheer for some.

MAKES 12 SANDWICH COOKIES

BUTTERCREAM

1/2 cup [122 g] pumpkin purée

1/4 cup [50 g] brown sugar

1 cup [2 sticks or 227 g] plus 1 tablespoon unsalted butter, at room temperature

1/2 teaspoon ground ginger

1/2 teaspoon ground cinnamon

1 teaspoon pure vanilla extract

Pinch salt

2 cups [240 g] confectioners' sugar

1 recipe Snickerdoodles (page 48)

1/2 cup [55 g] Caramel Shards (page 292), finely processed

FOR THE BUTTERCREAM

1) Combine the pumpkin purée, brown sugar, 1 tablespoon of the butter, the ginger, and cinnamon in a small saucepan over low heat, stirring continuously until the butter has melted and the sugar has dissolved. Increase the heat to medium and continue to heat the mixture, stirring constantly, until the mixture comes to a boil. Once the purée is bubbling, turn the heat down to medium-low and cook the mixture for about 5 minutes, still stirring. Remove the purée from the heat. For a fine consistency, blitz the purée with an immersion

blender. Let the purée cool to room temperature, then cover and chill in the refrigerator for 30 minutes before using. **2)** In the bowl of a stand mixer fitted with a paddle, beat the remaining 1 cup [2 sticks or 227 g] of butter on medium speed until very smooth and creamy, 2 to 3 minutes. Add the vanilla and salt, and beat again on medium speed until combined. Turn the mixer to low speed, and slowly add the confectioners' sugar, mixing until combined. Add the cool pumpkin purée to the buttercream 1 tablespoon at a time, mixing well on low speed after each addition. Keep adding until the desired pumpkin taste is reached, but no more than $1/2$ cup [128 g], which can make the buttercream runny. Scrape down the sides of the bowl and increase the mixer speed to medium; beat until the buttercream is light and smooth, 4 to 6 minutes.

NOTE If you end up adding too much pumpkin and your buttercream is runny, you can add either more butter or confectioners' sugar (1 tablespoon at a time) to help make it light and creamy again. Just remember that adding more confectioners' sugar will make it sweeter, and more butter will make it very buttery.

TO ASSEMBLE

Spread or pipe 1 tablespoon of filling over the bottom of half of the cookies. Sprinkle generously with the processed caramel shards. Top with the remaining cookies, pressing gently to adhere them together. Cookies can be stored in an airtight container at room temperature for 2 days.

94

Ginger Cookies with Salted Caramel Ice Cream

I think these sandwich cookies would be perfect on those early autumn days, where the leaves are falling and we are all ready for sweaters and fires but the afternoons are still clinging to those blazing hot summer moments. Gingery spices mixed with caramel ice cream will find the middle ground and set things right.

MAKES 11 SANDWICH COOKIES

1 recipe No-Churn Ice Cream, Salted Caramel variation (page 290)

1 recipe Ginger Cookies (page 51)

TO ASSEMBLE

Scoop a generous amount of the ice cream on the bottom of half of the cookies. Top with the remaining cookies, pressing gently to adhere them together. Eat immediately.

95

Oatmeal Cream Pies

Every year, my family took a vacation to the one and only Midwest hot spot: the Wisconsin Dells. It was an ungodly long car ride where my siblings and I dreamed of water slides and Tommy Bartlett's Robot World, and fought over the Walkman and *Garfield* comics. It was also the one time every year my mom didn't make a peep about what we ate, and my dad loaded the car with grocery bags full of every treat imaginable. One of those delicacies was a box of Oatmeal Cream Pies, my personal favorite. This is my made-from-scratch version—a softer, creamier version that is heads and tails above the original.

MAKES 10 SANDWICH COOKIES

1 recipe Marshmallow Fluff (page 286)

1 recipe Oatmeal Raisin Cookies, raisins omitted (page 52)

TO ASSEMBLE

Spread or pipe a generous amount of marshmallow fluff over the bottom of half of the cookies. Top with the remaining cookies, pressing gently to adhere them together. Cookies can be stored in an airtight container at room temperature for 2 days.

96

Sugar Cookies with Raspberry Ripple Ice Cream

Cool, creamy ice cream swirled with berries and sandwiched between sugar cookies. What could be better?

MAKES 10 SANDWICH COOKIES

1 recipe Sugar Cookies (page 38)

1 recipe No-Churn Ice Cream, Raspberry Ripple variation (page 290)

TO ASSEMBLE

Scoop a generous amount of the ice cream over the bottom of half of the cookies. Top with the remaining cookies, pressing gently to adhere them together. Eat immediately.

97

Brownies with Coffee Ice Cream

My birthday falls in late August, when the days are noticeably getting shorter and the kids start making whimpering noises about the possibility of school starting again. It's still hot and humid, and we're all secretly looking forward to cool autumn evenings and crumpled leaves under our feet. I barely turn the oven on those last few days of summer, but I will make an exception for these brownie sandwiches (and my birthday).

MAKES 12 LARGE OR 16 SMALL SANDWICH BROWNIES

1 recipe My Favorite Brownies (page 68)

1 recipe No-Churn Ice Cream, Coffee variation (page 290)

1) Adjust an oven rack to the middle of the oven. Preheat the oven to 350°F [180°C]. Grease two 9 by 13 in [23 by 33 cm] baking pans and line them with parchment slings. 2) Make the brownie batter as directed. Divide the batter equally between the prepared pans, and use an offset spatula to even out the tops. 3) Bake for 12 to 14 minutes, until a wooden skewer or toothpick inserted into the center comes out with quite a few crumbs. Transfer the pan to a wire rack and let cool completely. 4) Freeze the brownie layers for at least 1 hour (you can stack the layers on top of each other in the same pan, with parchment in between, if needed). 5) Make the ice cream as directed, but don't freeze it.

TO ASSEMBLE

1) Pour the mixed (but not frozen) ice cream over one of the brownie layers in the pan (make sure the parchment sling is still in place). Freeze the ice cream until solid, 2 to 3 hours. 2) Cover with the second brownie layer. Top the second layer with a piece of parchment paper or a piece of plastic, and place another 9 by 13 in [22 by 33 cm] baking pan on top (or some other gentle weight) to weight the bars down, then freeze for another 3 hours or overnight, until the ice cream is frozen through. 3) When ready to eat, move the pan to a workspace, and use the parchment sling to lift the brownies out of the pan. Cut into bars and eat immediately. Ice cream bars can also be wrapped individually and frozen for up to 1 week.

98

White Chocolate Brownies with Hazelnut Ice Cream

Here is my white chocolate take on brownie ice cream sandwiches. This one is extra fancy, with hazelnut ice cream and candied nuts.

MAKES 12 LARGE OR 16 SMALL SANDWICH BROWNIES

1 recipe White Chocolate Brownies (page 88)

1 recipe No-Churn Ice Cream, Salted Caramel variation (page 290)

1 cup [140 g] Candied Nuts, Hazelnut variation (page 291)

1) Adjust an oven rack to the middle of the oven. Preheat the oven to 350°F [180°C]. Grease two 9 by 13 in [23 by 33 cm] baking pans and line them with parchment slings. 2) Make the brownie batter as directed. Divide the batter equally between the prepared pans, and use an offset spatula to even out the tops. 3) Bake for 12 to 14 minutes, until a wooden skewer or toothpick inserted into the center comes out with quite a few crumbs. Transfer the pans to a wire rack and let cool completely. 4) Freeze the brownie layers for at least 1

hour (you can stack the layers on top of each other in the same pan, with parchment in between, if needed). 5) Make the ice cream as directed, but don't freeze it.

TO ASSEMBLE

1) Pour the mixed (but not frozen) ice cream over one of the brownie layers in the pan (make sure the parchment sling is still in place). Sprinkle the candied hazelnuts evenly over the ice cream. Freeze the ice cream until solid, 2 to 3 hours. 2) Cover with the second brownie layer. Top the second layer with a piece of parchment paper or a piece of plastic, and place another 9 by 13 in [22 by 33 cm] baking pan on top (or some other gentle weight) to weight the bars down, then freeze for another 3 hours or overnight, until the ice cream is frozen through. 3) When ready to eat, move the pan to a workspace, and use the parchment sling to lift the brownies out of the pan. Cut into bars and eat immediately. Ice cream bars can also be wrapped individually and frozen for up to a week.

99

Chocolate Chip Cookies with Ice Cream and Sprinkles

Ice cream sandwiches at their most basic. I like making these with the Brown Butter Chocolate Chip Cookies (page 30), but the Soft Chocolate Chip Cookies (page 29) would also be perfect here.

MAKES 10 SANDWICH COOKIES

1 recipe No-Churn Ice Cream, Vanilla or Chocolate variation (page 289)

1 recipe Brown Butter Chocolate Chip Cookies (page 30)

½ cup [90 g] sprinkles

TO ASSEMBLE

Scoop the ice cream and cover the bottom of half of the cookies with it. Top with the remaining cookies, pressing together gently to adhere. Roll the outside of the sandwich in the sprinkles, pressing gently into the ice cream. Serve immediately.

100

Chocolate Malt Ice Box Bars

It would have been my grandma's birthday the day I came up with this recipe, and while she's no longer here, they are a tribute to her love of chocolate and our late afternoon Bridgeman lunches, complete with chocolate malts with sweeping whipped cream tops. Eating a bar is bittersweet; even as the chocolate hits my tongue I can see her smiling as she takes the first bite, loudly exclaiming, "Oh, Sarah!" and then we both watch while the ice cream dribbles down our hands and arms. We laugh together, content and happy with our melty mess. *Our sweetest songs are those that tell of saddest thought.* —Percy Bysshe Shelley

MAKES 9 LARGE OR 12 SMALL BARS

ICE CREAM

One 14 oz [396 g] can sweetened condensed milk

3 oz [85 g] semisweet or bittersweet chocolate, melted and cooled

3 tablespoons malt powder

1 tablespoon pure vanilla extract

1/4 teaspoon salt

2 oz [57 g] cream cheese, at room temperature

2 1/2 cups [600 g] heavy cream

CARAMEL WHIPPED CREAM

1 cup [240 g] heavy cream

1/2 cup [170 g] Caramel (page 283), at room temperature

1 recipe Chocolate Sandwich Cookies (page 211), filling omitted, and cut into 1 in [2.5 cm] circles

FOR THE ICE CREAM

1) In a large bowl, whisk together the sweetened condensed milk, chocolate, malt powder, vanilla, and salt until completely combined. 2) In the bowl of a stand mixer fitted with a whisk, beat the cream cheese on medium speed until smooth. Turn the mixer to low speed and add the heavy cream in a slow, steady stream, mixing until combined. Increase the speed to medium-high and whisk until stiff peaks form, 3 to 4 minutes. 3) Add half of the whipped cream

mixture to the sweetened condensed milk mixture and whisk until completely combined. Using a rubber spatula, gently fold in the remaining whipped cream mixture until no streaks remain.

FOR THE WHIPPED CREAM

In the bowl of a stand mixer fitted with a whisk, add the heavy cream and caramel. Whisk on low speed for 30 to 45 seconds. Increase the speed to medium and beat for 30 to 45 seconds. Increase the speed to high and beat until the cream is smooth, thick, and nearly doubled in volume, 30 to 60 seconds. The whipped cream can be made 2 hours ahead of time and stored in the refrigerator.

TO ASSEMBLE

Line an 8 by 8 in [20 by 20 cm] pan with a parchment sling. Pour two-thirds of the ice cream into the pan. Gently press the chocolate cookies vertically into the ice cream, about 1 in [2.5 cm] apart, lining them in rows. You will get about 3 rows of 13 cookies in each row. Pour the remaining ice cream over the top and use an offset spaturla to smooth. Freeze the bars until firm, 4 hours or overnight. When ready to serve, remove the bars with the parchment sling, and cut into pieces. Top each piece with some of the caramel whipped cream. Eat immediately.

CHAPTER 8
Extras

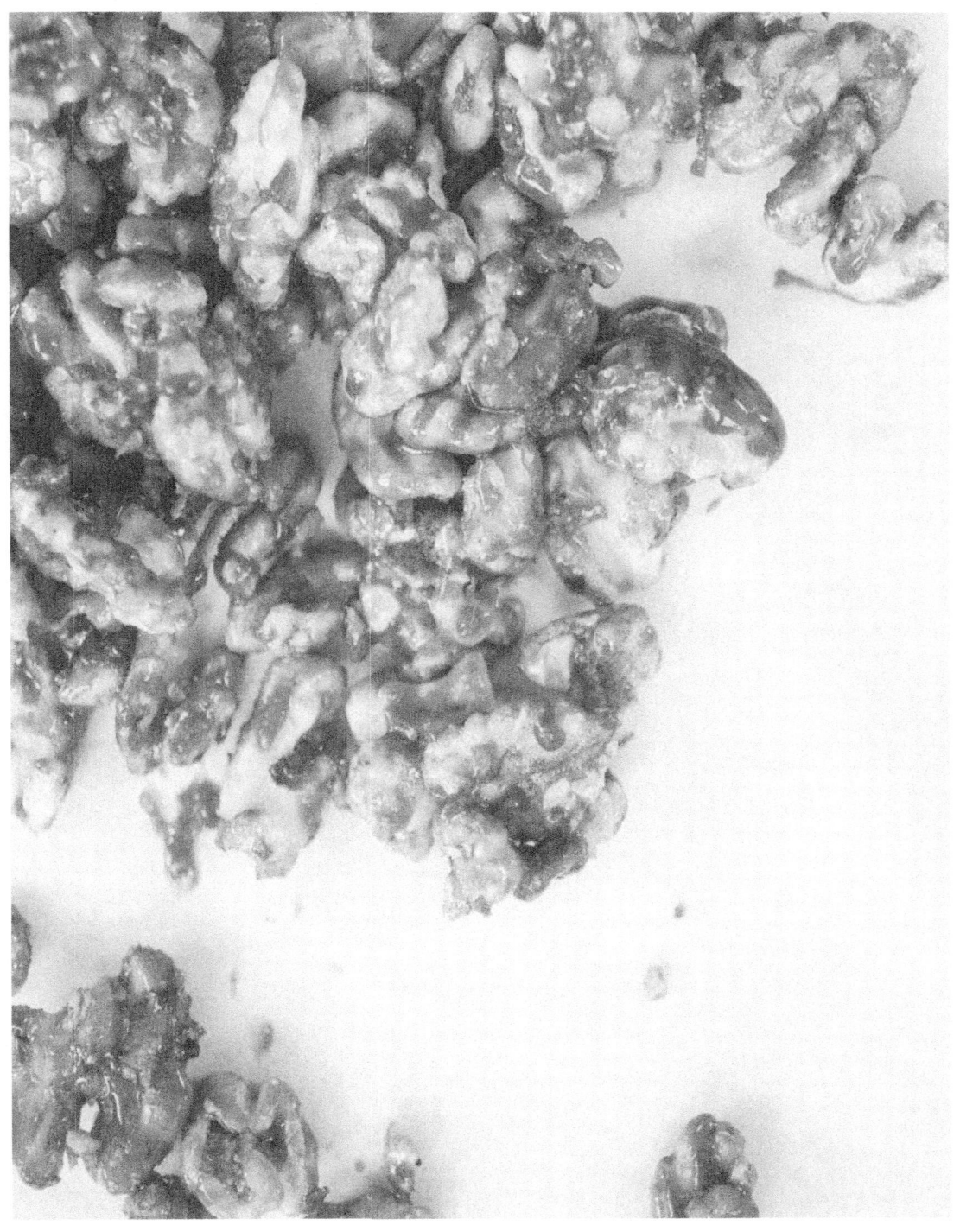

"My mum always said things we lose have a way of coming back to us in the end. If not always in the way we expect."

—J. K. Rowling, *Harry Potter and the Order of the Phoenix*

Pie Dough Base

My favorite pie dough makes a perfect base for several of the bars in this book, such as the French Silk Pie Bars (page 174) and Banana Cream Pie Bars (page 126).

MAKES A SINGLE OR DOUBLE 9 BY 13 IN [23 BY 33 CM] PIE CRUST

SINGLE

8 tablespoons [1 stick or 113 g] unsalted butter, cut into 16 pieces

1½ cups [213 g] all-purpose flour, plus more for dusting

1 tablespoon granulated sugar

½ teaspoon salt

DOUBLE

18 tablespoons [2¼ sticks or 255 g] unsalted butter, cut into 18 pieces

Ice water

2½ cups [355 g] all-purpose flour, plus more for dusting

2 tablespoons granulated sugar

1 teaspoon salt

1) Preheat the oven to 375°F [190°C]. 2) Put the sliced butter in a small bowl and place it in the freezer. Fill a medium liquid measuring cup with water and add plenty of ice. Let both the butter and the ice water sit and get very cold for 5 to 10 minutes. 3) In the bowl of a

stand mixer fitted with a paddle, mix the flour, sugar, and salt on low speed until combined. Add half of the chilled butter and mix on low speed until the butter is just starting to break down, about 1 minute. Add the rest of the butter and continue mixing until the butter is broken down in various sizes (some butter will be incorporated into the dough, some will be a bit large, but most should be about the size of small peas). Stop the mixer and use your hands to check for any dry patches of dough on the bottom of the bowl; incorporate the dry flour as best you can. With the mixer running on low speed, slowly add about $1/4$ cup [60 g] of the ice water and mix until the dough starts to come together but is still quite shaggy (if the dough is not coming together, add more water, 1 tablespoon at a time, until it does). 4) Dump the dough out onto a lightly floured work surface and flatten it slightly into a square. Gather any loose/dry pieces that won't stick to the dough and place them on top of the square. Gently fold the dough over onto itself and flatten again. Repeat this process three or four more times, until all the loose pieces are worked into the dough, being careful not to overwork the dough. Flatten the dough one last time into a 6 in [15 cm] disk. If making a double crust, form the dough into two 6 in [15 cm] disks.

BAKING A SINGLE CRUST

1) Make sure your work surface is lightly floured and roll the dough into a 9 by 13 in [23 by 33 cm] rectangle. Transfer the dough to a 9 by 13 in [23 by 33 cm] pan. Place pie weights on top of the dough (this helps keep the pie crust flat), and bake until the dough is golden brown, 20 to 28 minutes. (Start checking the dough at 20 minutes. The dough goes from light golden brown to dark golden brown very quickly.) 2) Remove the pan from the oven and place it on a wire rack. Remove the pie weights and let the crust cool to room temperature before using. Crust can be made 1 day in advance and

stored in an airtight container in the refrigerator. The crust can also be frozen for up to 3 weeks. Allow it to come to room temperature before using if frozen.

Rough Puff Pastry

Store-bought puff pastry will work in a pinch, but homemade puff pastry is exceptional. This "rough" version comes together more quickly than the traditional version.

MAKES ABOUT 2 LB [908 G] OF PUFF PASTRY

1 1/2 cups [3 sticks or 339 g] unsalted butter, cut into 20 pieces

Ice water

1/2 teaspoon lemon juice

2 cups [284 g] all-purpose flour, plus more for dusting

1 tablespoon granulated sugar

1/2 teaspoon salt

1) Put the butter in a small bowl and place it in freezer. Fill a medium liquid measuring cup with water and add plenty of ice. Let the butter and the ice water sit and get very cold, 5 to 10 minutes. **2)** In the bowl of another liquid measuring cup, combine 1/4 cup [60 g] of the ice water and the lemon juice. **3)** In the bowl of a stand mixer fitted with a paddle, mix the flour, sugar, and salt. Add the butter and mix on low speed until slightly incorporated. The butter will be smashed and in all different sizes, most about half the original size. **4)** Add the lemon juice mixture and mix on low speed until the dough just holds together and looks shaggy. If the dough is still really dry and not coming together, add ice water, 1 tablespoon at a time, until it just starts to hold. **5)** Transfer the dough to a lightly floured work surface and flatten it slightly into a square. Gather any loose/dry pieces and place them on top. Gently fold the dough over onto itself and flatten again. Repeat this process 5 or 6 times, until all the loose pieces are worked into the dough. Be very gentle with your movements, being careful not to overwork the dough. Flatten the dough one last time into a 6 in [15 cm] square. Transfer the dough to a floured sheet pan or plate and sprinkle the top of the dough with flour. Place the dough in the refrigerator and chill until firm, 20 minutes. **6)** Return the dough to the lightly floured work surface and roll it into an 8 by 16 in [20 by 40.5 cm] rectangle. If the dough sticks at all, sprinkle more flour underneath it. Brush any excess flour off the dough, and, using a bench scraper, fold the short ends of the dough over the middle to make three layers, similar to a business letter. This is the first turn. (If the dough still looks shaggy, don't worry, it will become smooth and will even out as you keep rolling.) **7)** Flip the dough over (seam-side down), give the dough a quarter turn, and roll away from you, this time into a 6 by 16 in [15 by 30.5 cm] rectangle. Fold the short ends over the middle, business-letter style. This is the second turn. 8) Sprinkle the top of the dough with flour and return it to the sheet pan and refrigerate for 20 minutes. 9) Return the dough to the work surface and repeat the process of folding the dough, creating the third and fourth turns. On the last turn, gently use a rolling pin to compress the layers together slightly. Wrap tightly in plastic wrap and chill for at least 1 hour before using; keep refrigerated for up to 2 days.

Brown Butter

Brown butter adds a nice, nutty flavor to many dishes, but please note, it's not a perfect swap for regular butter in most recipes, as some of the liquid evaporates from the butter as it cooks. You can use any amount of butter for this; the process will be the same.

Unsalted butter

In a light-colored, heavy-bottom skillet, melt the butter over medium-low heat. As the butter begins to melt, swirl it around the pan with a rubber spatula. When it starts to bubble, increase the heat to medium and keep stirring the butter until it boils and beings to foam, 3 to 5 minutes. You will start to see brown bits at the bottom of the skillet, and it will begin to smell nutty. Keep stirring, making sure to gently scrape the bottom of the pan with the spatula as you do so. The butter will quickly change from light brown to dark brown at this point, so keep a close eye on the pan. Once it is golden brown, remove it from the heat, and pour the butter and any flecks on the bottom of the pan into a heatproof bowl. The brown butter can be used immediately or cooled to room temperature and stored in the refrigerator for up to 5 days.

Pastry Cream

Pastry cream is a little time consuming, but the end result always makes it worthwhile. If you have leftover pastry cream, you can add room-temperature butter to it, whip it up in your stand mixer, and turn it into buttercream (this is known as German buttercream, or Crème Mousseline). Just use 1 cup [227 g] of butter to 2 cups [450 g] of pastry cream.

MAKES ABOUT 2 CUPS [450 G]

5 egg yolks, at room temperature

1 1/4 cups [250 g] granulated sugar

1/4 teaspoon salt

1 vanilla bean, seeds scraped

1/4 cup [28 g] cornstarch

1 cup [240 g] whole milk

1 cup [240 g] heavy cream

1 tablespoon unsalted butter

2 teaspoons pure vanilla extract

1) In the bowl of a stand mixer fitted with a paddle, beat the egg yolks on low speed. Slowly add the sugar, followed by the salt and vanilla bean seeds, and increase the speed to medium-high. Beat the egg-sugar mixture until very thick and pale yellow, about 5 minutes. Scrape down the sides of the bowl and add the cornstarch. Turn the

mixer to low speed and mix until combined. 2) In a small saucepan over medium-low heat, heat the milk, heavy cream, and vanilla bean pod until just about to simmer. Remove the pan from the heat and pour the mixture into a medium measuring cup with a pourable spout. 3) With the mixer running on low speed, very slowly add the hot milk mixture (along with the pod). Mix until completely combined. 4) Transfer the mixture to a medium, heavy-bottom saucepan. Cook over low heat, stirring constantly with a wooden spoon, until the pastry cream becomes very thick and begins to boil, 5 to 7 minutes. Switch to a whisk, and whisk the mixture until the pastry cream thickens and is glossy and smooth, 3 to 4 minutes. Remove the pan from the heat and strain the pastry cream through a fine-mesh sieve into a medium bowl. Stir in the butter and vanilla. Cover with plastic wrap, making sure the wrap sits directly on top of the cream (this will help keep it from forming a skin). Place in the refrigerator until well chilled. Pastry cream can be kept refrigerated in an airtight container for 4 to 5 days.

NOTE If the egg yolks are left alone with sugar, the sugar can burn the yolk, causing it to harden and form little egg yolk bits in whatever you are making. Make sure to continuously whisk the yolks while adding sugar in any recipe.

VARIATION
• *Chocolate Pastry Cream—Add 6 oz [170 g] of melted bittersweet chocolate to the saucepan just before straining the pastry cream. Whisk until fully incorporated, and strain the pastry cream as directed.*

Lemon Curd

I was never crazy about lemon curd until I made it for myself. It took me a few tries to get it just right, but I discovered that while I like my curd very yolky, I do prefer the addition of one whole egg. I leave out the zest for a smooth, not-too-tart curd, but you can add some to ramp up the lemon flavor.

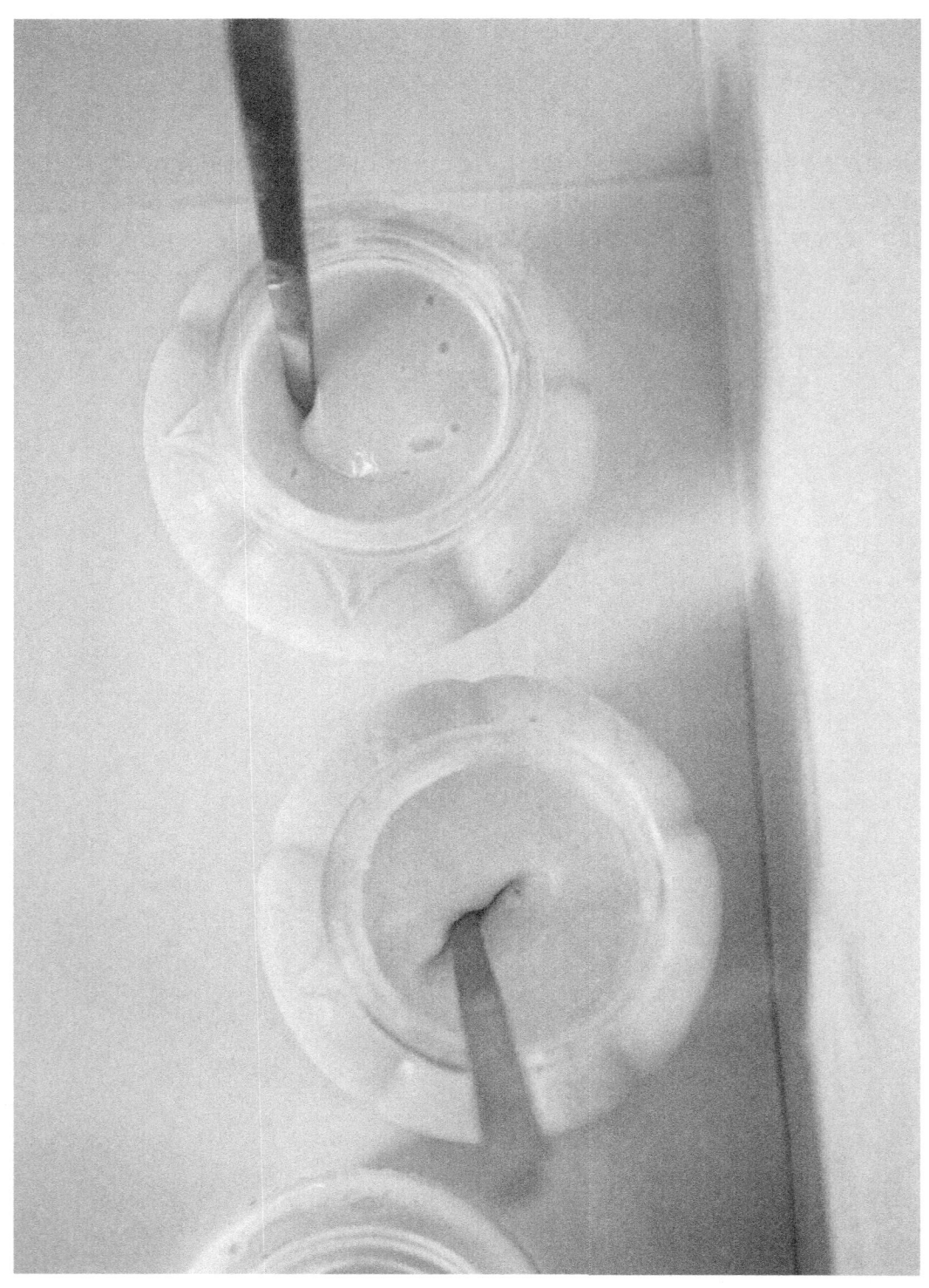

MAKES ABOUT 2 CUPS [640 G]

8 tablespoons [1 stick or 113 g] unsalted butter, at room temperature

1 1/2 cups [250 g] granulated sugar

1/4 teaspoon salt

5 large egg yolks plus 1 large egg

1/3 cup [80 g] lemon juice

1) In the bowl of a stand mixer fitted with a paddle, beat the butter on medium speed until creamy, about 1 minute. Add the sugar and salt and mix on medium speed until combined, another minute more. Scrape down the sides of the mixing bowl, and add the egg yolks on low speed. Increase the speed to medium and beat until smooth and light, 3 to 4 minutes. Add the whole egg and mix on low speed until combined, then add the lemon juice and mix on low speed until combined, scraping down the sides as needed. 2) Transfer the mixture to a medium, heavy-bottom saucepan. Cook over medium heat, stirring constantly with a spatula, until the curd becomes very thick, about 10 minutes, or registers 170°F [75°C] on a candy thermometer. The mixture should coat a spatula at this point. Strain the mixture through a fine-mesh sieve, then cover with plastic wrap, making sure the wrap sits directly on top of the curd (this will help keep it from forming a skin). Place in the refrigerator until well chilled. The curd can be stored in the refrigerator in an airtight container for 5 days.

NOTE Add 2 tablespoons of lemon zest to the mixing bowl with the granulated sugar for a lemon curd with a more tart, acidic flavor.

VARIATIONS

• *Passion Fruit Curd*—Replace the lemon juice with $1/2$ cup [120 g] of passion fruit pulp.

• *Lime Curd*—Replace the lemon juice with equal parts lime juice.

• *Lemon-Lavender Curd*—Put 1 tablespoon of culinary lavender buds into the saucepan along with the curd mixture. Discard the buds when straining the curd.

• *Grapefruit Curd*—Replace the lemon juice with $1/2$ cup [120 g] of grapefruit juice.

• *Blood Orange Curd*—Replace the lemon juice with $1/2$ cup [120 g] of blood orange juice.

Caramel

This is another staple that is fine store-bought, but so much better homemade. This also tastes delicious poured over any of the No-Churn Ice Creams (page 289).

MAKES 1½ CUPS [270 G]

1¼ cups [250 g] granulated sugar

¼ cup [60 g] water

½ teaspoon salt

½ cup [120 g] heavy cream

5 tablespoons [⅔ stick or 72 g] unsalted butter, cut into 8 pieces

1 tablespoon pure vanilla extract

In a large, heavy-bottom saucepan (the caramel will bubble up quite a bit once it starts cooking, so it's important to have a pan that is deep), combine the sugar, water, and salt, stirring very gently to combine while trying to avoid getting any sugar crystals on the sides of the pan. Cover the pot and bring to a boil over medium-high heat; cook until the sugar has melted and the mixture is clear, 3 to 5 minutes. Uncover and cook until the sugar has turned a pale golden brown and the temperature reaches 300°F [100°C]. Turn down the heat and cook until deep golden brown, about 340°F [170°C]. Remove the pot immediately from the heat and add the heavy cream. The cream will foam considerably, so be careful pouring it in. Add the butter next, followed by the vanilla, and stir to combine. Set aside to cool. Caramel can be refrigerated for 2 weeks.

VARIATION

• *Salty Caramel—When you take the caramel off the heat, add $1/2$ teaspoon fleur de sel.*

Crème Fraîche

Crème fraîche is similar to sour cream, but is less sour and often has a higher percentage of butterfat. It also endures heat much better than sour cream and doesn't break when introduced to high temperatures.

MAKES ABOUT 4 CUPS [960 G]

3 cups [720 g] heavy cream

¾ cup [180 g] buttermilk

In a large bowl, whisk together the cream and buttermilk. Cover the top of the bowl with several individual layers of cheesecloth. Place a rubber band or tie a string around the bowl to keep the cheesecloth in place. Let the bowl sit out at room temperature for 24 hours and up to 3 days, until it has thickened considerably. (The time it needs to sit depends on the temperature inside your home; cold winter days will take much longer than hot summer ones to thicken.) When it is thick and ready to use, gently stir the mixture and transfer it to an airtight container. Refrigerate the mixture for up to 1 week.

NOTE Buttermilk contains active cultures ("good" bacteria) that prevent the cream from spoiling, and is acidic enough to deter "bad" bacteria from growing.

Marshmallows

I didn't realize how superior homemade marshmallows were until I tried them; they are heads and tails above the supermarket versions. They also toast much better, with a deep amber char.

MAKES 24 LARGE OR 48 SMALL MARSHMALLOWS

3/4 cup [90 g] confectioners' sugar

1/4 cup [28 g] cornstarch

2 large egg whites

1/4 teaspoon cream of tartar

5 teaspoons gelatin

1/2 cup [120 g] cold water, plus 1/2 cup [120 g] room-temperature water

2 cups [400 g] granulated sugar

1/4 cup [85 g] corn syrup

1/4 teaspoon salt

1 tablespoon pure vanilla extract

1) Lightly grease a 9 by 13 in [23 by 33 cm] baking pan. 2) In a small bowl, whisk together the confectioners' sugar and the cornstarch. Set aside. 3) In the bowl of a stand mixer fitted with a whisk, whip the egg whites and cream of tartar on medium-high speed until soft peaks form, 2 to 3 minutes. 4) In a small bowl, combine the gelatin and the cold water. 5) In a medium, heavy-bottom saucepan fitted with a candy thermometer, combine the granulated sugar, corn syrup, salt, and the room-temperature water. Bring to a boil over medium-high heat, until the temperature reaches 240°F [120°C]; this will take a few minutes. Immediately remove the saucepan from the heat and whisk in the gelatin. 6) Turn the stand mixer on low speed, and carefully pour the hot sugar syrup along the side of the mixing bowl, being careful

not to hit the whisk attachment as you pour. When all the syrup is in the bowl, increase the speed to medium-high and continue whisking until the mixture has doubled in volume, is quite thick and glossy, and the sides of the bowl have cooled, 8 to 10 minutes. Add the vanilla and mix on low speed until combined. **7)** Scrape the marshmallow into the prepared pan. Use an offset spatula to smooth the top of the mixture. Sift 2 to 3 tablespoons of the confectioners' sugar mixture over the tops of the marshmallow. Let the marshmallow sit overnight at room temperature, uncovered, until firm. **8)** Remove the marshmallow from the pan and cut with a knife, scissors, or pizza wheel dusted with some of the confectioners' sugar mixture. Toss the cut marshmallows into the remaining confectioners' sugar mixture (a few at a time) and coat completely. Move the coated marshmallows to a fine-mesh sieve and shake off any excess coating. Transfer the marshmallows to an airtight container, and store at room temperature for up to 1 week.

VARIATIONS
• *Vanilla Bean Marshmallows*—Add the seeds from 1 vanilla bean to the marshmallows along with the vanilla.

• *Honey Marshmallows*—Replace the corn syrup with an equal amount of honey.

• *Raspberry Marshmallows*—Add $1/2$ cup [16 g] freeze-dried raspberries, processed into powder in a food processor fitted with a blade, to the filling along with the vanilla.

Marshmallow Fluff

Marshmallow fluff is the softer side of marshmallows, and while I love it in the middle of Oatmeal Cream Pies (page 267), I wouldn't object to it in the middle of chocolate chip cookies, either.

MAKES 3½ CUPS [490 G]

4 large egg whites

½ teaspoon cream of tartar

2 tablespoons cold water, plus ½ cup [120 g] room-temperature water

1 teaspoon gelatin

1 cup [336 g] corn syrup

1 cup [200 g] granulated sugar

¼ teaspoon salt

1 tablespoon pure vanilla extract

1) In the bowl of a stand mixer fitted with a whisk, whip the egg whites and cream of tartar on medium-high speed until soft peaks form, 2 to 3 minutes. **2)** In a small bowl, combine the cold water and the gelatin. **3)** In a medium, heavy-bottom saucepan fitted with a candy thermometer, combine the corn syrup, sugar, room-temperature water, and salt. Bring to a boil over medium-high heat, until the temperature reaches 240°F [120°C]; this will take a few minutes. Immediately remove the saucepan from the heat, and whisk in the gelatin. **4)** Turn the stand mixer on low speed, and carefully pour the hot sugar syrup along the side of the mixing bowl, being careful not to hit the whisk attachment as you pour. When all the syrup is in the bowl, turn up the speed to medium-high and continue whisking until the mixture has doubled in volume, is quite thick and glossy, and the sides of the bowl have cooled, 8 to 10 minutes. Add the vanilla and mix until combined. Scrape the mixture into an airtight container. Marshmallow fluff will keep in the refrigerator for 1 week.

Ermine Buttercream

This buttercream method is an old-school boiled flour frosting that I came across years ago and instantly fell in love with. It is a great way to infuse flavor into buttercream, and it is less sweet than traditional buttercreams. I like using it for the filling in Macarons (page 193), and you could also use one of the flavor variations in place of the Basil Buttercream in the Chocolate Basil Brownies (page 86).

MAKES ABOUT 2 CUPS [448 G]

3/4 cup [150 g] granulated sugar

1/4 cup [36 g] all-purpose flour

1/4 teaspoon salt

1/2 cup [120 g] whole milk

1/2 cup [120 g] half-and-half

1 cup [2 sticks or 227 g] unsalted butter, at room temperature

2 teaspoons pure vanilla extract

Food coloring (optional)

1) In a medium bowl, whisk together the sugar, flour, and salt until fully combined (the sugar will help keep the flour from lumping when it boils, so spend a good minute to really whisk it together). Put the mixture into a medium, heavy-bottom saucepan. Slowly pour the whole milk and half-and-half into the pan, whisking to combine as you pour. Cook over medium heat, stirring constantly, just until the mixture comes to a gentle boil (periodically run a spatula round the edges of the saucepan to remove any flour lurking there). Reduce the heat slightly, and continue to whisk constantly and stir the edges occasionally until the mixture has thickened considerably, 2 to 3 minutes. It should be glossy and leave streaks in the bottom of the pan when you drag a spatula through it. Remove from the heat and continue stirring for 30 seconds. 2) Transfer the mixture to a bowl and cover with plastic wrap, making sure the plastic sits directly on top of the cream (this will help keep it from forming a skin). Let cool to room temperature. 3) When the flour mixture has cooled, place the butter in the bowl of a stand mixer fitted with a paddle, and beat on

medium speed until smooth and creamy, scraping down the sides as needed. Start adding the cooled flour mixture a few spoonfuls at a time, mixing on low speed after each addition, until it is all incorporated. Scrape down the sides and mix on medium speed until the buttercream is light and fluffy, 2 to 3 minutes. Add the vanilla and food coloring, if using, and mix on low speed until combined. Buttercream can be stored in the refrigerator in an airtight container for up to 3 days.

VARIATIONS
• *Rosemary Buttercream—Combine the milk, half-and-half, and 2 rosemary sprigs in a medium saucepan. Heat gently over medium heat until just simmering, then remove from the heat. Let cool, then cover and refrigerate for at least 2 hours and up to overnight. Remove the rosemary from the milk and discard. Add the infused milk to the buttercream as directed above.*

• *Lavender Buttercream—Combine the milk, half-and-half, and 1 teaspoon of culinary lavender in a medium saucepan. Heat gently over medium heat until just simmering, then remove from the heat. Let cool, then cover and refrigerate for at least 2 hours and up to overnight. Remove the lavender from the milk and discard. Add the infused milk to the buttercream as directed above.*

• *Green Tea Buttercream—Combine the milk, half-and-half, and $1/2$ cup [16 g] of green tea leaves (or two bags of tea) in a medium saucepan. Heat gently over medium heat until just simmering, then remove from the heat. Let cool, then cover and refrigerate for at least 2 hours and up to overnight. Remove the tea leaves from the milk and discard. Add the infused milk to the buttercream as directed above.*

- Coffee Buttercream—Combine the milk, half-and-half, and $1/2$ cup [45 g] of whole coffee beans in a medium saucepan. Heat gently over medium heat until just simmering, then remove from the heat. Let cool, then strain the coffee beans and discard. Cover and refrigerate for at least 2 hours and up to overnight. Add the infused milk to the buttercream as directed above. Stir in 1 teaspoon of ground espresso with the vanilla (optional).

- Cardamom Buttercream—Combine the milk, half-and-half, and seeds from 10 cardamom pods in a medium saucepan. Heat gently over medium heat until just simmering, then remove from the heat. Let cool, then cover and refrigerate for at least 2 hours and up to overnight. Remove the cardamom seeds from the milk and discard. Add the infused milk to the buttercream as directed above. Add $1/2$ teaspoon ground cardamom along with the salt when making the buttercream.

No-Churn Ice Cream

I had a whole chapter of no-churn ice cream in my last book, and I find it a welcome alternative to churning homemade ice cream, as it takes less time and doesn't need fancy machinery. I've included my basic recipe here, as well as a few new variations.

MAKES ABOUT 4 CUPS [960 G]

One 14 oz [396 g] can sweetened condensed milk

1 tablespoon pure vanilla extract

1 vanilla bean, seeds scraped (optional)

¼ teaspoon salt

2 oz [57 g] cream cheese, at room temperature

2 cups [480 g] heavy cream

1) In a large bowl, whisk together the sweetened condensed milk, vanilla, vanilla bean seeds, if using, and salt until completely combined. 2) In the bowl of a stand mixer fitted with a whisk, beat the cream cheese on medium speed until smooth. Turn the mixer to low speed and add the heavy cream in a slow, steady stream, mixing until combined. Increase the speed to medium-high and whisk until stiff peaks form, 3 to 4 minutes. 3) Add half of the whipped cream mixture to the sweetened condensed milk mixture and whisk until completely combined. Using a rubber spatula, gently fold in the remaining whipped cream mixture until no streaks remain. Pour into a 9 by 4 by 4 in [23 by 10 by 10 cm] Pullman loaf pan with a lid and freeze until firm, 6 hours, or up to 1 week.

NOTE If you don't have a Pullman pan, a regular 9 in [23 cm] loaf pan covered with plastic wrap will work, too.

VARIATIONS

• *Coffee No-Churn Ice Cream*—Add 1/2 cup [120 g] of room-temperature brewed espresso or strong coffee and 1/2 teaspoon of ground espresso to the sweetened condensed milk mixture.

• *Chocolate No-Churn Ice Cream*—Melt 8 oz [226 g] of semisweet or bittersweet chocolate. Pour 5 oz [142 g] of the chocolate onto a sheet pan lined with parchment and freeze until firm, 10 to 15 minutes. Add the remaining 3 oz [85 g] of melted chocolate to the sweetened condensed milk mixture. Chop the cold chocolate into bite-size pieces and add it to the finished ice cream mixture before pouring it into the loaf pan.

• *Raspberry Ripple No-Churn Ice Cream*—Bring 2 cups [200 g] of raspberries (fresh or frozen), 1/3 cup [65 g] of granulated sugar, and a pinch of salt to a simmer in a medium saucepan over medium-high heat. Cook, stirring and pressing down on the berries occasionally until they have released their juices, about 5 minutes. Strain the berry mixture through a fine-mesh sieve, pressing on the solids to extract as much juice as possible. Discard the solids. Let the juice cool to room temperature, then place in the refrigerator to chill. Make the no-churn ice cream as directed above. Pour half of the ice cream mixture into the Pullman pan, then dollop half of the raspberry juice over the ice cream. Use the tip of a butter knife to swirl the juice into the ice cream. Pour the remaining ice cream on top, then dollop with the remaining raspberry juice, swirling it again with the butter knife. Freeze as directed above.

- *Salted Caramel No-Churn Ice Cream*—Make the no-churn ice cream as directed above. Pour half of the ice cream mixture into the Pullman pan, then dollop $1/2$ cup [180 g] of Caramel, Salted Caramel variation (page 283), over the ice cream. Use the tip of a butter knife to swirl the mixture into the ice cream. Pour the remaining ice cream on top, then dollop with another $1/2$ cup [180 g] of caramel. Swirl again with the butter knife. Freeze as directed above.

- *Hazelnut No-Churn Ice Cream*—Add $1/4$ cup [60 g] of Frangelico liqueur and $1/4$ cup [60 g] of room-temperature espresso or strong coffee to the sweetened condensed milk mixture.

Whipped Cream

Homemade whipped cream is so delicious and really simple to make.

MAKES ABOUT 3 CUPS [360 G]

$1^1/_2$ cups [360 g] heavy cream

2 tablespoons granulated sugar

2 teaspoons pure vanilla extract

Pinch salt

Ten minutes before whipping the cream, place the bowl and whisk from a stand mixer in the freezer and let chill. In the chilled bowl of the stand mixer fitted with the chilled whisk, whisk together the heavy cream, sugar, vanilla, and salt in the chilled bowl on low speed for 30 to 45 seconds. Increase the speed to medium and beat for 30 to 45 seconds. Increase the speed to high and beat until the cream is smooth, thick, and nearly doubled in volume, 30 to 60 seconds. The whipped cream can be made 2 hours ahead of time and stored in an airtight container in the refrigerator.

Candied Nuts

My first encounter with candied nuts was on a peanut butter pie that Zoë François posted on Instagram. I made them immediately and was hooked. Nuts are perfect by their lonesome, but adding some caramelized sugar and salt makes them extraordinary. They are a great addition to bars and cookies alike.

MAKES ABOUT 3 CUPS [420 G]

2 cups [280 g] walnuts, peanuts, hazelnuts, cashews, or almonds

1/2 cup [100 g] granulated sugar

1/4 teaspoon salt

In a large skillet over medium heat, stir together the nuts, sugar, and salt. Cook until the sugar begins to melt and the nuts begin to toast, stirring almost constantly. Once the sugar begins to melt, turn the heat down to low and cook until the nuts are lightly caramelized. Pour the nuts onto a sheet pan lined with parchment paper. Let them cool completely before chopping. Nuts can be stored in an airtight container for up to 1 week.

Candied Cacao Nibs

I first discovered candied cacao nibs in Tara O'Brady's wonderful book, *Seven Spoons*. They make a delicious addition to any of the brownie recipes, and are the perfect ice cream topping.

MAKES ABOUT 2 1/2 CUPS [300 G]

2 cups [240 g] cacao nibs

1/2 cup [100 g] granulated sugar

Pinch salt

In a large skillet over medium heat, stir together the cacao nibs, sugar, and salt. Cook until the sugar begins to melt and the cacao nibs begin to toast, stirring almost constantly. Once the sugar begins to melt, turn the heat down to low and cook until the cacao nibs are lightly caramelized. Pour the cacao nibs onto a sheet pan lined with parchment paper. Let them cool completely before chopping. Candied nibs can be stored in an airtight container at room temperature for 1 week.

Caramel Shards

I came across caramel shards in Pierre Hermé's book *Macaron*; he uses them finely processed as filling in his famous cookies. I love trying to sneak crunchiness into most of my desserts, and found this to be a clever way to do so.

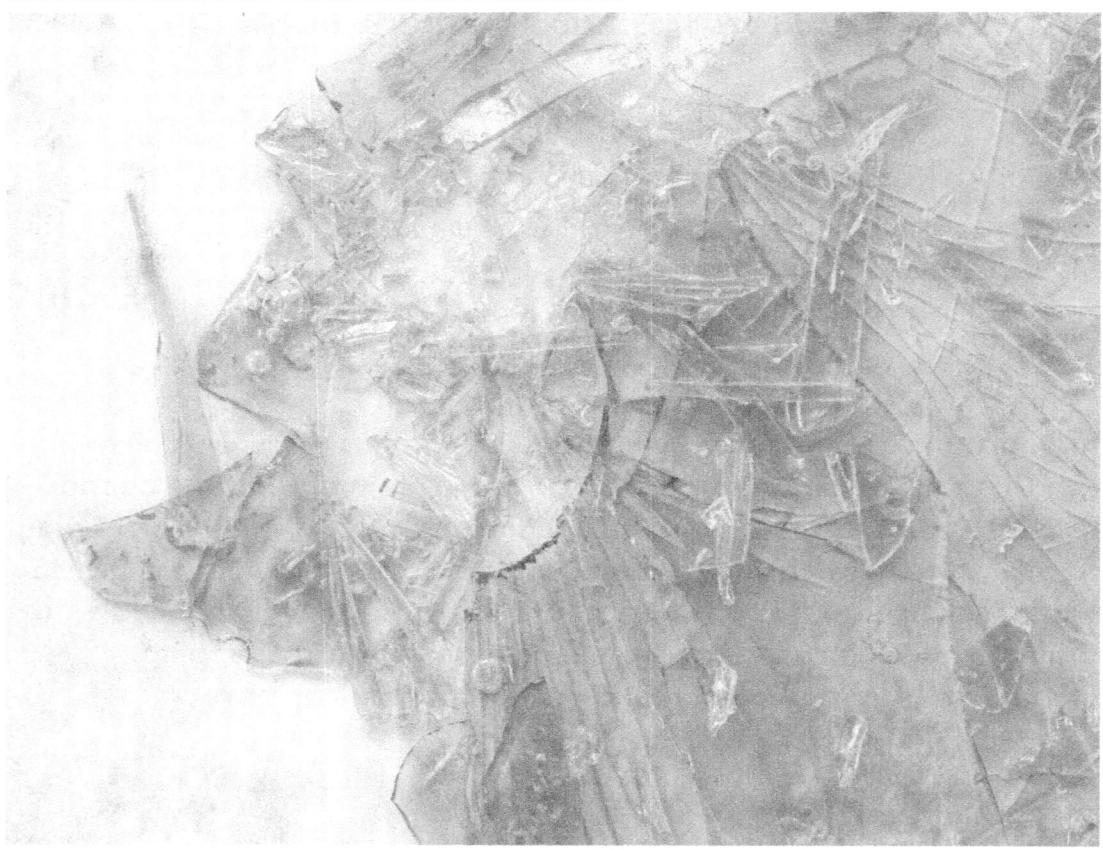

MAKES ABOUT 2 CUPS [220 G]

1/2 cup [100 g] granulated sugar

1/4 cup [85 g] corn syrup

2 tablespoons water

1/4 teaspoon salt

2 teaspoons pure vanilla extract

1) Line a sheet pan with parchment paper. **2)** In a large, heavy-bottom saucepan, combine the granulated sugar, corn syrup, water, and salt, stirring very gently while trying to avoid getting any sugar crystals on the sides of the pan. Cover the pot and bring to a boil over medium-high heat, until the sugar has melted and the mixture is clear, 3 to 5 minutes. Uncover, and then cook until the sugar has turned a pale golden color, 4 to 5 minutes more, and registers about 300°F [150°C] on a candy thermometer. Turn the heat down slightly, and cook for a few minutes more until the sugar is golden and registers 350°F [180°C]. Remove the pot immediately from the heat and add the vanilla, stirring to combine. **3)** Pour the caramel onto the prepared sheet pan, and tip the sheet pan back and forth until the caramel is in a thin, even layer, about $1/4$ in [6 mm] thick. Let the caramel harden, then cut with a knife for larger pieces, or process in a food processor for very small shards. Caramel shards can be stored in an airtight container at room temperature for 2 weeks.

"The world is a table
engulfed in honey and smoke...

The table is already set,
and we know the truth
as soon as we are called:
whether we're called to war
or dinner we will have to
choose sides, have to know...

whether we'll wear the pants
of hate or the shirt of love,
freshly laundered."

—Pablo Neruda, "Ode to the Table"

MUSIC TO BAKE TO

I included a music guide in my last cookbook, and got so many notes thanking me for it, I decided to make sure this book had a list, too. These albums were on constant rotation during the making of this book.

LOUIS ARMSTRONG
The Decca Singles, 1935–1946

CHET BAKER
Jazz in Paris

KEN BURRELL
Midnight Blue

MILES DAVIS
Bye Bye Blackbird

FEIST
Pleasure

ELLA FITZGERALD
Ella Fitzgerald Sings the Duke Ellington Songbook

GRAVEYARD CLUB
Goodnight Paradise

THE JAPANESE HOUSE
Good at Falling

LUXURY
Trophies

NAT KING COLE TRIO
The Complete Capitol Recordings

OVER THE RHINE
The Long Surrender

ST GERMAIN
Tourist

THE SWELL SEASON

Strict Joy

CAL TJADER
Soul Sauce

U2
Achtung Baby

VARIOUS ARTISTS
Banoffee Pies Beats 01 and *Banoffee Pies Beats 02*

100 Cookies Playlist on Apple Music: https://apple.co/2t3YYeH
100 Cookies Playlist on Spotify: https://spoti.fi/2RARFFn

Conversions

Commonly Used Ingredients	Oven Temperatures	Weights
1 cup flour = 142 g	300°F = 150°C	½ oz = 14 g
1 cup granulated sugar = 200 g	350°F = 180°C	1 oz = 28 g
1 cup brown sugar = 200 g	375°F = 190°C	1½ oz = 45 g
1 cup confectioners' sugar = 120 g	400°F = 200°C	2 oz = 57 g
1 cup cocoa powder = 100 g	425°F = 220°C	2½ oz = 71 g
1 cup butter (2 sticks) = 227 g	450°F = 230°C	3 oz = 85 g
1 egg white = 35 g		3½ oz = 99 g
1 cup whole milk = 240 g		4 oz = 113 g

1 cup heavy cream = 240 g	
1 cup sour cream = 240 g	
1 cup cream cheese = 226 g	

4½ oz = 128 g	
5 oz = 142 g	
8 oz = 226 g	
10 oz = 283 g	
12 oz = 340 g	
16 oz = 455 g	

Bibliography

Much of my baking training was hands-on experience that took place in the workplace, and many ideas, techniques, and recipe evolutions were picked up here and there over the years. It would be impossible to cite everything and everyone, but I must acknowledge (with so much gratitude) Larry and Colleen Wolner and Zoë François for their mentorship, guidance, and encouragement (you can sample the Wolners' amazing baked goods at The Blue Heron Coffeehouse in Winona, Minnesota. And Zoë offers help to all on her beautiful website, zoebakes.com, and her Instagram, @zoebakes).

Over the years, many books have both taught me new techniques and guided my baking knowledge. Here are some that have inspired a starting point or answered a baking question for this book.

Ansel, Dominique. *The Secret Recipes*. New York: Simon & Schuster, 2014.

Arefi, Yossy. *Sweeter Off the Vine*. Berkeley: Ten Speed Press, 2016.

Editors at America's Test Kitchen. *The Perfect Cookie*. Brookline, MA: America's Test Kitchen, 2017.

Editors at *Farm Journal*. *Homemade Cookies*. New York: Doubleday & Company, Inc, 1971.

Greenspan, Dorie. *Dorie's Cookies*. Boston, New York: Houghton Mifflin Harcourt, 2016.

Hay, Donna. *Modern Baking*. Sydney: HarperCollins, 2018.

Hermé, Pierre. *Macaron*. New York: Abrams, 2015.

Hoffler, Alex, and Stacey O'Gorman. *Meringue Girls*. San Francisco: Chronicle Books, 2014.

Huff, Tess. *Icing on the Cake*. New York: Abrams, 2019.

Kaldunski, Shelly. *The Art of the Cookie*. San Francisco: Weldon Owen, 2010.

Keller, Thomas. *Bouchon Bakery*. New York: Artisan, 2012.

Lewis, Matt, and Renato Poliafito. *Baked Explorations*. New York: Stewart, Tabori & Change, 2010.

Lin, Irvin. *Marbled, Swirled, and Layered*. Boston, New York: Houghton Mifflin Harcourt, 2016.

O'Brady, Tara. *Seven Spoons*. Berkeley: Ten Speed Press, 2015.

Ottolenghi, Yotam, and Helen Goh. *Sweet*. New York: Ten Speed Press, 2017.

Page, Karen, and Andrew Dorenburg. *The Flavor Bible*. New York: Little, Brown and Company, 2008.

Park, Stella. *Bravetart*. New York, London: W. W. Norton & Company, 2017.

Ptak, Claire. *The Violet Bakery Cookbook*. Berkeley: Ten Speed Press, 2015.

Reed, Jessica. *The Baker's Appendix*. New York: Clarkson Potter, 2017.

Segal, Mindy, with Kate Leahy. *Cookie Love*. Berkeley: Ten Speed Press, 2015.

Tosi, Christina. *Milk*. New York: Clarkson Potter, 2011.

Resources

BREVILLE
breville.com
Kitchen equipment and essentials

EMILE HENRY
emilehenryusa.com
Ceramic cookware

GUITTARD CHOCOLATE COMPANY
guittard.com
Chocolates and cocoa powder

KING ARTHUR FLOUR
kingarthurflour.com
Specialty flours and baking items

LAND O'LAKES
landolakes.com
Unsalted and European butter

MATERIAL
materialkitchen.com
Beautiful and functional kitchen knives

MAUVIEL
mauvielusa.com
Copper cookware

NORDIC WARE
nordicware.com
Baking pans and kitchen necessities

PENZEYS SPICES
penzeys.com
Spices and vanilla beans

SWEETAPOLITA
sweetapolita.shop.com
Sprinkles and baking supplies

VALRHONA
valrhona-chocolate.com
Chocolates and cocoa powder

VOLLRATH
vollrath.com
Disher scoops that don't break

WILLIAMS-SONOMA
williams-sonoma.com
Bakeware, baking utensils, and decorating tools

You can also find my favorite kitchen items at my Amazon storefront: amazon.com/shop/sarah_kieffer

Acknowledgments

First, a huge thank-you to all of *The Vanilla Bean Blog* readers and pan-bangers of the world. I really wouldn't be here without all of you, and I am eternally grateful for each and every one of you.

Thank you to Chronicle Books, and my amazing editors Sarah Billingsley and Deanne Katz, for giving this book a chance, and for being so dedicated to making sure it turned out beautifully in every respect. I appreciate your quick and thoughtful responses, your attention to detail, and your expertise. Thank you to Lizzie Vaughan for the book design—I love all you've done with this book. And thanks to Margo Winton Parodi for your time and thoroughness copyediting.

Thanks to my literary agent, Jane Dystel, who gently prodded me to try another book. I appreciate your help and guidance through this whole process, as well as your constant reassurance when my anxiety got the best of me.

To all my recipe testers: First and foremost, Kelsey Tenney, who just may have baked all the recipes in this book for me. Also to Lindsay Reine, Heidi Smith, Molly Yeh, Tara O'Brady, Joel Peck, Molly Hayes, Mark Neufang, Linda Mueller, Scott Beck, Jaci McKay, Melanie Murray, Mandy Tensen-Woolery, Heather Meyen, Amy Wyland, Clair Anderson, Summer McCall, and Michelle Westmark Wingard, for your help and feedback. You all helped shaped this book into what it is.

To Kate Peck and Melody Heide, for all your encouragement, help, and support, and for our endless text message thread that keeps me sane.

A big thank-you to Zoë François for always answering texts and emails, reassuring my anxiety, making me laugh, and teaching me so much. I am grateful for your friendship.

To Larry and Colleen Wolner, thank you for giving me a chance in your kitchen so many years ago, even when I didn't know what I was doing. You continue to teach and inspire me, and I'm thankful for both of you.

To Mom and Dad, thank you for all the babysitting and nice texts, buying sooooo many copies of my book(s), and always supporting me over the years. I love you both.

Winter and River, I appreciate your patience and encouragement, even though I know you didn't always like me working so much. I'm so glad you're mine, and I look forward to so many years of baking together.

Adam: Aimee Nezhukumatathil wrote, "Flour on the floor makes my sandals slip and I tumble into your arms," and somehow that image sums us up quite nicely. I'm so thankful for your love, friendship, and support. You're my favorite one.

Index

almond flour, 19
    Banana–Espresso–Cacao Nib Cookies, 249–50
    Chocolate Macarons, 197–99
    Macarons, 193–96
    Peanut Butter Cookies, 240
    Strawberry Crème Fraîche Bars, 137–38

almonds
    Orange Almond Shortbread Cookies, 118–19
    Rocky Road Cookies, 237
    toasting, 20

apples
    Danish Pear-Apple Bars, 133–34
    Mixed Berry Crumble Bars, 135–36

apricots
    Palmiers with Apricot and Cardamom, 159
    White Chocolate, Rosemary, and Apricot Cookies, 122

baking powder, 19–20
baking soda, 20
baking tips, 15–17
bananas
    Banana Cream Pie Bars, 126–28
    Banana Crunch Blondies, 105–6
    Banana–Espresso–Cacao Nib Cookies, 249–50
    Banana Poppy Seed Cookies, 125

bark
    Caramelized White Chocolate Pistachio Bark, 221
    Chocolate–Peanut Butter Pretzel Bark, 219–20

basil
    Basil Buttercream, 86–87

    Chocolate Basil Brownies, 86–87
Black and White Cheesecake Bars, 170–71
Blondies, 96
    Bourbon S'mores Blondies, 108
    Brown Butter Blondies, 99
    Cinnamon Roll Blondies, 102–3
    Espresso Caramel Blondies, 100–101
    S'mores Blondies, 107–8
blood oranges
    Blood Orange Curd, 283
    Blood Orange Glaze, 114–15
blueberries
    Mixed Berry Crumble Bars, 135–36
Boston Cream Pie Bars, 183–84
bourbon
    Bourbon Sablés with Chocolate, 59
    Bourbon S'mores Blondies, 108
Brown Butter, 280
    Brown Butter Blondies, 99
    Brown Butter Chocolate Chip Cookies, 30–31
Brownie Cookies, 45
    Brownie Cookies with Cardamom Buttercream Filling, 258
    Brownie Cookies with Peanut Butter, 45
brownies
    Brownies with Coffee Ice Cream, 270
    Cakey Brownies, 71–72
    Chocolate Basil Brownies, 86–87
    Coconut Cream Swirl Brownies, 80
    Cream Cheese Brownies, 75
    Dark Chocolate Swirl White Chocolate Brownies, 90
    Fudgy Brownies, 70
    Marshmallow Peanut Butter Brownies, 82
    Milk Chocolate Cacao Nib Crunch Swirl Brownies, 81
    Milk Chocolate Candied Nut Swirl Brownies, 81
    Milk Chocolate Swirl Brownies, 81
    My Favorite Brownies, 68
    Peanut Butter Crunch Brownies, 85
    Raspberry Swirl White Chocolate Brownies, 91

Rocky Road Brownies, 78–79
  Turtle Brownies, 76
  White Chocolate Brownies, 88–89
  White Chocolate Brownies with Hazelnut Ice Cream, 272
  White Chocolate Brownies with Toasted Sesame Caramel, 95
  White Chocolate Red Velvet Brownies, 92–93

brown sugar, 19
  Brown Sugar Cookies, 41

butter, 16, 17–18

buttercreams. *See frostings and buttercreams*
  butterscotch
  Kitchen Sink Cookies, 209–10
  Scotcharoos, 215
  Smoky Butterscotch Cookies, 156–57

cacao nibs, 21
  Banana Crunch Blondies, 105–6
  Banana–Espresso–Cacao Nib Cookies, 249–50
  Brownie Cookies with Cardamom Buttercream Filling, 258
  Candied Cacao Nibs, 291
  Coffee Cacao Nib Filling, 199
  Meringues with Cacao Nibs and Caramel Swirl, 163
  Milk Chocolate Cacao Nib Crunch Swirl Brownies, 81
  Peanut Butter Crunch Brownies, 85

Cakey Brownies, 71–72

Candied Cacao Nibs, 291

Candied Nuts, 291

canola oil, 18

Caramel, 283
  Caramel Bars with Candied Peanuts, 216–17
  Caramelized White Chocolate Pistachio Bark, 221
  Caramel Shards, 292
  Espresso Caramel Blondies, 100–101
  Meringues with Cacao Nibs and Caramel Swirl, 163
  Rhubarb Caramel Filling, 195

    Salty Caramel, 283
    Toasted Sesame Caramel, 95

cardamom
    Cardamom Buttercream, 289
    Cardamom Chocolate Sugar Cookies, 42

Carrot Cake Bars with Meringue, 185–86

cherries
    Cherry Almond Cheesecake Swirl Bars, 142
    Red Wine Cherry Cheesecake Swirl Bars, 141–42

chocolate
    Banana Crunch Blondies, 105–6
    Banana–Espresso–Cacao Nib Cookies, 249–50
    Black and White Cheesecake Bars, 170–71
    Blondies, 96
    Boston Cream Pie Bars, 183–84
    Bourbon Sablés with Chocolate, 59
    Brown Butter Blondies, 99
    Brown Butter Chocolate Chip Cookies, 30–31
    Brownie Cookies, 45
    Brownie Cookies with Cardamom Buttercream Filling, 258
    Brownie Cookies with Peanut Butter, 45
    Brownies with Coffee Ice Cream, 270
    Cakey Brownies, 71–72
    Caramel Bars with Candied Peanuts, 216–17
    Cardamom Chocolate Sugar Cookies, 42
    Chocolate Basil Brownies, 86–87
    Chocolate Chip Cookies, 228
    Chocolate Chip Cookies with Ice Cream and Sprinkles, 273
    Chocolate Crinkle Cookies, 46–47
    Chocolate Ganache, 85, 86–87, 105–6, 167–68, 170–71, 183–84
    Chocolate Ganache Crunch Filling, 199
    Chocolate Hazelnut Bars, 173
    Chocolate Macarons, 197–99
    Chocolate Malt Ice Box Bars, 274–75
    Chocolate Mint Sugar Cookies, 42
    Chocolate Mousse, 177–78
    Chocolate Pastry Cream, 281
    Chocolate–Peanut Butter Pretzel Bark, 219–20

Chocolate Roll-Up Cookies, 203–5
Chocolate Sandwich Cookies, 211–12
Chocolate Sugar Cookies, 42
Coconut Cream Swirl Brownies, 80
Cream Cheese Brownies, 75
Double Chocolate Espresso Cookies, 164–66
Double Chocolate Sugar Cookies, 42
Espresso Caramel Blondies, 100–101
Espresso Cheesecake Bars, 167–68
French Silk Pie Bars, 174–76
Fudgy Brownies, 70
Kitchen Sink Cookies, 209–10
Marshmallow Peanut Butter Brownies, 82
melting, 20–21
Milk Chocolate Cacao Nib Crunch Swirl Brownies, 81
Milk Chocolate Candied Nut Swirl Brownies, 81
Milk Chocolate Swirl Brownies, 81
Mud Pie Bars, 177–78
My Favorite Brownies, 68
Neapolitan Cookies, 200–202
Oatmeal Chocolate Cookies, 231
Peanut Butter Cookies, 240
Peanut Butter Cookies with Peanut Butter Filling, 260
Peanut Butter Crunch Brownies, 85
Rocky Road Brownies, 78–79
Rocky Road Cookies, 237
Scotcharoos, 215
S'mores Blondies, 107–8
S'mores Cookies, 251–52
Soft Chocolate Chip Cookies, 29
Sugar Cookies with Chocolate and Sprinkles, 247
tempering, 16
Thin and Crispy Chocolate Chip Cookies, 32
Thin and Crispy Double Chocolate Cookies, 35
Thin Mints, 212
Toasted Sesame Cookies, 238
Triple Chocolate Cookies, 234
Turtle Brownies, 76

types of, 20, 21
White Chocolate Red Velvet Brownies, 92–93

cinnamon
Cinnamon Roll Blondies, 102–3
Cinnamon Roll-Up Cookies, 203–5

Citrus Pie Bars, 148–49

cocoa powder, 21

Coconut Cream Swirl Brownies, 80

coffee
Banana–Espresso–Cacao Nib Cookies, 249–50
Coffee Buttercream, 289
Coffee Cacao Nib Filling, 199
Double Chocolate Espresso Cookies, 164–66
Espresso Caramel Blondies, 100–101
Espresso Cheesecake Bars, 167–68
Espresso Meringues, 160
Espresso Shortbread, 61

confectioners' sugar, 19

conversions, 296

cookies. *See also individual recipes*
baking tips for, 15–17
flattening, 17
giving, 17
pan-banging method for, 226–27
size of, 16–17
storing, 17

corn syrup, 19

cream, heavy, 18

cream cheese, 18
Banana Cream Pie Bars, 126–28
Black and White Cheesecake Bars, 170–71
Carrot Cake Bars with Meringue, 185–86
Cherry Almond Cheesecake Swirl Bars, 142
Chocolate Malt Ice Box Bars, 274–75
Cinnamon Roll Blondies, 102–3
Citrus Pie Bars, 148–49
Cream Cheese Brownies, 75
Cream Cheese Buttercream, 185–86

    Cream Cheese Frosting, 92–93
    Cream Cheese Pumpkin Pie Bars, 129–30
    Crème Brûlée Cheesecake Bars, 181–82
    Danish Pear-Apple Bars, 133–34
    Espresso Cheesecake Bars, 167–68
    French Silk Pie Bars, 174–76
    No-Churn Ice Cream, 289–90
    Red Wine Cherry Cheesecake Swirl Bars, 141–42

Crème Brûlée Cheesecake Bars, 181–82

Crème Fraîche, 18, 284

curds
    Blood Orange Curd, 283
    Grapefruit Curd, 283
    Lemon Curd, 281–83
    Lemon-Lavender Curd, 283
    Lime Curd, 283
    Passion Fruit Curd, 283

Cut Out Cookies, 62–63

D

Danish Pear-Apple Bars, 133–34

dark chocolate
    Chocolate Ganache Crunch Filling, 199
    Dark Chocolate Swirl White Chocolate Brownies, 90

Double Chocolate Espresso Cookies, 164–66

Double Chocolate Sugar Cookies, 42

E

eggs
    separating, 18
    size of, 18
    temperature of, 18
    wash, 16

equipment, 21–22

Ermine Buttercream, 287–89

espresso. *See coffee*

fleur de sel, 18
flour
    measuring, 15
    types of, 19
French Meringues, 160
French Silk Pie Bars, 174–76
frostings and buttercreams
    Basil Buttercream, 86–87
    Cardamom Buttercream, 289
    Coffee Buttercream, 289
    Cream Cheese Buttercream, 185–86
    Cream Cheese Frosting, 92–93
    Ermine Buttercream, 287–89
    Green Tea Buttercream, 289
    Lavender Buttercream, 289
    Pumpkin Buttercream, 263
    Rhubarb Caramel Filling, 195
    Rosemary Buttercream, 289
Fudgy Brownies, 70

ganache
    Chocolate Ganache, 85, 86–87, 105–6, 167–68, 170–71, 183–84
    Chocolate Ganache Crunch Filling, 199
ginger
    Ginger Cookies, 51
    Ginger Cookies with Salted Caramel Ice Cream, 265
    Ginger Molasses Cookies, 243
glazes
    Blood Orange Glaze, 114–15
    Lemon–Poppy Seed Glaze, 115
    Simple Glaze, 62–63

White Chocolate–Crème Fraîche Glaze, 154–55

graham crackers
Citrus Pie Bars, 148–49
Cream Cheese Pumpkin Pie Bars, 129–30
Crème Brûlée Cheesecake Bars, 181–82
Red Wine Cherry Cheesecake Swirl Bars, 141–42
S'mores Cookies, 251–52

grapefruit
Grapefruit Cake Bars, 143–44
Grapefruit Curd, 283

Green Tea Buttercream, 289

Half-and-Half Cookies, Two Ways, 206–8
hazelnut flour, 19
Chocolate Hazelnut Bars, 173
Thumbprints, 55

ice cream
Brownies with Coffee Ice Cream, 270
Chocolate Chip Cookies with Ice Cream and Sprinkles, 273
Ginger Cookies with Salted Caramel Ice Cream, 265
No-Churn Ice Cream, 289–90
Sugar Cookies with Raspberry Ripple Ice Cream, 268
White Chocolate Brownies with Hazelnut Ice Cream, 272

Kitchen Sink Cookies, 209–10

lavender

Lavender Buttercream, 289
Lavender Cookies with White Chocolate–Crème Fraîche Glaze, 154–55
Lemon-Lavender Curd, 283

lemons
Citrus Pie Bars, 148–49
Lemon Curd, 281–83
Lemon-Lavender Curd, 283
Lemon-Lime Sugar Cookies, 117
Lemon Oat Bars, 146–47
Lemon–Poppy Seed Glaze, 115
Lemon–Poppy Seed Sugar Cookies, 117
Lemon Shortbread, 61
Lemon Sugar Cookies, 117
Strawberry Lemonade Cookies, 206–7

limes
Citrus Pie Bars, 148–49
Lemon-Lime Sugar Cookies, 117
Lime Curd, 283
Lime-Mint Pie Bars, 149

Macarons, 193–96
Chocolate Macarons, 197–99
M&M Cookies, 29
Marshmallows, 284–86
Kitchen Sink Cookies, 209–10
Marshmallow Fluff, 286–87
Marshmallow Peanut Butter Brownies, 82
Oatmeal Cream Pies, 267
Rocky Road Brownies, 78–79
Rocky Road Cookies, 237
S'mores Blondies, 107–8
S'mores Cookies, 251–52

measuring, 15–16, 21, 296

meringues
French Meringues, 160

Meringues with Cacao Nibs and Caramel Swirl, 163
milk, 18
milk chocolate
Milk Chocolate Cacao Nib Crunch Swirl Brownies, 81
Milk Chocolate Candied Nut Swirl Brownies, 81
Milk Chocolate Swirl Brownies, 81
S'mores Blondies, 107–8
S'mores Cookies, 251–52
Triple Chocolate Cookies, 234
mint
Chocolate Mint Sugar Cookies, 42
Lime-Mint Pie Bars, 149
Mint Sandwich Cookies, 212
Thin Mints, 212
Mixed Berry Crumble Bars, 135–36
Mousse, Chocolate, 177–78
Mud Pie Bars, 177–78
music, 295
My Favorite Brownies, 68

Neapolitan Cookies, 200–202
No-Churn Ice Cream, 289–90
nuts. *See also individual nuts*
Candied Nuts, 291
toasting, 20

oats
Espresso Cheesecake Bars, 167–68
Kitchen Sink Cookies, 209–10
Lemon Oat Bars, 146–47
Mixed Berry Crumble Bars, 135–36
Oatmeal Chocolate Cookies, 231
Oatmeal Cream Pies, 267

    Oatmeal Raisin Cookies, 52
    Rum Raisin Cookies, 232–33
    Strawberry Crème Fraîche Bars, 137–38
    White Chocolate, Rosemary, and Apricot Cookies, 122

olive oil, 18
    Olive Oil Sugar Cookies with Blood Orange Glaze, 114–15
    Olive Oil Sugar Cookies with Lemon–Poppy Seed Glaze, 115

oranges
    Blood Orange Curd, 283
    Blood Orange Glaze, 114–15
    Citrus Pie Bars, 148–49
    Orange Almond Shortbread Cookies, 118–19
    Orange Dreamsicle Cookies, 208
    Orange Dreamsicle Pie Bars, 149

oven temperature, 17, 22

Palmiers with Apricot and Cardamom, 159
pan-banging method, 226–27
pans
    lining, 16, 17
    size of, 17, 22
    tapping vs. banging, 16

parchment paper, 16, 22
Passion Fruit Curd, 283
Pastry Cream, 280–81
    Chocolate Pastry Cream, 281

peanut butter
    Brownie Cookies with Peanut Butter, 45
    Chocolate–Peanut Butter Pretzel Bark, 219–20
    Kitchen Sink Cookies, 209–10
    Marshmallow Peanut Butter Brownies, 82
    Peanut Butter Cookies, 37, 240
    Peanut Butter Cookies with Peanut Butter Filling, 260
    Peanut Butter Crunch Brownies, 85
    Scotcharoos, 215

peanuts
    Caramel Bars with Candied Peanuts, 216–17
    Milk Chocolate Candied Nut Swirl Brownies, 81

Pear-Apple Bars, Danish, 133–34

pecans
    Blondies, 96
    Brown Butter Blondies, 99
    Carrot Cake Bars with Meringue, 185–86
    Rocky Road Brownies, 78–79
    toasting, 20
    Turtle Brownies, 76

Pie Dough Base, 278

pistachios
    Caramelized White Chocolate Pistachio Bark, 221
    Pistachio Sablés, 56

poppy seeds
    Banana Poppy Seed Cookies, 125
    Lemon–Poppy Seed Glaze, 115
    Lemon–Poppy Seed Sugar Cookies, 117

potato chips
    Kitchen Sink Cookies, 209–10

pretzels
    Chocolate–Peanut Butter Pretzel Bark, 219–20
    Kitchen Sink Cookies, 209–10

puff pastry
    Palmiers with Apricot and Cardamom, 159
    Rough Puff Pastry, 279

pumpkin
    Cream Cheese Pumpkin Pie Bars, 129–30
    Pumpkin Buttercream, 263

raisins
    Oatmeal Raisin Cookies, 52
    Rum Raisin Cookies, 232–33

raspberries

Mixed Berry Crumble Bars, 135–36
Raspberry Rye Cookies, 121
Raspberry Swirl White Chocolate Brownies, 91
Red Velvet Cookies, 247
Red Wine Cherry Cheesecake Swirl Bars, 141–42
Rhubarb Caramel Filling, 195
rice cereal, crisped
Scotcharoos, 215
Rocky Road Brownies, 78–79
Rocky Road Cookies, 237
Roll-Up Cookies, Two Ways, 203–5
Rosemary Buttercream, 289
Rough Puff Pastry, 279
Rum Raisin Cookies, 232–33
Rye Cookies, Raspberry, 121

Sablés, 56
Bourbon Sablés with Chocolate, 59
Pistachio Sablés, 56
salt, 16, 18
Salty Caramel, 283
sanding sugar, 19
Scotcharoos, 215
sesame oil, toasted, 18
sesame seeds
Toasted Sesame Cookies, 238
White Chocolate Brownies with Toasted Sesame Caramel, 95
Shortbread, 60–61
Caramel Bars with Candied Peanuts, 216–17
Espresso Shortbread, 61
Lemon Shortbread, 61
Orange Almond Shortbread Cookies, 118–19
Simple Glaze, 62–63
Smoky Butterscotch Cookies, 156–57
S'mores Blondies, 107–8

S'mores Cookies, 251–52

Snickerdoodles, 48, 244
    Snickerdoodle Cookies with Pumpkin Buttercream, 263

Soft Chocolate Chip Cookies, 29

spices, 18

strawberries
    Mixed Berry Crumble Bars, 135–36
    Neapolitan Cookies, 200–202
    Strawberry Crème Fraîche Bars, 137–38
    Strawberry Lemonade Cookies, 206–7
    Strawberry Sandwich Cookies, 212
    Thumbprints, 55

sugar
    beet vs. cane, 19
    organic, 19
    types of, 19

Sugar Cookies, 38, 246–47
    Cardamom Chocolate Sugar Cookies, 42
    Chocolate Mint Sugar Cookies, 42
    Chocolate Sugar Cookies, 42
    Double Chocolate Sugar Cookies, 42
    Lemon-Lime Sugar Cookies, 117
    Lemon–Poppy Seed Sugar Cookies, 117
    Lemon Sugar Cookies, 117
    Olive Oil Sugar Cookies with Blood Orange Glaze, 114–15
    Olive Oil Sugar Cookies with Lemon–Poppy Seed Glaze, 115
    Red Velvet Cookies, 247
    Sugar Cookies with Chocolate and Sprinkles, 247
    Sugar Cookies with Raspberry Ripple Ice Cream, 268

Swirl Brownies, Two Ways, 80–81

Tea Buttercream, Green, 289
Thin and Crispy Chocolate Chip Cookies, 32
Thin and Crispy Double Chocolate Cookies, 35
Thin Mints, 212
Thumbprints, 55

Toasted Sesame Cookies, 238
Triple Chocolate Cookies, 234
Turtle Brownies, 76

vanilla, 21

walnuts
    Banana Crunch Blondies, 105–6
    toasting, 20
Whipped Cream, 290
white chocolate, 21
    Black and White Cheesecake Bars, 170–71
    Blondies, 96
    Caramelized White Chocolate Pistachio Bark, 221
    Dark Chocolate Swirl White Chocolate Brownies, 90
    Espresso Cheesecake Bars, 167–68
    Raspberry Swirl White Chocolate Brownies, 91
    Turtle Brownies, 76
    White Chocolate Brownies, 88–89
    White Chocolate Brownies with Hazelnut Ice Cream, 272
    White Chocolate Brownies with Toasted Sesame Caramel, 95
    White Chocolate–Crème Fraîche Glaze, 154–55
    White Chocolate Red Velvet Brownies, 92–93
    White Chocolate, Rosemary, and Apricot Cookies, 122

Printed in Great Britain
by Amazon